Comparative Literature in the Age
of Multiculturalism

Parallax 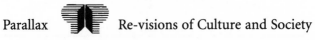 Re-visions of Culture and Society

Stephen G. Nichols, Gerald Prince, and Wendy Steiner,
Series Editors

COMPARATIVE LITERATURE
IN THE AGE OF
MULTICULTURALISM

EDITED BY

Charles Bernheimer

THE JOHNS HOPKINS UNIVERSITY PRESS

BALTIMORE AND LONDON

© 1995 The Johns Hopkins University Press
All rights reserved. Published 1995
Printed in the United States of America on acid-free paper
04 03 02 01 00 99 98 97 96 95   5 4 3 2 1

The Johns Hopkins University Press
2715 North Charles Street
Baltimore, Maryland 21218-4319
The Johns Hopkins Press Ltd., London

Library of Congress Cataloging-in-Publication Data will be found
at the end of this book.
A catalog record for this book is available from the British Library.

ISBN 0-8018-5004-5
ISBN 0-8018-5005-3 (pbk.)

CONTENTS

Preface   ix

Introduction: The Anxieties of Comparison   1
CHARLES BERNHEIMER

PART ONE
Three Reports to the American Comparative Literature Association

1. The Levin Report, 1965   21

2. The Greene Report, 1975   28

3. The Bernheimer Report, 1993   39

PART TWO
Three Responses to the Bernheimer Report at the
MLA Convention, 1993

4. *Geist* Stories   51
K. ANTHONY APPIAH

5. Comparative Literature and Global Citizenship   58
MARY LOUISE PRATT

6. On the Complementarity of Comparative Literature and Cultural
Studies   66
MICHAEL RIFFATERRE

PART THREE
Position Papers

7. The Function of Criticism at the Present Time:
The Promise of Comparative Literature   77
ED AHEARN AND ARNOLD WEINSTEIN

8. Comparative Exile: Competing Margins in the History of Comparative
Literature   86
EMILY APTER

9. Must We Apologize?   97
PETER BROOKS

10. In the Name of Comparative Literature   107
REY CHOW

11. Comparative Literature, at Last!   117
JONATHAN CULLER

12. Literary Study in an Elliptical Age   122
DAVID DAMROSCH

13. Between Elitism and Populism: Whither Comparative Literature?   134
ELIZABETH FOX-GENOVESE

14. Their Generation   143
ROLAND GREENE

15. Comparative Literature on the Feminist Edge   155
MARGARET R. HIGONNET

16. Spaces of Comparison   165
FRANÇOISE LIONNET

17. "Literature" in the Expanded Field   175
MARJORIE PERLOFF

CONTENTS

18. Telling Tales out of School: Comparative Literature and Disciplinary Recession   187
MARY RUSSO

19. Sincerely Yours   195
TOBIN SIEBERS

Notes on Contributors   205

PREFACE

The story of this collection begins in the summer of 1992 when Stuart McDougal, then president of the American Comparative Literature Association (ACLA), asked me to appoint and chair a committee charged to write a so-called Report on Standards for submission to the association. The bylaws of the ACLA, Stuart told me, mandated that such a report be prepared every ten years. The first report was submitted in 1965 by a committee chaired by my thesis director, Harry Levin; the second was submitted in 1975 by a committee chaired by Tom Greene. A third report was written ten years thereafter, but, Stuart disclosed, the chair of that committee was so dissatisfied with the document that he exercised a pocket veto and never submitted it.

Before deciding whether or not to accept this challenging task, I asked Stuart to send me copies of the first two reports. After reading them, I knew that this was an opportunity not to be missed. These reports are impressively strong articulations of a view of comparative literature which, in my view, no longer applies to actual practices in the field. To write a report as forceful as the earlier ones which would indicate new goals and methods for the discipline, this, I decided, would be an exciting and instructive enterprise.

So I accepted Stuart's invitation and set about immediately constituting my committee. I wanted a diverse group of top scholars from diverse institutions. The group that agreed to serve included Jonathan Arac from Pittsburgh, a specialist in theory and nineteenth-century studies, especially American; Marianne Hirsch, a feminist critic from Dartmouth, with a particular interest in narrative and genealogy; Ann Rosalind Jones from Smith, who works in the Renaissance from the perspective of feminism and cultural studies; Ronald Judy from Carnegie-Mellon, a recent Ph.D. in comparative literature with interests in black studies and critical theory; Arnold Krupat from Sarah Lawrence, who has authored books on ethnic studies and Native American literature; Dominick LaCapra from Cornell, a historian who has written extensively about intellectual and literary history and theory; Sylvia Molloy from New York University, a leader in the field of Latin American studies; Steve Nichols from Johns Hopkins, a scholar of medieval literature with strong interests in iconography and music; and Sara Suleri from Yale, whose work has focused on issues of colonialism and postcolonialism.

In the fall I wrote up a preliminary version of a report, sketching out ideas, and sent this document around to all committee members. We then met as a group at the 1992 MLA convention in New York and engaged in a spirited debate on the issues. We agreed that we wanted to write a report that would stir up controversy, not one that would try to find a comfortable middle ground. We felt uneasy about being asked to establish "standards" and decided to give more importance to our ideas about the intellectual mission of the discipline than to spelling out requirements (in this spirit, the bylaws were amended at the last ACLA meeting to rename the report the Report on the State of the Discipline). Despite our differences, a surprising consensus emerged about the directions in which we felt comparative literature should move. After this stimulating discussion, I revised the report to include many of the observations made at the meeting and circulated this draft to the committee, asking for precise suggestions on wording and presentation. I also distributed this version at the ACLA meeting in Bloomington in March and received valuable feedback from many interested colleagues. Integrating this feedback with the comments of committee members, I then produced the final version of the report.

Since part of our purpose in giving our report a distinct polemical edge was to produce what we regarded as much-needed disciplinary self-analysis, we wanted to publicize the document as widely as possible. With this goal in mind, Stuart McDougal suggested that one of the ACLA's two sessions at the 1993 MLA convention be dedicated to a discussion of the report and asked me to select and chair the panel. Looking for a spectrum of responses from leaders in the profession, I invited Michael Riffaterre, Mary Louise Pratt, and K. Anthony Appiah to participate, and they graciously accepted. Around four hundred people came to the session, which Professor Appiah unfortunately missed because of bad weather in Boston. Afterward, debate continued in the hallways and at the cash bars. I felt that we had made an excellent first step toward the goal of stimulating a fundamental examination of the discipline's identity and goals at the end of the century.

But more needed to be done. In particular, I thought that the issues raised by the report, and the debate generated by it, should not dissipate into thin air. So when Michael Riffaterre suggested that the three MLA talks warranted publication in a more widely disseminated medium than the in-house organ of the ACLA, its *Bulletin,* I began to entertain the idea of a collection of essays which would print the three reports, the three MLA papers, and short position papers by major figures in the profession. I drew up a list of potential contributors, looking for diversity in critical perspective and institutional affiliation and ruling out members of the ACLA committee, and began making phone calls. Almost everyone I contacted declared that he or she had been thinking for some time about the questions I was raising and welcomed the opportunity to put these ideas onto paper. I sent each contributor copies of the three reports and the three MLA talks. Eric Halpern, the editor at the Johns Hopkins University Press, where the project had been accepted, agreed that we would try to have books available for the 1994 MLA convention. This would be something of a coup in academic publishing: a debate generated at one MLA would have a book of original essays dedicated to it available for purchase at the next MLA. Although the contributors, all busy scholars, had very limited time in which to prepare their papers, they met the strict deadlines I had to impose. The result is a volume that offers an extraordinary range of passionate insights and engaged opinions about the theory and practice of comparative literature at the turn of the century.

Comparative Literature in the Age
of Multiculturalism

INTRODUCTION

The Anxieties of Comparison

CHARLES BERNHEIMER

Comparative literature is anxiogenic. The eager graduate student—let's assume she's a woman, since today the majority of students in comparative literature programs and departments are women—begins her course of study with an excited sense of broad horizons opening before her. A year or two later, she discovers that she has no firm ground underfoot. More is expected of her than of her peers in the national literature departments—more knowledge of languages, more reading of literatures, more expertise in theory—but it is not clear that she will benefit professionally from all this extra work. She's told early on that there are very few jobs in comparative literature departments, so she will have to compete head-on with her friends whose studies have been less arduous but more specialized. Won't national literature departments prefer someone with her skills and training over a more narrowly educated scholar? she queries hopefully. Not necessarily, answers her advisor. It depends on the intellectual and political climate of the particular department and on how that department interprets its needs. Sometimes the comparatist's ability to wear different hats is just what is wanted—"hey, she can teach a film course for us . . . and that survey of eighteenth-century French lit . . . and she could even pinch-hit in twentieth-century!" At other times this multifacetedness is viewed as a sign of dilettantism.

Comparison of herself with her peers in the national literature departments makes the graduate student feel anxious about her calling to compare literatures. Or is that really her calling? Some of the most exciting courses on campus don't focus on literature at all. Professors assign readings in sociology, anthropology, philosophy, history. The hottest debates are about theory rather than literature. So what's supposed to be compared to what and how? "The most serious sign of the precarious state of our study is the fact that it has not been able to establish a distinct subject matter and a specific methodology," declared René Wellek back in 1958 in a paper entitled "The Crisis of Comparative Literature."[1] Thirty-seven years later the same could still be said, reflects our anxious graduate student. So is this field constantly in crisis? she wonders. How does this jibe with comparative literature's being, by all accounts, an elite discipline? Is one of the qualifications of this elite the ability to sustain the anxiety of an academic field whose identity is perpetually precarious?

Peter Brooks' confession in his essay for this volume suggests an affirmative answer to this question: "Although I hold a Ph.D. in comparative literature," writes Brooks, "I have never been sure I deserved it, since I've never been sure what the field, or the discipline, is and never sure that I could really claim to be teaching it or working in it".[2] Had Brooks somehow become clear about his field and convinced of his right to practice it, he probably would not be chair today of Yale's Comparative Literature Department. Yet, according to his own account, he did not accommodate easily to his anxiety. He rid himself of some of it, he says, when he "managed to stop worrying about 'comparing the literature,' about that adjective *comparative*." Teaching in the Yale undergraduate program called, simply, The Literature Major, he could study and teach "literariness and the literary phenomenon" without having to worry about what to compare it to. But this "liberation" was short-lived, he remarks regretfully, for The Literature Major was combined with the graduate program, and he found himself once again identified with that anxiogenic, "still only vaguely defined enterprise," comparative literature.

Comparison is indeed the . . . what is it?—activity, function, practice? all of these?—that assures that our field will always be unstable, shifting, insecure, and self-critical. Ten years after Wellek spoke of the field's lack of specific subject matter and methodology, Harry Levin criticized his colleagues for spending too much time talking about comparative literature, its organization and methodology, and, as he put it, "not enough [energy] comparing the literature."[3] But this is to assume that, if we were to stop dawdling and feeling anxious, we could just go ahead and staunchly compare, whereas comparison is just what makes us productively anxious, generates the interesting questions, probes thought beyond traditional boundaries, and, at its best, justifies our being considered an elite group. And these days it is not only comparison that is at issue. The very identity of literature as an object of study is no longer clear. Many scholars today would consider Brooks' conviction that he can teach "literariness and the literary phenomenon" a questionable ideological position.

Changes in the discipline's focus since World War II can be viewed as a series of attempts to cure, contain, or exploit the anxiety of comparison. In the fifties and sixties, the possibility of cure seemed to be held out by the projection of a unifying, consolidating goal to the comparatist's endeavors. "The comparatist's effort and reward," writes François Jost, "is to perceive the literary world in its fundamental unity."[4] This desire for totalization was a response to the violent rending of European cultures during the war and is the subject of comment by a number of contributors to this volume. During this period, definitions of the discipline were offered with relative confidence and always stressed supranationalism and cross-disciplinarity. Typical is the definition offered in 1969 by Owen Aldridge in his introduction to a collection of essays entitled *Comparative Literature: Matter and Method*: "Briefly defined, comparative literature can be considered the study of any literary phenomenon from the perspective of more than one national literature or in conjunction with another intellectual discipline or even several."[5] Aldridge then presents his collection under five headings, "literary criticism and theory," "literary movements," "literary themes," "literary forms," and "literary relations" (which include sources and influences). Generally speaking, these categories, widely accepted at the time, serve to highlight continuities and analogies in each insistently labeled "literary" category across national boundaries. Division promotes unity. "Method is less important than matter," Aldridge remarks in his introduction (5). His point is that the matter, literature itself, is a reassuring given, whereas methods are "at best ambiguous" (5)—hence anxiogenic, hence in need of cure.

In 1969 I was a graduate student finishing my studies at Harvard. Protest against the Vietnam War reached a high point that year and affected even Harvard's staid Comparative Literature Department. We had a meeting of faculty and students to talk about the structure and goals of the program. I recommended that the required proseminar not take as its textbook Warren and Wellek's *Theory of Literature* but read Nietzsche, Freud, Marx, and other such seminal thinkers, in an effort to stimulate the students to ask fundamental questions and to disorient them from their received assumptions about literary study. In effect, I was recommending the anxiety of comparison. From the other side of the room, Harry Levin, in a kindly tone, corrected me: "Charlie, I am sure you mean orient, don't you?" and he spread his hands apart to indicate the distance between the student, here, and "the body of knowledge," there. The proper orientation, he said, put one on a straight path on which, as one advanced, one gained ever more knowledge, ever more matter. The implication was that this advance would also make me less anxious and less upset about the war. But I wasn't buying.

In any case, Levin's orientation was about to be superseded by the epoch of theory, when method became more important than matter and anxiety was no longer considered a symptom to be cured but rather a textual function to be appreciated and analyzed. Across the country, comparative literature departments became known as hotbeds of theory, and theory became identified with what many took to be its most rigorous practice, deconstruction. In a certain sense, the goal of comparison did not change, "to perceive the literary world in its fundamental unity." "There is absolutely no reason why analyses of the kind suggested here for Proust," claimed Paul de Man in 1979, "would not be applicable, with proper modifications of technique, to Milton or to Dante or to Hölderlin."[6] But, of course, the unity of literature meant something very different for de Man than it did for Jost, Aldridge, or Levin. They were humanists. Literature for them was a repository of values, in conflict and contestation to be sure, and all the more relevant to the moral education of men and women because of this dynamic interplay. In contrast, de Man, a Ph.D. in comparative literature from Harvard and only seven years Levin's junior, was an antihumanist. His technique of reading, to whatever text it is applied, always shows values to be delusive, cognition to be erroneous, agency to be illusory, and motivations to be aberrant. The social or psychological subject is revealed to be an equivocal effect of rhetorical displacements. Textuality itself is anxiogenic according to de Man, hence the unity of the literary world in its deconstruction and the centrality of comparative literature to the project of rhetorical reading.

The appeal of deconstruction can partially be understood, I think, in relation to the prevailing post-Vietnam mood of cynicism and distrust. Deconstruction as a technique of demystification requires systematic suspicion. One of the most frequently used phrases in its lexicon is the claim that such and such "is not innocent," a point of view whose appeal in the Nixon years is not hard to understand. Of course, this claim does not mean simply that guilt can be assumed but that the distinction between guilt and innocence is undecidable. Comparison in this high-theoretical practice collapses the distinctions on which the comparative process relies and demonstrates how each element is contaminated by the other. When applied in the political arena, for instance on the Cold War rhetoric of opposition, this strategy has a strong subversive effect, undermining the moral claims of both sides, showing that the two opponents are both engaged in deceit masking violence. Deconstructors argue that this demonstration is itself a political intervention. But it is so, in my view, only in a very limited sense. The intervention is basically inert. It amounts to saying, "a plague on both your houses." Viewed from the deconstructive abyss, engagement on either side involves mystification and blindness. Abysmal wisdom resides in disengagement and reading.

Reading what? Nietzsche, Freud, Marx for starters, just those authors I had wanted to put on the comparative literature proseminar syllabus at Harvard. And Hegel, Heidegger, Rousseau, Plato, Proust, Mallarmé, Poe, Lacan—it was one of the great accomplishments of deconstruction's heyday that literary scholars and other intellectuals felt stimulated to read these difficult texts, and to study the languages in which they were originally written, so as to have a better understanding of the brilliant analyses de Man and Derrida had made of them. In those years, the study of comparative literature at some of the best graduate schools gave priority to theory over literature, to method over matter. The trend that Harry Levin had deplored in 1968 was intensifying: we weren't comparing the literatures so much as we were comparing theories about comparison. Anxiety was fashionable. Indeed, it was de rigueur, rigor being the fetish of theory.[7]

But, as the Reagan-Bush years gradually eroded the liberal social agenda, it became more and more painful for many professors in literature departments to continue in an attitude of skeptical detachment and sophisticated alienation. The inevitable aporia of deconstructive undecidability began to seem too much like the indecipherable double-talk of the politicians we detested. Even those, myself included, who had been deeply influenced by deconstruction were feeling tired of systematic, suspicious vigilance, tired and demoralized by the work of displacing the ground from under our own feet, tired of being mortally rigorous, tired of comparisons that always collapsed into indifference. This mood was no doubt in part responsible for what Hillis Miller calls "a massive shift of focus in literary study since 1979 [the publication date of de Man's *Allegories of Reading*] away from the 'intrinsic,' rhetorical study of literature toward study of the 'extrinsic' relations of literature, its placements within psychological, historical or sociological contexts."[8]

The essay from which this sentence is taken, "The Function of Literary Theory at the Present Time," published in 1989, is an interesting effort by an influential advocate of deconstruction to deal with its loss of influence in the academy. Miller adopts a mocking tone about the shift he discerns: "It is as if a great sigh of relief were rising from all across the land. The era of 'deconstruction' is over. It has had its day, and we can return with a clear conscience to the warmer, more human work of writing about power, history, ideology, the 'institution' of the study of literature, the class struggle, the oppression of women, and the real lives of men and women in society as they exist in themselves and as they are 'reflected' in literature" (103). Clarity of conscience, Miller suggests, derives from a naive trust in the mimetic transparency of words, in their capacity to reflect the world. The shift away from the rhetorical study of literature is motivated, he claims, by a refusal to live with the anxiety caused by "an indefinite delay or postponement of our desire to turn our attention to the relations of literature to history, to society, to the self" (103).

This sounds like a version of the objections made by the establishment to the students protesting the Vietnam War: you are impatient and irresponsible, you are grounding your dissent in the body rather than in reason, you are driven by desire where rigor is called for. Miller goes on to declare his admiration for the honorable motives underlying the shift in interest toward history and society, gender and power, but argues that these motives should not come into play until a text has been subjected to "a rhetorical analysis of the most vigilant and patient sort" (104). The task of criticism in the coming years, he declares, will be to mediate between this kind of analysis and the study of the extrinsic relations of literature. But no sooner has he used the word *mediation* than he qualifies it and explains that the specific literariness of a text cannot be understood "by historical, sociological, or psychological methods of interpretation" (105) and hence cannot enter into a comparative process such as mediation. When he declares in the next paragraph that the extrinsic relations with which the intrinsic ones were to be mediated are actually intrinsic themselves, Miller has offered a vivid demonstration of the kind of logic whose abandonment produced that "great sigh of relief" he evoked earlier in his essay.

That essay was written, Miller tells us in a note, before the discovery and publication of de Man's wartime collaborationist writings. As the essay attests, the tide had already turned against deconstruction before the de Man affair broke, but the affair—as much because of a widely felt aversion to the tortured exercises in "reading" used by Derrida and others to construct exculpatory scenarios as because of moral outrage at de Man's youthful sympathy with Nazi ideology—signaled for many the end of high theory's domination.[9] Lack of innocence seemed discredited as a textual quality when it could be seen to apply referentially to its preeminent advocate. Anxiety no longer seemed containable in the space of comparison's collapse when the motive to deny there being anything extrinsic to textuality could be thought to be strategically self-serving.

Now, to be sure, comparative literature departments had never been completely taken over by deconstructive theory, even at its apogee. Although many feminist critics integrated deconstructive insights into their work—indeed, no one working seriously in the literary field could ignore the powerful force of these insights—the major impact of feminist critique involved a renewal of moral analysis in the arena of social practices. In the seventies and eighties feminism presented an increasingly sophisticated, diverse, and energetic challenge to efforts to divorce textual analysis from the material conditions and contexts—social, historical, and political—of literature's production and reception. As more and more women entered the profession, their concerns with the marginalization or suppression of women's voices in such diverse contexts as narrative representations, social arrangements, publishing practices, and academic policies generated a complex of questions concerning the relations of literature to experience, of aesthetics to ideology, of gender to power, which challenged the poetics of rhetoricity propounded in high theory.

These questions intersected fruitfully with those being asked from a number of related points of view. Under the influence of Foucault, the analysis of discourse, associated with the regulatory mechanisms of power, displaced the study of rhetoric, felt to be too self-contained. Under the influence of Bakhtin, language came to be seen less as an autonomous structure à la Saussure and more as a highly variable set of discourses produced through, and productive of, social differentiation and conflictual interaction. Under the influence of the Frankfurt school, especially of Benjamin, material social practices were seen to express complex psychopoetic dynamics. And younger critics exercised significant influence by showing how literary forms are embedded in collective histories and ideological structures—to name only a prominent few, Edward Said and Gayatri Spivak helped generate interest in the now rapidly developing field of colonial and postcolonial studies; Fredric Jameson showed that Marxist analysis could make productive use of poststructuralist insights for literary and cultural critique; Stephen Greenblatt sent students scouring the archives in search of materials that would offer startlingly new historical contexts for reading literary texts.

This extremely rapid survey brings us up to the present, when the critical field is fragmented into a multiplicity of diverse theoretical perspectives. Yet it appears today that contextualization has become the watchword of the most influential approaches to literature. History, culture, politics, location, gender, sexual orientation, class, race—a reading in the new mode has to try to take as many of these factors as possible into account. The trick is to do so without becoming subject to Miller's criticism, without, that is, suggesting that a literary work can be explained as an unmediated reflection of these factors. The slipperiness of the evidentiary status of anecdotes in much new historicist writing testifies to the difficulty of successfully performing this trick of contextualizing without reifying.

The politics of multiculturalism have not facilitated the task. Advocates of multicultural canon revision wish to extend the ethical demand for recognition of marginalized cultural groups and expressive traditions, which began with the civil rights and women's movements, to include both minority ethnic cultures in this country and non-Western cultures globally. Fundamental to this demand is a liberal notion of representation, which operates on two levels. First, the canon should be representative not just of European high culture but also of the diversity of literary productions throughout the world. Second, the works chosen to be included in a revised canon should be representative of the cultures in which they were created. Both parts of this program assume a "reflectionist" view of literature's relation to the cultural site of its production. The work's value is perceived as residing primarily in the authenticity of the image it conveys of the culture it is taken to represent, politically and mimetically.

This program raises many problems. For instance, how is authenticity to be judged? How is one to avoid the mistake, to which Rey Chow draws attention in her contribution to this book, of substituting for a canon of European masterpieces another canon of non-European works? These works, moreover, may well be representative only of the dominant traditions in cultures that are themselves hegemonic in their geopolitical contexts. And isn't the entire multiculturalist model flawed by its tendency to essentialize those cultures, attributing to them far more unity, regularity, and stability than they actually have? And isn't the model of reflection, for all its good intentions, also flawed? A literary work can never authentically mirror a culture not only because that culture is not at one with itself but also because the work is a *literary* representation and hence not a transparent medium but a formal structure. Furthermore, the criterion of authenticity tends to equalize all cultures in a relativist haze and thereby destroys any possibility of differential judgment and comparison.

Comparison . . . I come back to that word and to the anxieties it raises in our contemporary age of multiculturalism. On the face of things, it would appear that multiculturalism, inherently pluralistic, would have a natural propensity toward comparison. But this propensity has been checked by the mimetic imperatives of an essentialist politics. Henry Louis Gates, Jr., observes that "the culturalist model normally imagines its constituent elements as cultural bubbles that may collide but that could, in principle, exist in splendid isolation from one another."[10] The anxiety of the comparatist who proposes to break down this isolation and bring some bubbles into collision is manifold. There is first of all the issue of entitlement. Do I have the right to speak about these cultures to which I don't belong? Even though I am fascinated by African literatures, do I have any chance of getting a job to teach them if my skin is white? Is it not desirable these days to be able to offer the construction of one's own subjectivity as a particularly telling context through which to perform a reading of so-called foreign or ethnic texts? It seems that it is no longer enough for comparatists to speak different tongues: now they have to put on different skins as well.

Identity politics are particularly anxiogenic for the comparatist who ventures beyond the European arena or gets involved with ethnic cultures at home. No matter how many years you may have given to the study of a culture, if it is not yours "in the blood," it will always be possible for you to be found lacking in some quality of authenticity. The more literatures you try to compare, the more like a colonizing imperialist you may seem. If you stress what these literatures have in common—thematically, morally, politically— you may be accused of imposing a universalist model that suppresses particular differences so as to foster the old humanist dream of man's worldwide similarity to man. If, on the other hand, you stress differences, then the basis of comparison becomes problematic, and your respect for the uniqueness of particular cultural formations may suggest the impossibility of any meaningful relation between cultures.

I am, of course, oversimplifying the dilemma. I do so in order to highlight the ethical and political contexts within which some of the most pressing questions facing comparative literature are currently being framed. These contexts reflect the vicissitudes of recent history. On the one hand, events such as the demolition of the Berlin Wall, the end of the Cold War, the fall of communism in Russia and central Europe, and the democratic elections in South Africa have seemed to open the world to the processes of globalization, democratization, and decolonization which Mary Louise Pratt welcomes as creating for comparative literature "an especially hospitable space for the cultivation of multilingualism, polyglossia, the arts of cultural mediation, deep intercultural understanding, and genuinely global consciousness." On the other hand, as Marjorie Perloff reminds us, the nationalist aspirations of ethnic groups are producing fierce conflicts on just about every continent, making the world seem an ever more fractious and fragmented place. As to intercultural understanding, Tobin Siebers finds that, even after years of study, a culture as apparently familiar as that of France remains fundamentally alien (a perception that Peter Mayle has exploited for all its worth in his best-selling books about Provence).

Should the comparatist work to unify our sense of the essential nature and function of literature cross-culturally, or should he or she work to promote our understanding of the diverse constructions of the category of the literary in different cultures? The contributors to this volume seem to divide into two camps on this question. Jonathan Culler suggests that the national literature departments should become departments of national cultural studies, clearing the space for comparative literature to study and teach literature "as such." Just how this study should proceed Culler does not spell out, but presumably he would agree with Peter Brooks that its foundation should be the study of poetics. "To place the study of literature in the context of 'cultural studies,'" writes Brooks in a recent essay in *Critical Inquiry* which complements his piece in this volume, "will be a mistake if thereby the specificity of the aesthetic domain is lost."[11] Citing Schiller, Brooks associates that specificity with the *Spieltrieb,* the play-drive, which has the salutary function of promoting the illusion that one can be free from materiality. He castigates as moralistic wielders of a "rhetoric of virtue" (AI 514) those materialist critics who would associate such freedom with irresponsible elitism. "The realm of the aesthetic needs to be respected," Brooks insists, "by an imperative that is nearly ethical" (AI 522). This imperative is similar to the one that leads Michael Riffaterre to declare in this volume that a text becomes properly literary only when it is decontextualized and that it is the task of theory to assure that a text "survives the extinction of the issues, the vanishing of the causes, and the memory of the circumstances to which [it] responded."

These critics agree that the work of comparison involves first and foremost a reflection on the aesthetic phenomenon of literariness in a cross-national context. Despite significant differences, their arguments belong in the same tradition as those put forward in more explicitly rhetorical terms by de Man and Derrida. Literature can be taught "as literature" (Brooks), with its "invariant features" (Riffaterre), without worrying about the historical contingency of this category. That worry belongs with cultural studies, which for these critics constitutes an approach to literature from without, not a theory of reading but an ideologization of aesthetic values for the purpose of political critique. Hence they see the 1993 ACLA report as an abandonment of the true forms of literary study. (Culler does not say as much, but his sweeping aside of cultural studies so that comparative literature can at last preside over the study of literature in itself is eloquent.)

On the other side of the spectrum of opinion are those critics who agree with the general thrust of the report. Precisely because this agreement involves the advocacy of a pluralized and expanded contextualization of literary study, it is less focused than the formalist advocacy of poetics. These critics accept the challenge of what Françoise Lionnet calls "the messiness of globalization and the risk of contamination that might result from the democratization of the idea of literature as an intersubjective practice." Part of what could be thought of as disorderly in this practice is its overt concern with values other than the aesthetic, or, put differently, with situating aesthetics in a broad spectrum of values. Brooks feels uneasy, not to say anxious, about literary criticism's engaging in acts of evaluation whose basis is, finally, the critic's moral and political convictions. Those convictions, he argues, referring to Keats and Eliot, need to be tempered by a depersonalizing appeal to tradition, so that the critic's voice echoes with those of his or her cultural inheritance.

Brooks, of course, does not want to be seen as advocating the conservative notion of a traditional canon embodying transcendent values, so he is quick to stress that "traditions are really constructions" (AI 521), historically contingent and politically biased. But tradition in this sense cannot be appealed to, it can only be interpreted, and that interpretation entails an inquiry into particular historical, cultural, institutional, and political contexts. By allowing these contexts to echo in his or her own voice, I would say, contra Brooks, that the comparatist is not so much depersonalized as made aware of his or her subjectivity as a construction requiring interpretation, which is quite a different matter.

I am suggesting that multiculturalist comparatism begins at home with a comparison of oneself to oneself. This process precludes the cultural essentialism of identity politics, while it sensitizes the comparatist to the extremely difficult issues involved in evaluating cultural differences. The "productive discomfort" that Lionnet describes as arising from being brought up on an island where French and English cultures intersect with African and Indian traditions vividly evokes the hybrid constitution of the comparatist subject. Here the cultural bubbles of which Gates speaks are not closed off from one another. Rather, they are systems of knowledge and interpretation which coexist and interpenetrate within us, creating a mobile, fluid space of intersecting class and family allegiances, clan and religious traditions, historical and political pressures, inherited traits, unconscious drives, geopolitical locales, and so forth.

Interest in the subject's constitution as a hybrid, multicultural conjuncture has led certain critics toward autobiography. Although this move might be seen as narcissistic—which it may be, in part—it can be viewed more positively as complementary, rather than hostile, to a global broadening of perspective. The critic's autobiography—I think, for instance, of Alice Kaplan's *French Lessons*—is typically the story of the traces of cultural otherness discovered within and of ambivalent interactions with otherness confronted without. Even when these traces and confrontations do not go beyond the purview of European cultures and histories, the critic's autobiography— especially if he or she is a comparatist—tends to describe a subject who "travels cultures," in the sense recently expounded by James Clifford.[12] As Clifford remarks, for such a subject the question is not so much "where are you from?" as "where are you between?" (109). For instance, in my own case I could say that my origins are between my mother's father's birthplace, Neuchâtel, Switzerland, with its stern Calvinist traditions and repressed libido, and Munich, Germany, center of anti-Semitism, where my father's family were successfully assimilated Jewish antique dealers. I associate each of these sites with many others between which my intercultural itinerary has moved in dynamic—and sometimes traumatic—shifts, interferences, and translations: "a history of locations and a location of histories," in Clifford's phrase (105).

As Emily Apter argues in her contribution to this volume, exilic consciousness, "the material and psychic legacy of dislocation," is more definitively formative of the discipline of comparative literature than of any other field in the humanities. I agree with her that the voice of comparative literature is "unhomely" and that this very quality of dispossession—a kind of haunting by otherness—is that voice's great strength. To date, our haunting has been most often by culturally familiar ghosts, even if they originated in an imaginary Transylvania. The challenge facing us now is to increase the scope of our haunting, to broaden the space of those sites we are between. For many of us this entails a stretch beyond the European contexts of our cultural heritage and of our professional training. Such a stretch is at once exciting, in that it expands our horizons, and anxiogenic, in that it takes us outside the fields of our certified authority.

Certain pragmatic measures may help relieve this anxiety about expertise. Those of us trained in European languages and literatures could team-teach courses with colleagues trained in, for instance, Asian, African, Indian, or Near Eastern languages and literatures. This would enable works read in translation to be presented by teachers able to explain the specific linguistic qualities of the original texts. But collaboration could well reach beyond literary fields to include interested colleagues in such departments as history, anthropology, sociology, music, art history, folklore, media studies, philosophy, architecture, and political science. The search for more cosmopolitan, transcultural approaches is being actively pursued by innovative thinkers in all these domains, many of whom share a common set of theoretical readings. To encourage such collaborations is not to abandon literature as an object of study—which, pace Riffaterre, is not what the authors of the Bernheimer report intended to advocate—but rather to suggest a fundamentally relational and dynamic approach to cultural forms, including literary texts.

Another way of dealing with the issue of expertise is to subject it to pressing inquiry, asking just what constitutes expert knowledge, what authority qualifies an expert as such, what assumptions about authenticity sustain notions of local expertise, and so forth. Expertise, Kristin Ross has argued, is an ideology, and it often serves to dominate and silence rather than to teach and stimulate.[13] If we are careful about positioning ourselves in relation to the cultural differences embedded in the works we are teaching, then that act of positioning can become an important part of what the student learns in a course. Our objects of study are in important ways creations of the terms we use to study them. To have some intellectual distance from those terms is not necessarily a bad thing. We don't need to be experts in everything we teach, as long as we don't pretend to be and our effort to understand is in good faith. But neither should we act as tourists, having read a few guidebooks to faraway places. The tourist regurgitates information about "native" cultures while ignoring his or her own nativeness. In contrast, the comparatist in the age of multiculturalism reads herself or himself as a site of contradiction and contamination, distrusts all guides that offer to decode the exotic other, and refuses to become a detached observer exercising a free-floating, disengaged intelligence.[14] The comparatist's perspective cannot be mapped on a model of center and margin; rather, as David Damrosch proposes here, it is elliptical, generated from two foci, each engaging other overlapping ellipses. Such a dynamic model always puts centralizing authority in question and underlines the struggles between dominant and resisting social and ethnic groups.

Team-teaching offers an easily implemented way to promote a responsibility to global perspectives in pedagogical practice. Changes in institutional formations are harder to realize, given the entrenched interests defending current departmental structures and disciplinary boundaries. Nevertheless, certain groupings already exist within the academy which could potentially serve as models for new disciplinary configurations with a multicultural comparative outlook. I will mention just two, period studies and area studies.

Faculty at many institutions have formed research groups in medieval studies, Renaissance studies, and eighteenth-century studies. These groups usually include professors from four or five literature departments, often joined by colleagues from history and art history. Founded on the study of the interconnections between European literary and cultural texts and their common classical heritage, these groups have a coherent raison d'être in the task of tracing what Anthony Appiah here calls the life of the Western *Geist*. But, as Appiah acknowledges, this coherence has a number of elliptical second foci that explode its autonomy—literally, with gunpowder brought in from China, figuratively with the influence of Islamic and African traditions, and economically with the growth of distant markets and the spread of empires. If the research groups were to explore the dynamics of the elliptical approach, their comparative work could intersect with that of scholars of non-Western cultures in the same or similar periods, and the result could be a broadened and revitalized conception of literary and cultural history, still centered in Europe but also crucially decentered. These transnational and transdisciplinary groups could eventually become degree-granting entities.

Because the interconnections between the West and the rest of the world become so multiple, complex, and conflicted in the nineteenth and twentieth centuries, and because the fund of knowledges becomes so huge, the comparative period studies model is impracticable for this time frame. An area studies model may be more suitable, but only if the premises that have sustained such models in the past are reviewed and revised. In some cases, area studies programs—which typically bring historians, political scientists, and economists together with literary scholars and students of popular culture—were Cold War creations intended to help the government know its enemy. In other cases, the programs served to bunch together Third World countries so that they could be studied on the model of a colonial territory.[15] In the case of a field like German studies, the problem, as Peter Hohendahl argued recently, was that there was no coherent basis to the program of study, students being encouraged to take courses in a variety of disciplines, literature being only one option among many.[16] Still, the area studies model could be reconceptualized to foreground literature and to undo, via an elliptical bifocus, the notion of a stable geographical area. Here the experience of American studies programs may be instructive, both in terms of the conflicts in that field about the place of literary studies and in terms of the multicultural pluralization of its constituency (Native American, African American, Asian American, Chicano, Hispanic, and more).

Just how to foreground literature in the new contextualized modes of comparison is, of course, not evident. The fact that the 1993 ACLA report was read by many as an attack on literature is perhaps a sign of how vulnerable literary scholars feel in today's academic atmosphere. Although some of the phrases in the document may seem to imply otherwise, its authors, if I may speak for them, wanted to suggest not literature's diminished role in an evolution toward cultural studies but rather literature's expanded horizon in a multicultural, multimedia world. Peter Brooks notes the many "shoulds" in the report and wonders what kind of imperatives they express, whether they be "intellectual, pedagogical, institutional, ethical?" Speaking as one of the authors of the report, I would say that we felt that the work of comparison demonstrates that such distinctions maintain the separation of domains that actually interpenetrate. We wanted to suggest that literary study as a form of intellectual critique should be ethically motivated both in its pedagogical practice and in its institutional formation.

To claim, as we do, that literature is one discursive practice among many is not to attack literature's specificity but to historicize it.[17] Literature's identity, its difference from the nonliterary, cannot be established according to absolute standards. If some kind of transcendental justification for literary value is desired, such as access to eternal verities or to the essence of human nature, then it is true that literature as we speak of it in the report fails to perform. But to say that literature is embedded in networks of material practices and that it is constructed differently in different contexts and at different historical moments is not to say that what is constructed in those contexts and at those moments is so relative that it can best be viewed as a deceptive illusion.

Literature is no more or less deceptive than other forms of cultural knowledge, but it constructs its knowledge otherwise, in a peculiar way. The report's statement that "the term 'literature' may no longer adequately describe our object of study" has suggested to some colleagues that we were ready to abandon this cherished peculiarity. Admittedly, the statement is poorly phrased, for our goal was not to jettison "literature" in favor of "culture" but rather to shift the boundaries of what is construed as peculiarly literary in our culture. Insofar as that shift broadens what we call "the space of comparison" to include many contexts in which literature is produced and consumed, certain colleagues have expressed apprehension lest the positivities of contexts be used to resolve the ambiguities of texts. But contexts can be just as ambiguous as texts, from which, given that contexts are to a large extent textually mediated, their difference is not clearcut.

That a context can, and should, be read and interpreted does not mean, however, that it has the same kind of highly wrought complexity as a literary work (though its degree of complexity may be comparable). Love of the text's dynamic complexity in its many modes of expression—rhetorical, narrative, moral, psychological, social—is what attracted most of us to the profession of teaching literature. Conviction that this complexity can only be fully appreciated and understood in the text's original articulation is what led us comparatists to immerse ourselves in the study of foreign languages. As the influence of social science models of gathering and reporting knowledge continues to grow, it becomes all the more important to defend the value of literature's peculiar ways of knowing and unknowing—such as indirection, paradox, fantasy, passion, irony, contradiction, extremity. One of the major tasks facing literary scholars today is a renewed articulation of the value of literature which respects both its individual, subjective aspects—among them, the sensual pleasure of verbal craftsmanship; the delightfully inconsequential play of reality and illusion; the temporary liberation from time and the entry into what Maurice Blanchot calls the space of one's own death—and its social and political implications and imbrications. Recent emphases on the latter modes have sometimes made the former seem almost suspect—too private, irresponsible, hedonistic. An effective defense of literature's value to the individual and to society will have to show that the two modes are inextricably and productively bound together.

Comparatists are best equipped to undertake this important task because of the breadth of their knowledge of literature's construction and function in different cultures. In the age of multiculturalism, the comparatist's anxiety has finally found a field adequate to the questions that generated it.[18]

Notes

1. René Wellek, "The Crisis of Comparative Literature," in *Concepts of Criticism*, ed. Stephen Nichols (New Haven: Yale University Press, 1963), 282.

2. Brooks is not alone among chairs unsure of just what they are chairing: Thomas Rosenmeyer, former chair of the Berkeley Comparative Literature Department, admits in a recent autobiographical essay that he is "not even sure what a comparatist is or does"

("Am I a Comparatist?" in *Building a Profession: Autobiographical Perspectives on the Beginnings of Comparative Literature in the United States*, ed. Lionel Grossman and Mihai I. Spariosu [Albany: State University of New York Press, 1994], 49).

3. Harry Levin, "Comparing the Literature," in *Grounds for Comparison* (Cambridge: Harvard University Press, 1972), 89.

4. François Jost, *Introduction to Comparative Literature* (New York: Bobbs-Merrill, 1974), xi.

5. A. Owen Aldridge, *Comparative Literature: Matter and Method* (Urbana: University of Illinois Press, 1969), 1.

6. Paul de Man, *Allegories of Reading* (New Haven: Yale University Press, 1979), 16.

7. In his provocative book *Cultural Capital: The Problem of Literary Canon Formation* (Chicago: University of Chicago Press, 1993), John Guillory argues that, in the context of a decline in the market value of the cultural capital that the old bourgeoisie had invested in literature, a rigorous deconstructive reading was rewarded because it involved technical work analogous to that undertaken by the new professional-managerial class that was dominating bureaucracies at all levels of governance, including the university.

8. J. Hillis Miller, "The Function of Literary Theory at the Present Time," in *The Future of Literary Theory*, ed. Ralph Cohen (New York: Routledge, 1989), 102.

9. See *Responses: On Paul de Man's Wartime Journalism*, ed. Werner Hamacher, Neil Hertz, and Thomas Keenan (Lincoln: University of Nebraska Press, 1989).

10. Henry Louis Gates, Jr., "Beyond the Culture Wars: Identities in Dialogue," in *Profession '93*, ed. Phyllis Franklin (New York: MLA, 1993), 6.

11. Peter Brooks, "Aesthetics and Ideology: What Happened to Poetics?" *Critical Inquiry* 20 (Spring 1994): 519. Hereafter abbreviated AI.

12. James Clifford, "Traveling Cultures," in *Cultural Studies*, ed. Lawrence Grossberg, Cary Nelson, and Paula Treichler (New York: Routledge, 1992), 96–112.

13. Kristin Ross, "The World Literature and Cultural Studies Program," *Critical Inquiry* 19 (Summer 1993): 666–76.

14. A good description of such a point of view is offered by Bruce Robbins, "Comparative Cosmopolitanism," *Social Text* 31–32 (1992): 168–86.

15. See Rey Chow, *Writing Diaspora: Tactics of Intervention in Contemporary Cultural Studies* (Bloomington: Indiana University Press, 1993), 133–34.

16. Peter Uwe Hohendahl, "*Germanistik* Past, Present, and Future," talk given at the Stanford colloquium "Disciplining Literature," May 6, 1994.

17. A similar point of view toward literary study is eloquently articulated in Stephen Greenblatt and Giles Gunn, introduction to *Redrawing the Boundaries: The Transformation of English and American Literary Studies* (New York: MLA, 1992), 1–11.

18. I would like to thank Charlie Altieri, Jonathan Arac, Howard Bloch, and Olga Matich for their helpful readings of this introduction in its first draft.

PART ONE

Three Reports to the American Comparative Literature Association

1

THE LEVIN REPORT, 1965

Report on Professional Standards

The recent proliferation of Comparative Literature, in colleges and universities throughout the country, could hardly have materialized without the support of the National Defense Education Act; but it marks the coming-of-age of a movement which has been spurred for some time by the revival of interest in language teaching, the introduction of programs and courses in great books, and the international cross-currents and exchanges of postwar years. It appears that our subject is now represented in the catalogues of about eighty academic institutions within the United States, according to the canvass of our Secretary, which continues to enlarge from term to term. More than half of these manifestations seem to have emerged within the last five to ten years, and may therefore still be considered as in a formative stage, though it is obvious that whatever trend they take will have great influence over the field as a whole. Members of the ACLA profess, broadly speaking, a set of common objectives. What is needed with some urgency, before our subject gets too thinly spread, is a set of minimal standards. A preliminary question arises as to whether it is necessarily desirable or practical that Comparative Literature be represented in every institution; whether it does not make special demands, in the way of linguistic preparation and intellectual perspective, which ought to reserve it for the more highly qualified students; and whether it does not presuppose an existing strength in language departments and libraries to which not very many colleges, and indeed not every university, can be fairly expected to measure up. At this point we venture to suggest that, where it is not yet represented in a curriculum, it should not be introduced without a good deal of institutional heart-searching and a careful scrutiny of the facilities and requirements elsewhere.

This brings us to a second question, instrumental in character and multiform in its possible answers: whether the representation of Comparative Literature within a faculty ought to take the form of a department, a subdepartment, or a committee. So far as these distinctions are merely nominal, they do not much matter; and there are many differences in local organization or specific personnel which justify a variety of approaches. What matters is to recognize that courses and programs in Comparative Literature are not designed to compete with those in the other departments of languages and literatures, but rather to augment and bridge them, and that there must consequently be a certain amount of departmental interdependence. In this sense, Comparative Literature must always be embodied in a kind of interdepartment, since it must draw upon the cooperation of specialists, generally through a member or members of a department of English, or modern languages, especially concerned with interrelationships; but this would seem to be a transitional pattern, leading toward some less ancillary arrangement. The interdepartmental committee would seem to be the most practical arrangement in the early years of a new program. There are at present very few professorial chairs which are wholly in Comparative Literature, and it may well be mutually helpful for the holder of such a chair—or for other appointees —to retain some footing in another department. However, an autonomous department may bring with it budgetary advantages, while administrative convenience may profit from the pattern of a central professor flanked by a number of cooperating colleagues. Perhaps we also need to consider here the relevance of other than literary disciplines: notably linguistics, folklore, art, music, history, philosophy, and possibly psychology, sociology, and anthropology. Our rigor in defining our own position should help us to clarify our interdisciplinary relationships.

Further clarification would also be helpful with regard to the course-offering. It is evident that, in many institutions where our official rubric is not used, courses that might otherwise be so designated are in the curriculum nonetheless—courses which cross the usual boundaries interposed by language, in dealing with such genres as the novel or such movements as the Renaissance. Now, where the approach is by way of a technique, such as the drama, or through the history of ideas, as in a course on the Enlightenment, there may be good excuse for studying works from a number of languages in translation. It is an exceptional undergraduate who can be expected to read works from more than one or two foreign languages in the original, albeit we should do as much as we can to cultivate such exceptions. Yet is it too much to expect that the teacher of literature, while not professing to be an expert in everything he teaches, should have some access to all the original languages involved? We need not be too much concerned with the problem of foreign literature in translation, if we distinguish clearly between such courses and courses in Comparative Literature; and, if the latter courses include a substantial proportion of work with the originals, it would be unduly puristic to exclude some reading from more remote languages in translation. A further distinction might conceivably by drawn between Humanities or World Literature or Great Books at the undergraduate level and Comparative Literature as a graduate discipline.

On the graduate level, it seems clear that much of the course-work in programs toward advanced degrees would have to be taken under the cooperating departments, where the sequences of literary history and the explication of individual texts can most relevantly be pursued. Far from seeking to replace such courses, we need them to build upon. On the other hand, these studies need to be integrated at some point by a series of seminars which bring together our students working in different literatures and focus on literary problems transcending national limits. For example, the history of criticism can help the student to define his terms and organize his knowledge, while exercise in translation, comparative metrics, and stylistic analysis could give him the most concrete experience in the relation of one language to another. Given the spread of our graduate students through differing courses and departments, according to their combination of interests in each case, it may be advisable to provide them all with one or two basic courses—let us say, proseminars in theory of literature and in textual methods or technical problems. Such courses often seem to attract, and profit from the presence of, the more adventurous students in other graduate fields. Comparative Literature performs a service for the other literary departments, and repays its incidental obligations to them, by widening the critical orientation of their students.

As to the desirability of an undergraduate major, there would seem to be more disparity here than anywhere else. The fact that the option is now available at about twenty places would seem to suggest that it is here to stay. There would seem to be general agreement that it should be relatively tough, admitting fit company even if few. The principal objection has been the language limitation for undergraduates; but even where the title of Comparative Literature is reserved for work at a more professional level, majors are sometimes open which involve a combination of languages—e.g., the Classics—or of an extra language with other relevant disciplines. More graduate programs in Comparative Literature would prefer that their candidates have solid training in a few languages, rather than that they have skimmed through a great many works in translation or literary history second hand. One or two universities still require the M.A. in a single field as a prerequisite to the Ph.D. in Comparative Literature; this implies an even dimmer view of the undergraduate major, and makes it rather difficult for the candidate to progress from the one-or-two language stage to the three-or-four. At the other extreme, it is noteworthy that a number of institutions have thus far been concentrating their efforts on a meaningful master's degree in the field of Comparative Literature itself.

At the doctoral level, most of us seem to agree that every candidate ought to have a strong major field around which to develop his comparative interests. Since there are not many posts in Comparative Literature, he should be competent enough to teach Spanish or Russian or whatever is taught in the particular department of his specialization. In other words, he should know one literature as a chronological whole and have some acquaintance with its philological background—i.e., the history of the language and a reading knowledge of its earlier texts. Then he should likewise know, within the limits of his special period or chosen concern, at least one and probably two minor fields. And, of course, we count on his curiosity regarding additional fields which he cannot be asked to master so fully, plus an informed concern with the methodology of criticism and scholarship. The value of a critical approach and the attractions of the modern period should not obscure the importance of sound historical training; a truly comparative method, after all, finds many points of reference in the past as well as among contemporaries. Certain auxiliary languages—notably French and German—will be important to the student, even if he does not specialize in their literatures; Greek and Latin are still of unique value to all exponents of Western culture, though Sanskrit or some other classical language has been relevantly substituted in the increasing number of programs where a span is attempted between Occidental and Oriental literature.

In a subject which thrives upon the diversity of the minds it attracts, no single canon ought to be laid down as the qualifications of candidates. Ideally speaking, they ought to possess both linguistic competence and critical aptitude to a high degree; in practice they often tend to be weighted somewhat more on one side or the other. We should seek for balance in this respect, just as we balance the counterclaims of coverage and depth. It should be frankly recognized that a Ph.D. in Comparative Literature may take longer to acquire than one in most of the separate areas of language and literature; and if a candidate has any hesitations between the straight degree and ours, he may well be encouraged to make the more traditional choice. If we profess to cover more ground than our sister departments we should honestly acknowledge that we must work harder, nor should we incur their suspicion by offering short-cuts. It almost goes without saying that our students should also be encouraged to take advantage of whatever opportunities come their way for study abroad. Still further, we may look forward to a time of development when they find it advantageous to move about more freely among the Comparative Literature programs in various American universities.

Since there has been some talk about an American school of Comparative Literature, we should like to reaffirm our belief in the internationalism of our field. For historic reasons which must be respected, certain countries have figured prominently in its pioneering investigations, as indeed have certain periods and types of relationship. In attempting to extend its scope and to utilize newer methods of interpretations, there is no reason why we should neglect what has been validly established by our predecessors and colleagues across the sea. On the contrary, it is largely because of America's cultural pluralism, above all its receptivity to Europeans and European ideas, that we have been enabled to develop centers for the study of Comparative Literature since the last war. A generation ago, this would have been looked upon as at best a supplement to the national literary histories, and as such a luxury for most academic communities. However, as the literary and linguistic disciplines have reconsidered their criteria and reorganized their curricula, it has been moving from the periphery toward a more and more centralizing role. We can scarcely overemphasize that our relationship with the sister departments should be one of close collaboration, rather than rivalry; that we should not be living up to our standards unless we are also fulfilling theirs; and that, if we succeed, we shall be realizing together the richest potential of the humanities.

Appendix: The Undergraduate Major

While recognizing that Comparative Literature is primarily a graduate discipline, we cannot help observing the steady growth of undergraduate programs in a variety of institutions across the country. The need for minimal standards in undergraduate programs in Comparative Literature is no less urgent than in the graduate area, but the circumstances and problems are basically different and warrant separate consideration.

We believe that, properly conceived and directed, undergraduate programs in Comparative Literature can make a useful contribution to the educational experience and growth of the student and can also serve as a sound basis for graduate study in Comparative Literature. It should be recognized, however, that not all institutions may or should wish to offer such programs, just as not every institution may wish to offer graduate training in Comparative Literature. A number of institutions may prefer, as at present, to represent the subject in the curriculum without making it available as a field of concentration. Where undergraduate programs in Comparative Literature are contemplated or already exist, we believe that certain minimal standards should be met:

I. *The Institution*
   1. It should have strong departments in both classical and modern languages and literatures. Variety and balance of specialization are particularly important.
   2. It should have at least one staff member with the doctorate in Comparative Literature or with equivalent training, who is directly connected with the program.
   3. It should have substantial library holdings in several languages and literatures.

II. *The Programs*
   1. An undergraduate program in Comparative Literature should meet the needs of students preparing for graduate work in Comparative Literature, as well as of other students interested in literary study.
   2. A sound program of offerings should include courses in the major periods, movements, and genres, and in special topics. For the latter, independent study is recommended.

III. *Minimum Requirements for the Undergraduate Major in Comparative Literature*
   1. Work of upper division caliber in at least two literatures, ancient or modern (one of which may be English), studied in the original languages.
   2. Study in depth of at least one literature.
   3. Where one of the literatures studied is English, students who plan to continue in graduate school will be expected to acquire a reading knowledge of a second language.
   4. Advanced undergraduate courses in Comparative Literature demanding considerable reading in original texts. These courses should provide training in the study of literature from an international perspective, and should be offered by a staff member trained in Comparative Literature.

5. Some acquaintance with the major writings of western literature from classical antiquity to the present.

IV. *Comparative Literature for the Non-Major*

1. As service courses, undergraduate courses in Comparative Literature are a legitimate and valuable part of liberal education.

2. The instructor should have the doctorate in Comparative Literature or a comparable background, and should be able to deal with all of the readings in their original text. Frequent recourse to the original text in class is strongly recommended.

3. The courses should be genuinely comparative. Courses exclusively in a single national literature should not be designated as courses in Comparative Literature.

4. Whenever possible, majors in Comparative Literature should be separated for instructional purposes from students who read exclusively in translation. When such separation is not possible, measures should be taken to insure reading in original texts by majors in Comparative Literature. It is particularly important for the instructor to make special provisions so that the presence of majors and of students without any foreign language ability in the same classroom will not affect standards of instruction.

We believe that, under proper circumstances, the undergraduate major in Comparative Literature can provide a solid foundation for graduate study. Its special advantage lies in its early inculcation of a comparative outlook and its emphasis on both breadth and depth as part of the student's undergraduate training. Students often come to Comparative Literature relatively late in their career; a strong undergraduate program can reinforce and support graduate training in comparative studies. It cannot be sufficiently emphasized, however, that study in Comparative Literature must proceed hand in hand with intensive work in the individual national literatures, at undergraduate as well as graduate levels.

A. O. Aldridge; Chandler B. Beall; Haskell Block; Ralph Freedman; Horst Frenz; J. C. La Drière; Alain Renoir; René Wellek; Harry Levin, *Chairman*

2

THE GREENE REPORT, 1975

A Report on Standards

I. When the Comparative Literature movement gathered strength in the U.S. during the two decades following World War II, it was dedicated to high goals. It wanted to stand, and in large part did stand, for a new internationalism: for broader perspectives on works and authors, for a European grasp of historical movements, for larger contexts in the tracking of motifs, themes, and types as well as larger understandings of genres and modes. It aimed also at the clarification of the great theoretical issues of literary criticism from a cosmopolitan vantage point. Within the academy, it wanted to bring together the respective European language departments in a new cooperation, reawakening them to the unity of their common endeavor, and embodying that unity in various ways, both customary and creative, which could mingle faculty and students across disciplinary boundaries. Beyond even these boundaries, the Comparative Literature movement wanted to explore the relationships of literature with the other arts and humanities: with philosophy, history, history of ideas, linguistics, music, art, and folklore among others. It did not of course minimize the strenuous sweep of its aspirations, and it did not perceive itself to be available to all students or even all universities. It defined itself as a discipline appropriate only to institutions endowed with excellent libraries, with consistently strong foreign language departments, and with gifted students combining linguistic depth with literary aptitude. This vision of a fresh and central academic discipline was ambitious in the noblest sense. It remains our common inheritance.

This seminal conception of Comparative Literature received a classic expression in a "Report on Professional Standards" written in 1965 and submitted to the ACLA by a committee of scholars chaired by Professor Harry

Levin. The Levin Report is notable for its balance, its judgment, and its elegance, yet its authors did not hesitate to defend a certain elitism which they perceived to be inherent in the nature of their subject. The Comparative Literature undergraduate major, they wrote, "should be relatively tough, admitting fit company even if few." They counselled against too rapid or too broad an expansion:

> A preliminary question arises as to whether it is necessarily desirable or practical that Comparative Literature be represented in every institution; whether it does not make special demands, in the way of linguistic preparation and intellectual perspective, which ought to reserve it for the more highly qualified students; and whether it does not presuppose an existing strength in language departments and libraries to which not very many colleges, and indeed not every university, can be fairly expected to measure up. At this point we venture to suggest that, where it is not yet represented in a curriculum, it should not be introduced without a good deal of institutional heart-searching and a careful scrutiny of the facilities and requirements elsewhere.

Significantly for the seventies, the report also distinguished between courses in Comparative Literature and courses in translation:

> We need not be too much concerned with the problem of foreign literature in translation, if we distinguish clearly between such courses and courses in Comparative Literature; and, if the latter courses include a substantial proportion of work with the originals, it would be unduly puristic to exclude some reading from more remote languages in translation. A further distinction might conceivably be drawn between Humanities or World Literature or Great Books at the undergraduate level and Comparative Literature as a graduate discipline.

The report called for competence in the teaching of a foreign language on the part of each Ph.D. It called for doctoral programs requiring harder work and longer study than those of neighboring departments, and it foresaw for us "a more and more centralizing role" within the university. It reflected, of course, a discipline which had bound its feet in the graduate schools of a few large universities and expected essentially to remain there. This has not in fact been the case. The "elitism", the pursuit of the highest standards within a few, small departments,—this ideal which seemed so desirable and so feasible ten years ago has been challenged for better or worse by rapid historical change. The Comparative Literature movement must now ask itself how much of its original vision it wants to preserve, how much change it wants to resist, how restrictive it should try to remain. These questions and others have prompted the present Report on Standards.

II. The evidence of change is everywhere about us, but it may be worth-while to survey a few determining facts. First, the fact of rapid growth. There are now "entities" (departments, programs, committees) administering Comparative Literature at 150 institutions in this country, a figure twice that when the Levin Report was submitted, and rising every year. A second fact is the heavy swing toward undergraduate teaching and indeed toward colleges with no graduate training. A third fact is the growth of Comparative Litera-ture programs whose staff contains no Ph.D. trained in the subject, programs depending on libraries whose holdings are modest, and supported by lan-guage departments not fully equipped for Comparative purposes. A fourth fact is the growth of the large lecture course teaching literature in translation which makes no linguistic demands upon its undergraduate audiences but seems to establish an equation between "World Literature" and "Comparative Literature." A fifth fact is the admission into graduate school of larger num-bers of matriculants than ever before, a fact that remains valid, so far as we can judge, despite the deteriorating job market. At least a few institutions number over a hundred students in residence. A sixth fact is the erosion, if not the withering, of the strength of foreign language departments in the wake of abolished requirements, an erosion which in some places may actually stem in part from the growing popularity of Comparative Literature courses. This trend is deeply ironic, since in fact Comparative Literature can only exist if it enjoys the support of neighboring disciplines and depends upon a continuing intimate relationship with them.

A final fact of a somewhat different order is the growth of interdisciplin-ary programs (American Studies, Medieval Studies, and so on) which like Comparative Literature attempt to bring together several traditional subjects but from a single dominant perspective. There has also arisen widespread and growing interest in the non-European literatures—Chinese, Japanese, San-skrit, Arabic, and many others less familiar, as well as those oral "literatures" of illiterate communities which are not properly described by our most basic term but for which we have no alternative. A new vision of *global* literature is emerging, embracing all the verbal creativity during the history of our planet, a vision which will soon begin to make our comfortable European perspec-tives parochial. Few Comparatists, few scholars anywhere, are prepared for the dizzying implications of this widening of horizons, but they cannot be ignored.

Against the challenging or disturbing signs of change can be set of course those trends and those continuities in which most Comparatists would rightfully take pride. Gifted young scholars have been trained, and well trained; valuable books have been written; first-rate departments flourish; the literary outlook of the American academy has become far more cosmopolitan. The Comparative Literature movement has not shamefully betrayed its origins. Yet there is cause, we believe, for serious concern lest the trends now transforming our discipline, taken in the aggregate, not debase those values on which it is founded. The slippage of standards, once allowed to accelerate, would be difficult to arrest. The causes of this transformation are not all of our own making. But we have reached a juncture which behooves us, singly and collectively, to take cognizance of a threat and to search our consciences.

The forthcoming "Nichols Report" on undergraduate programs refers to the extremely wide gap "in almost all instances" between the number of majors and the number of students enrolled in Comparative Literature courses. (In the examples there cited, the ratios range from 1–10 to 1–90.) This state of affairs is probably a given fact for the near future, and it allows for many interpretations. It may testify first of all to the rigor of the Comparative Literature major. But it may possibly also testify to a compromise with that rigor in the education of the less committed student. Reflecting on programs like that which reports 6 majors and 500 enrollments, we are tempted to discern there two faces of contemporary Comparative Literature—the one demanding and severe, the other accommodating, searching for its own place in the sun at its own institution. Apparently many comparatists throughout the country have tacitly accepted a trade-off in which large scale popularization with minimal requirements is accepted in exchange for the right to provide rigorous training for a small number of students. Much of the recent expansion of Comparative Literature, especially at the undergraduate level, seems to be based on an uneasy compromise between qualitative and quantitative norms, with the balance shifting more and more toward the quantitative rationale of large enrollments and relatively low instructional costs. In at least some colleges and universities Comparative Literature seems to be purveyed in the style of a smorgasbord at bargain rates.

The burgeoning of Comparative Literature in the colleges is potentially a development to give us satisfaction; it also mitigates the problems of placing our students. But the growth of undergraduate programs imposes responsibilities which are not always being met. Courses in translation are potentially of great value to the student, but if no one in the classroom, including the instructor, is in touch with the original language, then something precious has been lost to the learning experience, and something also of our Comparatist integrity. An examination of several college catalogues suggests that, at more than one institution, the titles of Comparative Literature course offerings do not exclude the dilettantish, the modish, even the frivolous.

The shift in our discipline's center of gravity was doubtless inherent from its beginnings in the logic of our academic and economic worlds. Our effort now is to absorb this shift without slackening our dedication to the best of our heritage. All of the changes we face raise questions about *standards* in the broadest sense: about the value of what we are doing and should be doing, about our function in the academic community and the larger intellectual community, about our responsibilities to our students, our colleagues, and ourselves. Standards are admittedly difficult to define; they permit finally no quantification; they depend ultimately on the judgment of each scholar. The scholar, in turn, sets the level of his standards primarily during his graduate training. By definition, any crisis of undergraduate training would be a crisis of graduate training. The authors of the present report cannot of course hope to resolve any of the issues facing our discipline. But they can hope to alert their colleagues to what they see as dangers; they can recommend academic norms and goals for the present which in their judgment perpetuate the best of the past; and they can suggest means by which the American Comparative Literature Association might affect the direction of standards in the future.

III. The first requisite for a healthy department or program in Comparative Literature is an adequate staff, and the second, following close upon it, is the department's relationship to other literature departments. Every department or program ought to include at least one and preferably two trained Comparatists on its staff, normally in positions of responsibility. Normally, the staff is enlarged by recourse to the strength of neighboring departments. One useful means of promoting collegiality between departments is the joint appointment, an arrangement which commonly promotes communications and properly supplies a structural basis for a spirit of co-operation.

Such a spirit is indeed crucial. Any Comparative Literature program must depend heavily on its neighboring departments of national literatures, indeed on all the Humanities departments at its institution. Without a strong English department and strong foreign language teaching, Comparative Literature cannot itself be strong. The present deterioration of support encountered by many graduate programs in the languages threatens our discipline with grave consequences. It is by no means certain that the enlargement of Comparative Literature programs can offset the decline of departments of foreign languages and literatures even when serious efforts are made to assume their specific functions. The decay of programs in foreign languages and literatures is bound to affect standards in Comparative Literature. Our relationships with our colleagues in these programs must in fact be symbiotic. Cooperation should occur at almost every level of departmental activity, both major and minor, central and modest, and it should occur in two directions. It goes without saying that cross-departmental freedom of enrollment is a necessary guarantee of vitality. Other examples include: the cross-listing of course offerings; the exchange of instructors to teach courses in neighboring departments; the borrowing of instructors for oral examinations; their use as co-directors of dissertations; their assistance in administering language examinations; their participation in colloquia, panel discussions, conferences, and similar activities. These are a few examples, but only examples; the crucial element is that spirit of collegiality which is implicit in the very term *university* as well as *college*. Without this spirit of fraternal participation in a common humane endeavor, Comparative Literature cannot thrive; indeed it cannot exist as a dynamic enterprise.

A major responsibility of a graduate program in Comparative Literature is to admit only that number of capable students it can truly educate as they deserve, as the discipline requires, and as available fellowship funds permit. Wholesale admission of students by institutions with little or no fellowship support is, we believe, reprehensible. Few universities in the seventies can offer blanket four-year support, as some did in the sixties, but some assistance toward the most needy and most gifted abbreviates the long test of stamina which graduate study can become. It is wiser to admit a realistic number of students among whom available support can be meaningfully distributed, than a number so large that a sense of community is lost and study becomes associated with penury.

Overpopulation in our graduate schools will be reduced if we weigh scrupulously the credentials of each applicant for admission. A critical criterion of each applicant's preparation is his acquaintance with foreign languages. Normally, he or she should bring to graduate study considerable knowledge of at least two languages; after one or two years, this number should rise to three. Of these, one should be an ancient language. Thus, by the time the student begins his dissertation, he should be capable of dealing with texts in at least four literatures, including English. In addition to these

linguistic requirements, which should be stringently maintained, some philological training is highly desirable. Most graduate programs, moreover,
continue to require a single major language and literature, and in view of the
present job market this requirement seems to rest on solid logic. Since it tends
to direct students toward positions in single language departments and thus
toward the teaching of elementary language courses, it further increases the
need for strong linguistic training.

To be admitted into a graduate program, a candidate ought to be able to
offer two other acquirements in addition to linguistic proficiency. He or she
must have had extensive undergraduate instruction in at least one literature,
and preferably in two. Such instruction should include training in the analysis
of texts, as well as in the forms, meters, traditions, genres,—the idiom and
particularity of the literature or literatures he has chosen to learn. This ac-
quirement already implies a second: a lively awareness of the past itself.
Despite some tendencies to permit students a nearly exclusive engagement
with the present century, Comparative Literature as a discipline rests unalterably on the knowledge of history. The student who wants to specialize in
Twentieth Century literature needs to know just as much about the past as his
fellow students, if he is truly to understand his chosen period. Arguably, he
needs to know more, since the cultural inheritance of our century is in the
nature of things richer than any earlier period's.

These strictures also apply of course to the actual list of courses offered by
the department itself. Any such list will inevitably depend on the interests and
competencies of those instructors who are available. But gifted students do
deserve certain minimal elements in their graduate study: a course or series of
courses in methodology and theory; a range of period courses which includes
the remote as well as recent past; the opportunity to encounter various critical
and scholarly approaches; the opportunity to work with various literary
genres and sub-genres; the opportunity to study linguistics, philology, and
esthetics. No single student will be able to pursue all his options, especially if
he is encouraged to select courses in other literature departments, but a
judiciously rich sampling of available courses will facilitate his preparation
for his oral examination during the third year and for his dissertation that
follows.

At some point during his graduate career, the student's performance
needs to be evaluated, not only for its mere adequacy but also for its real
promise. It is unfair to the student, to the department, and to a profession
afflicted with unemployment, to retain in the academy the weak and the
mediocre. We urge the directors and staff of graduate programs to give this

question of retention serious periodic scrutiny. Mediocrity in our student population is clearly bound to affect in time the quality of undergraduate as well as graduate study. If the requirement of the dissertation keeps its appropriate stringency—that is, if the dissertation is held to firm standards of scope, substance, and originality—then the weak student is likely to discover too late that the degree is beyond him. The risk, all too often, once the mediocre student has reached this stage, is to tailor the project to his abilities. Editions of texts are acceptable as dissertations in our view, only when accompanied by introductions of substantial length and substance: a minimum might be seventy five pages. We perform no favor either to the student, the institution, or the profession if we allow work of questionable quality to be rewarded with a doctorate. Here is an area where the judgment of colleagues in neighboring departments is especially useful.

At the undergraduate level, the most disturbing recent trend is the association of Comparative Literature with literature in translations. Many courses taught today under the rubric of Comparative Literature are not in fact properly labeled. The college lecturer who is truly a Comparatist should at the very least have read the text he is teaching in the original, and should *use* this experience to advantage in the classroom. He should also draw on the insights of those members of the class who are able to dispense with translations. Indeed, by his frequent references to the original, he should make the remaining students aware of the incompleteness of their own reading experience. Beyond the individual classroom, however, a larger problem lies in the narrowing assumptions about undergraduate Comparative Literature increasingly shared by dean, chairman, instructor, and student alike. No response to this situation would be more effective, in our judgment, than to reaffirm our support for the Appendix to the Levin Report on "The Undergraduate Major." This important document, never more pertinent than today, makes the crucial distinctions:

> Whenever possible, majors in Comparative Literature should be separated for instructional purposes from students who read exclusively in translation. When such separation is not possible, measures should be taken to insure reading in original texts by majors in Comparative Literature.

We would recommend the dissemination of this Appendix by whatever means are available, including publication in the Newsletters of the American Comparative Literature Association and the Modern Language Association. It should be of particular use to institutions which are now organizing or reorganizing their programs. Not all directors of doctoral programs are convinced that the undergraduate major is the best preparation for graduate study in Comparative Literature, however admirable it may be for general and liberal education.

As for the burgeoning of cross-disciplinary programs, we believe that Comparatists should welcome them. They have a salutary role to play in re-organizing our patterns of knowledge; we should be able to learn from them as well as contribute our own perspectives. But we must also be alert lest the crossing of disciplines involve a relaxing of discipline. Misty formulations, invisible comparisons, useless ingenuities, wobbly historiography plague all fields in the Humanities, including our own: cross-disciplinary programs are not immune from them. As participants, we need to muster the theoretical sophistication, the methodological rigor, the peculiar awareness of historical complexities our special training affords us.

The growth of interest in the non-European literatures is another devel-opment we can welcome, while cautiously searching for ways to accommo-date this interest to our own traditions. In the cases of literatures produced by peoples in contact with Europe, this accommodation is easy. Many depart-ments allow the substitution of Hebrew for Latin or Greek as a required foreign language; the acquisition of Arabic is logical for those with Hispanic interests. But for the study of those literatures further-flung from Europe and the Americas, perhaps all that can reasonably be said today is that meth-odological prudence must be tempered with flexibility. We are still lacking the concepts and tools that will permit us truly to study literature at the global level. These concepts and tools will gradually materialize. While waiting and searching for them, we must beware of ever again confusing "world litera-ture" with the literature of our inherited culture, however rich; conversely, while working toward global perspectives, we will still need the virtues of precision and integrity our inherited culture has taught us. It goes without saying that we cannot begin to absorb the wealth of exotic literatures before firmly possessing our own.

IV. Because Comparative Literature is inherently an arduous discipline, because some of the trends threatening to alter it will probably continue to gather strength, and because we believe the American Comparative Literature Association cannot ignore the danger of diluted excellence, we recommend the creation of a permanent Evaluation Committee. Such a committee should be chaired by a senior scholar of outstanding reputation, and it should in-clude as many as fifteen Comparatists chosen for their distinction, their judgment, their fairness, and their geographical distribution across the country. Each member might be asked to serve for a renewable term of three years. The existence of this committee would be publicized by the ACLA Newsletter, by the MLA Newsletter, by letters from the ACLA Secretariat to chairmen and deans, and possibly by other means. A small number—perhaps two—of the committee's members could be delegated to visit a given department or program of Comparative Literature, *when and only when* the committee was invited by the institution in question. The delegation would normally spend two days at the host institution, considering such matters as curriculum, staffing, the design of the undergraduate major (if one exists) and of the graduate program, enrollments, relations with other literature departments, and other relevant matters. After deliberating, the visitors would submit a thorough report to the appropriate chairman and dean, a second copy would be retained by the Chairman of the Evaluation Committee, who would be expected to submit periodic reports of the activity of the Committee to the Secretariat for publication in the *Newsletter*. There is reason to believe that funding for this committee might be available from the National Endowment for the Humanities. If not, the expenses of the evaluators would be paid by the host institution. Many public and private universities seek out such authoritative evaluations periodically as a matter of course. The creation of the standing Evaluation Committee we recommend might increase the number of such invitations; it would ensure the solid professional calibre of the visitors; and it would provide the ACLA Secretariat with information about specific programs. It ought to be particularly useful in assisting those institutions which want to initiate new programs, not a few of which come to the Secretary's attention every year.

Other means of preserving standards will occur to members of the ACLA. However subtle or however stringent they may be, we venture to suggest they ought to be understood as assisting institutions and departments and individual scholars, toward an excellence whose vision is shared almost everywhere if seldom achieved anywhere. For the individual teacher-scholar, the hard requirement is to be responsible in so many directions: to his profession, to the institution and department that hired him, to his students, to the past, to the texts he is entrusted with, and to himself. In the face of so many various and sometimes counter obligations, it is difficult to stay humane. The professional society can perhaps hope to help that individual scholar and his chairman toward a more humane pedagogy despite assorted barbarisms; ultimately the society will have to depend on the scholar's respect for the men and ideals that preceded him and that he himself re-evaluates, continuously and creatively.

Submitted to the American Comparative Literature Association by the Committee on Professional Standards: Haskell Block; Nan Carpenter; Frederic Garber; François Jost; Walter Kaiser; Elizabeth Trahan; Herbert Weisinger; Thomas Greene, *Chairman.*

3

THE BERNHEIMER REPORT, 1993

Comparative Literature at the
Turn of the Century

Of Standards and Disciplines

This is the third Report on Standards written for the ACLA and distributed in accordance with its bylaws. The first report, published in 1965, was prepared by a committee chaired by Harry Levin; the second, published in 1975, was the product of a committee chaired by Thomas Greene. The visions of comparative literature set out in these two documents are strikingly similar. Indeed, Greene's report does not so much articulate new goals and possibilities for comparative literature as it defends the standards proposed by Levin against perceived challenges. Together, the Levin and Greene reports strongly articulate the conception of the discipline which prevailed through much of the 1950s, 1960s, and 1970s. Many of the current members of the ACLA received their doctorates from departments that adhered to the standards defined in these reports. But the historical, cultural, and political contexts in which these same comparatists are now working, and the issues many of them are addressing, have changed so markedly from the time of their professional training that actual practices in the field have transformed it. Our report will address the issue of standards in the context of this profound transformation.

In order to clarify what we perceive to be the direction of this disciplinary evolution, we will begin with a brief analysis of the previous two reports. Both attribute the rapid growth of comparative literature in this country after World War II to a new internationalist perspective that sought, in Greene's phrase, "larger contexts in the tracking of motifs, themes, and types as well as larger understandings of genres and modes." This impulse to expand the horizon of literary studies may well have derived from a desire to demonstrate the essential unity of European culture in the face of its recent violent disruption. The broadened perspective, in any case, did not often reach beyond Europe and Europe's high-cultural lineage going back to the civilizations of classical antiquity. Indeed, comparative literary studies tended to reinforce an identification of nation-states as imagined communities with national languages as their natural bases.

This focus on national and linguistic identities is apparent in the way both the Levin and Greene reports address the notion of standards. High standards are necessary, they argue, in order to defend the elite character of the discipline, which, says Levin, "ought to reserve it for the more highly qualified students" and restrict it to large research universities with excellent language departments and libraries. Noting that "this ideal which seemed so desirable and so feasible ten years ago has been challenged for better or worse by rapid historical change," Greene goes on to argue the case for resistance to change. "There is cause," he writes, "for serious concern lest the trends now transforming our discipline, taken in the aggregate, not debase those values on which it is founded. The slippage of standards, once allowed to accelerate, would be difficult to arrest."

The greatest perceived threat is to the very basis of comparative literature's elite image, the reading and teaching of foreign language works in the original. Greene criticizes the increasing use of translations by professors in world literature courses who do not know the original languages. The use of translations is condemned in both the Levin and Greene reports, though Levin admits that, as long as comparative literature courses "include a substantial proportion of work with the originals, it would be unduly puristic to exclude some reading from more remote languages in translation." This statement illustrates the extent to which the traditional internationalist notion of comparative literature paradoxically sustains the dominance of a few European national literatures. Europe is the home of the canonical originals, the proper object of comparative study; so-called remote cultures are peripheral to the discipline and thence can be studied in translation.

Another threat to comparative literature, according to Greene, is the growth of interdisciplinary programs. Although he says we should welcome this development, Greene's emphasis is cautionary: "We must also be alert," he writes, "lest the crossing of disciplines involve a relaxing of discipline." "Crossing" here plays the same role in respect to disciplinary rigor as does "translation" in respect to linguistic purity. There is an effort to restrict the work of comparison within the limits of a single discipline and to discourage any potentially messy carrying over or transference from discipline to discipline. Just as comparative literature serves to define national entities even as it puts them in relation to one another, so it may also serve to reinforce disciplinary boundaries even as it transgresses them.

A third major threat to the founding values of comparative literature may be read between the lines of the Greene report: the increasing prominence in the seventies of comparative literature departments as the arenas for the study of (literary) theory. Although the theory boom was fostered in English and French departments as well, the comparatist's knowledge of foreign languages offered access not only to the original texts of influential European theoreticians but also to the original versions of the philosophical, historical, and literary works they analyzed. The problem in this development for the traditional view of comparative literature was that the diachronic study of literature threatened to become secondary to a largely synchronic study of theory. "Comparative Literature as a discipline rests unalterably on the knowledge of history," writes Greene in an implicit rebuke to the wave of theorizing overtaking the field.

The anxieties about change articulated in the Greene report suggest that, already in 1975, the field was coming to look disturbingly foreign to some of its eminent authorities. Their reaction tended to treat the definition and enforcement of standards as constitutive of the discipline. But the dangers confronting the discipline thus constructed have only intensified in the seventeen years since the publication of the Greene report, to the point that, in the opinion of this committee, the construction no longer corresponds to the practices that currently define the field. We feel, therefore, that our articulation of standards can be undertaken responsibly only in the context of a redefinition of the discipline's goals and methods. We base this redefinition not on some abstract sense of the discipline's future but rather on directions already being followed by many departments and programs around the country.

Renewing the Field

The apparent internationalism of the postwar years sustained a restrictive Eurocentrism that has recently been challenged from multiple perspectives. The notion that the promulgation of standards could serve to define a discipline has collapsed in the face of an increasingly apparent porosity of one discipline's practices to another's. Valuable studies using the traditional models of comparison are still being produced, of course, but these models belong to a discipline that by 1975 already felt defensive and beleaguered. The space of comparison today involves comparisons between artistic productions usually studied by different disciplines; between various cultural constructions of those disciplines; between Western cultural traditions, both high and popular, and those of non-Western cultures; between the pre- and postcontact cultural productions of colonized peoples; between gender constructions defined as feminine and those defined as masculine, or between sexual orientations defined as straight and those defined as gay; between racial and ethnic modes of signifying; between hermeneutic articulations of meaning and materialist analyses of its modes of production and circulation; and much more. These ways of contextualizing literature in the expanded fields of discourse, culture, ideology, race, and gender are so different from the old models of literary study according to authors, nations, periods, and genres that the term "literature" may no longer adequately describe our object of study.

In this unstable and rapidly evolving sociocultural environment, many of the scholars involved in rethinking the field of comparison have an increasingly uneasy relation to the practices called "comparative literature." They feel alienated because of the continued association of these practices, intellectually and institutionally, with standards that construct a discipline almost unrecognizable in the light of their actual methods and interests. One sign of this disaffection is that many colleagues whose work would fit into an expanded definition of the field do not have an institutional affiliation with comparative literature and are not members of the ACLA. Another sign is the discussion that has occurred on some campuses about the possibility of adding a phrase such as "and Cultural Studies," "and Cultural Critique," or "and Cultural Theory" to the departmental or program title in order to suggest ways in which the old designation may be inadequate. But such name changes have not been widely adopted, largely, we feel, because of a general belief that these new ways of reading and contextualizing should be incorporated into the very fabric of the discipline. In the rest of this report we hope to give a sense of how this incorporation will enable comparative literature to position itself as a productive locus for advanced work in the humanities.

The Graduate Program

1. Literary phenomena are no longer the exclusive focus of our discipline. Rather, literary texts are now being approached as one discursive practice among many others in a complex, shifting, and often contradictory field of cultural production. This field challenges the very notion of interdisciplinarity, to the extent that the disciplines were historically constructed

to parcel up the field of knowledge into manageable territories of professional expertise. Comparatists, known for their propensity to cross over between disciplines, now have expanded opportunities to theorize the nature of the boundaries to be crossed and to participate in their remapping. This suggests, among other fundamental adjustments, that comparative literature departments should moderate their focus on high-literary discourse and examine the entire discursive context in which texts are created and such heights are constructed. The production of "literature" as an object of study could thus be compared to the production of music, philosophy, history, or law as similar discursive systems.

Our recommendation to broaden the field of inquiry—already implemented by some programs and departments—does not mean that comparative study should abandon the close analysis of rhetorical, prosodic, and other formal features but that textually precise readings should take account as well of the ideological, cultural, and institutional contexts in which their meanings are produced. Likewise, the more traditional forms of interdisciplinary work, such as comparisons between the sister arts, should occur in a context of reflection on the privileged strategies of meaning making in each discipline, including its internal theoretical debates and the materiality of the medium it addresses.

2. The knowledge of foreign languages remains fundamental to our raison d'être. Comparatists have always been people with an exceptional interest in foreign languages, an unusual ability to learn them, and a lively capacity to enjoy using them. These qualities should continue to be cultivated in our students. Moreover, they should be encouraged to broaden their linguistic horizons to encompass at least one non-European language.

Precise language requirements will vary from department to department. We feel that the minimum to be expected is the study of two literatures in the original language, a good reading knowledge of two foreign languages, and, for students of older fields of European, Arabic, or Asian cultures, the acquisition of an ancient "classical" language. Some departments still require as many as three foreign languages plus a classical language. Many require a knowledge of three literatures. In any case, the context for these requirements should extend beyond their value for the analysis of literary meaning to their value for understanding the role of a native tongue in creating subjectivity, in establishing epistemological patterns, in imagining communal structures, in forming notions of nationhood, and in articulating resistance and accommodation to political and cultural hegemony. Moreover, comparatists should be alert to the significant differences *within* any national culture, which provide a basis for comparison, research, and critical-theoretical inquiry. Among these are differences (and conflicts) according to region, ethnicity, religion, gender, class, and colonial or postcolonial status. Comparatist research is ideally suited to pursue ways in which these differences are conjoined with differences in language, dialect, and usage (including jargon or slang) as well as with problems of dual- or multiple-language use and modes of hybridization.

3. While the necessity and unique benefits of a deep knowledge of foreign languages must continue to be stressed, the old hostilities toward translation should be mitigated. In fact, translation can well be seen as a paradigm for larger problems of understanding and interpretation across different discursive traditions. Comparative literature, it could be said, aims to explain both what is lost and what is gained in translations between the distinct value systems of different cultures, media, disciplines, and institutions. Moreover, the comparatist should accept the responsibility of locating the particular place and time at which he or she studies these practices: Where do I speak from, and from what tradition(s), or countertraditions? How do I translate Europe or South America or Africa into a North American cultural reality, or, indeed, North America into another cultural context?

4. Comparative literature should be actively engaged in the comparative study of canon formation and in reconceiving the canon. Attention should also be paid to the role of noncanonical readings of canonical texts, readings from various contestatory, marginal, or subaltern perspectives. The effort to produce such readings, given prominence recently in, for example, feminist and postcolonial theory, complements the critical investigation of the process of canon formation—how literary values are created and maintained in a particular culture—and vitalizes the attempt to expand canons.

5. Comparative literature departments should play an active role in furthering the multicultural recontextualization of Anglo-American and European perspectives. This does not mean abandoning those perspectives but rather questioning and resisting their dominance. This task may necessitate a significant reevaluation both of our self-definition as scholars and of the usual standards for comparative work. It may be better, for instance, to teach a work in translation, even if you don't have access to the original language, than to neglect marginal voices because of their mediated transmission. Thus we not only endorse Levin's remark, quoted earlier, that it would be "unduly puristic" to require all reading in comparative literature courses to be done in the original, we would even condone certain courses on minority literatures in which the majority of the works were read in translation. (Here it should be

acknowledged that minority literatures also exist within Europe; Eurocentricity in practice entails a focus on English, French, German, and Spanish literatures. Even Italian literature, with the exception of Dante, is often marginalized.) Similarly, anthropological and ethnographic models for the comparative study of cultures may be found as suitable for certain courses of study as models derived from literary criticism and theory. Department and program chairs should actively recruit faculty from non-European literature departments and from allied disciplines to teach courses and to collaborate in broadening the cultural scope of comparative literature offerings. In all contexts of its practice, multiculturalism should be approached not as a politically correct way of acquiring more or less picturesque information about others whom we don't really want to know but as a tool to promote significant reflection on cultural relations, translations, dialogue, and debate.

Thus conceived, comparative literature has some affinities with work being done in the field of cultural studies. But we should be wary of identifying ourselves with that field, where most scholarship has tended to be monolingual and focused on issues in specific contemporary popular cultures.

6. Comparative literature should include comparisons between media, from early manuscripts to television, hypertext, and virtual realities. The material form that has constituted our object of study for centuries, the book, is in the process of being transformed through computer technology and the communications revolution. As a privileged locus for cross-cultural reflection, comparative literature should analyze the material possibilities of cultural expression, both phenomenal and discursive, in their different epistemological, economic, and political contexts. This wider focus involves studying not only the business of bookmaking but also the cultural place and function of reading and writing and the physical properties of newer communicative media.

7. The pedagogical implications of the points previously outlined should be explored in courses, colloquia, and other forums sponsored by departments and programs of comparative literature. Professors from different disciplines should be encouraged to join faculty in comparative literature to team-teach courses that explore the intersections of their fields and methodologies. Active support should be given to colloquia in which faculty and students discuss interdisciplinary and cross-cultural topics. In such contexts, the cultural diversity of both the student body and faculty can usefully become a subject of reflection and an agent promoting increased sensitivity to cultural differences.

8. All of the above suggests the importance of theoretically informed thinking to comparative literature as a discipline. A comparatist's training should provide a historical basis for this thinking. Early in their careers, probably in their first year, graduate students should be required to take a course in the history of literary criticism and theory. This course should be designed to show how the major issues have developed and been modified through the centuries and to give students the background necessary to evaluate contemporary debates in their historical contexts.

The Undergraduate Program

1. As the discipline evolves at the graduate level, more undergraduate courses will naturally reflect these changes in perspective. For instance, comparative literature courses should teach not just "great books" but also how a book comes to be designated as "great" in a particular culture, that is, what interests have been and are invested in maintaining this label. More advanced courses might occasionally focus class discussion on current controversies about such matters as Eurocentrism, canon formation, essentialism, colonialism, and gender studies. The new multicultural composition of many of our classrooms should be actively engaged as a pedagogical stimulus for discussion of these matters.

2. Requirements for the major should offer a flexible set of options. One way of defining these, now adopted at many institutions, is: (a) two foreign literatures, with two languages required; (b) two literatures, one of which may be anglophone; and (c) a nonanglophone literature and another discipline. In order to move with some concrete preparation into issues of translation beyond the European cultural matrix, students should be encouraged to study languages such as Arabic, Hindi, Japanese, Chinese, or Swahili. Comparative literature departments and programs will need to argue for courses in such languages and will have to find ways in which their literatures can be included in the undergraduate major.

3. Undergraduate programs should offer a range of courses that study relations between Western and non-Western cultures, and all majors should be required to take some of these. These and other comparative literature courses should engage students in theoretical reflection on the methods of accomplishing such study. There is also a need for undergraduate courses in contemporary literary theory.

4. Whenever they have knowledge of the original language, teachers in comparative literature courses should refer frequently to the original text of a

work they assign in translation. Moreover, they should make discussion of the theory and practice of translation an integral part of these courses.

5. Comparative literature faculty need to alert themselves and their students to related subject areas in their institutions outside the discipline— linguistics, philosophy, history, media studies, film studies, art history, cultural studies—and to encourage extradisciplinary migrations and crossovers.

Conclusion

We feel that comparative literature is at a critical juncture in its history. Given that our object of study has never had the kind of fixity which is determined by national boundaries and linguistic usage, comparative literature is no stranger to the need to redefine itself. The present moment is particularly propitious for such a review, since progressive tendencies in literary studies, toward a multicultural, global, and interdisciplinary curriculum, are comparative in nature. Students of comparative literature, with their knowledge of foreign languages, training in cultural translations, expertise in dialogue across disciplines, and theoretical sophistication, are well positioned to take advantage of the broadened scope of contemporary literary studies. Our report puts forward some guiding ideas about the way curricula can be structured in order to expand students' perspectives and stimulate them to think in culturally pluralistic terms.

A word of caution is in order, however. Although we believe that "comparison" as defined here represents the wave of the future, the economic uncertainties of the present are currently holding that wave back at many universities and colleges. Budgetary restrictions have caused literature departments to define their needs in conservative ways, making it all the more important that comparative literature students be able to demonstrate solid training in their primary national literature. Given the unpredictable character of the current job market, it is more important than ever that students begin to think early in their graduate careers about the professional profile they will present and that professors offer them counsel at every stage of their studies about the shaping of their professional identity. This recommendation does not represent a cynical giving in to market forces but a recognition that we are in a transitional period and that comparatists need to be alert to the shifting economic and sociopolitical landscape in which they are operating.

This said, we feel that the new directions we have advocated for the field will keep it in the forefront of humanistic studies, and we look forward to the challenges future developments will bring.

Respectfully submitted,
Charles Bernheimer, *Chair*; Jonathan Arac; Marianne Hirsch; Ann Rosalind
Jones; Ronald Judy; Arnold Krupat; Dominick LaCapra; Sylvia Molloy; Steve
Nichols; Sara Suleri
May 1993

PART TWO

Three Responses to the
Bernheimer Report at
the MLA Convention, 1993

4

GEIST STORIES

K. ANTHONY APPIAH

When I first came to this continent, the Yale Afro-American Studies office where I hung out was in a building that also contained the office of Professor Emeritus René Wellek. From time to time the great man was pointed out to me by one colleague or other. Prompted by the reverential tone adopted by those who drew him to my notice, I acquired and read a volume of his essays and browsed his monumental history of criticism. And then one day I heard he was to give a lecture in the Sterling Library. For some reason—I think I had a class to attend, but perhaps I had some other pressing obligation—I was unable to arrive at the start of the lecture. But I rushed over as soon as I was free. As I pushed gently on the swing doors at the end of the hall, I heard—or, at least, I think I heard—a voice that sounded Mittel Europäisch pronouncing a dozen or so words. These words have stuck with me since, even though I can no longer be sure that I really heard them. What I think I heard was: " . . . the life of reason, which is the life of the spirit." That was it. The last words of the peroration. Tumultuous applause followed. I never had a chance to hear Wellek again.

I remember thinking, at the time, as my irritation at arriving late for the feast subsided, that "spirit" was not the right word for what was obviously "*Geist*." But I admired (if I did not share) the confidence that allowed Wellek to characterize the life of the *Geist*, even if I had missed the substance of the characterization.

I suppose the life of the *Geist*, in this technical sense, is, indeed, almost by definition the life of Reason. And for Wellek, I imagine, both literature and its criticism are expressions of the life of the *Geist*. But I confess that I think of the life of what we now call literature as having as little to do with reason as most of the rest of our lives; and while the criticism of literature may often have claimed to be the home of reason in the past, I do not think of reflection on reason as a central part of criticism's task. In this I imagine myself typical of our academy in our age.

Wellek's *Geist*—no one, I hope, will take very seriously my pinning this fantasy on Wellek's eleven words—was, I imagine, somewhat like Hegel's. It was singular: it had flown from Greece to Rome and then on into the northern forests, residing eventually in what might once have been called the heartlands of the Saxon and Romance races. To follow the poets and philosophers through whom the *Geist* made itself manifest—here in our interpretative dusk with Minerva's owl—you would therefore ideally know Greek and Latin, German and French. Italian would be easy enough if you knew Latin and French, and the *Geist*'s rare trips to the Iberian Peninsula probably wouldn't necessitate a knowledge of Spanish, never mind Portuguese. Hebrew, Sanskrit, and Arabic might be interesting because their literary and philosophical traditions were connected in interesting ways at various points with Europe's. Something very like the *Geist* may have traveled also through the long literate history of China and its cultural heirs in Japan and the Korean peninsula, but this spirit, the shadow-*Geist* of East Asia, had its own life and one could responsibly follow the Western *Geist* without much attention to it.

Following that *Geist* was already, then, a pretty demanding vocation. When, in 1965, Wellek signed off on the first of the American Comparative Literature Association's Reports on Professional Standards, he endorsed a document that was actually quite clear in insisting on the difficulty of the task, the special election of those who pursued it, and the high standards they must meet. ("It should be frankly recognized that a Ph.D. in Comparative Literature may take longer to acquire than one in most of the separate areas of language and literature; and if a candidate has any hesitations between the straight degree and ours, he may well be encouraged to make the more traditional choice.") But it was also rather vague about what the task exactly was.

Comparative literature involved the study of ancient languages: Greek and Latin ("of unique value to all exponents of Western culture"); Sanskrit for those interested in attempting "a span" between Occidental and Oriental literature; but no mention of Hebrew. It required, for an anglophone, some modern languages other than English: "Spanish or Russian or whatever is taught in the particular language of his [*sic*] specialization," along with French and German, not simply for their literatures and cultural histories, but as languages of scholarship. (Note that while the ideal scholar in the field met these polyglot desiderata, he or she might nevertheless have a single language of specialization. Adequate knowledge of the literature in *this* language should involve—and I'm quoting now—its history "as a chronological whole and . . . its philological background.") Finally, comparative literature entailed, also, an openness not only to the English and foreign language departments but to "linguistics, folklore, art, music, history, philosophy, and possibly psychology, sociology, and anthropology."

If these linguistic and disciplinary tools might all be relevant, it was because what distinguished the comparative literature specialists from some others who teach literature from a comparable range of sources was that they addressed texts in their original languages and in the context of the cultural histories of their authors and would, for example, certainly never teach texts (save the occasional "more remote" item) in translation which they had not read in the original. This was in part because, where the student could not read the original, he or she needed to be told about features of the text in the original language. The paraphrasable—the translatable—content would never be enough.

For graduate education, both the history of criticism and the theory of literature, on the one hand, and such necessarily interlinguistic activities as translation, comparative metrics, and stylistic analysis, on the other, would provide the common core of knowledge, the disciplinary language, of the field.

It seems to me that despite its abstractness, the first Report on Standards defines an identifiable project. It is not intellectual history, because it focuses on the "literariness" of texts—the property which, in Paul de Man's formula, "emerges" in a reading that "foregrounds the rhetorical over the grammatical and the logical function" (*The Resistance to Theory* [Minneapolis: University of Minnesota Press, 1986], 14). It is not English (or Spanish or Russian or whatever) literary study, because it demands a context of literary writings in other languages, while they merely permit such multilingualism. Nor, finally, is it the study of literariness as such—what de Man, in an influential formulation, saw as the project of theory—because if (as I myself doubt) that can be explored, its exploration can (at least in principle) go on in a single language; whereas the study of literariness is a universal project, engaging, if it is correct, texts in any human language, and it is not inherently a comparative project. Theory may be useful in comparative literary study, but it is not the goal of it.

As the third and most recent Report on Standards indicates, the second report is fundamentally in tune with the first, in its conception of the task of comparative literature. Its authors seem more conscious, however, of the pressure of the world outside the West. Where the first report gestures toward Sanskrit and the Oriental, the internationalism of which it boasts is the internationalism of the Treaty of Rome: the nations in question are largely those of western Europe, with the occasional diversion into literatures, like those of Russia, which have for some time been part—if only in translation—of the reading of the educated western European bourgeoisies. In the second report, in the mid-seventies, the "new vision of *global* literature is emerging, embracing all the verbal creativity during the history of our planet, a vision which will soon begin to make our comfortable European perspectives parochial." Nevertheless, the authors went on, "Our effort now is to absorb this shift without slackening our dedication to the best of our heritage."

The "we" whose heritage is here in question encompasses, of course, all the heirs of Western civilization, because, as the most recent report rightly observes, the older comparative literature, in stressing its inter-*nation*-alism, "paradoxically sustains the domination of a few European national literatures." The paradox, for me, is not so much that it is *European* literatures whose domination it sustains, but that it sustains them *as national* literatures. Shakespeare's cultural context is, of course, English; but his literary context includes, as we all know, classical and Italian Renaissance sources. Goethe's world contains Newton as much as it contains Heine. The connections between and among Europe's literatures which make comparative literature of the old sort possible depend on these sorts of interconnections, on the fact that the *Geist* has wended its way through this space. To insist on Newton's *Opticks* as part of the context for Goethe's *Farbenlehre* isn't to compare two distinct things: it is, rather, to enter into a world in which they were already connected.

How do you become an heir to this interconnected body of texts? Not, of course, as an older model would have suggested, by being of the European race but by studying just such texts and the cultures and histories that sustain them. This civilization, in my view, is much more the possession of Nigerian and Indian and Japanese scholars who have mastered some part of that vastly extended web of textuality than it is of many of those Europeans and Americans who imagine themselves as the heirs of Western civilization—what Du Bois said of the Bard is as true of the *Geist*: "I sit with Shakespeare and he winceth not."

So, to begin to respond now to the third report, which was my brief, I am not sure that I share the view that there is a problem in the Eurocentrism of the older comparative literature. Study these interconnected European literatures, I say. They make sense together. They were made for each other. But study also somewhere such interconnected bodies of writing as cohere in the same way around, for example, the travels of the Asiatic shadow-*Geist* I mentioned earlier.

What was absurd, I think, in the talk of comparative literature, *tout court*, in a world that contains, at the present, thousands of languages, was the hubris, the chutzpa, the cheek, of the label. A franker labeling—literatures of Western civilization, say—would have identified something more like what was going on. And I would have no problem in continuing that study, at least insofar as it relates to the period up until the Enlightenment.

A small digression is unfortunately necessary at this point. I do not mean, in this formulation, to ignore the very longstanding role of people and products from outside the West in the shaping of this intellectual heritage. We do not need to agree with the more extreme Afrocentrists to notice that the Greece to which the West looks back was at the crossroads of culture of North Africa and the Near East; the Spain that began the conquest of the New World had been deeply shaped by Islam; the Renaissance rediscovery of ancient learning owed a great deal to the Arabs who had preserved that tradition through the European Dark Ages; and the economic basis of modern capitalism depended on the labor of Africans, the gold and silver of the New World Indians, and the markets of Asia.

The West acquired gunpowder—at the military heart of the modern European state—from China and the astronomical data on which was based the beginnings of the Scientific Revolution from the ancient Near East. Or, to use an example I learned of only recently: musicologists now argue, as I learned in passing from reading a recent conference paper by Susan McClary, that the rhythmic structure of Monteverdi's *ciaconna* may derive either from Peruvian Indian music or from Africa. If the latter is correct, the first European dance craze with an Afro beat may have been a few centuries earlier than most of us had realized.

These facts are important: the West has no hard edges. But that doesn't mean that there isn't a history to be told in which, for example, the constant reflection on a few ancient texts—the Bible, Plato's dialogues, Aristotle's Ethics—is central to something called Western civilization in a way in which Sufi poetry is simply not.

When we come to the nineteenth and twentieth centuries, it seems to me that studying literature in the languages of western Europe without exploring questions of empire, colony, and postcolony is about as sensible as refusing to read Newton when one is studying the *Farbenlehre* because Newton, after all, contributed to literature in Latin and English, not German. At this point,

Western civilization becomes difficult to disentangle from global civilization, not because Western civilization becomes the culture of the World, but because the West as a category for literary culture makes as little sense as the nation did in the European Enlightenment. (And to see modern American literature as simply the tail end of this story of Western civilization is to make the same profound intellectual error.)

The new report, then, in my view, rather than responding to its plausible account of what was really done in the name of comparative literature by calling it what it was—the study of a particular, well worth studying, humanly interesting, and important body of high-cultural texts—proposes that we generalize the move from poesy to literature to encompass all of symbolic culture, or, as they say, "the production of music, philosophy, history, or law as similar discursive systems" as well as "television, hypertext, virtual realities." Since the "sister arts" have long been thought appropriate sources of comparison, this leaves hardly anything out. The range of phenomena we may study thus broadened, we should then take the word *comparative* for all it is worth:

> The space of comparison today involves comparisons between artistic productions usually studied by different disciplines; . . . between Western cultural traditions, both high and popular, and those of non-Western cultures; between the pre- and postcontact cultural productions of colonized peoples; between gender constructions defined as feminine and those defined as masculine, or between sexual orientations defined as straight and those defined as gay; between racial and ethnic modes of signifying; between hermeneutic articulations of meaning and materialist analyses of its modes of production and circulation; and much more.

More is going on here than the inevitable agglomeration of committee reports. All these things really are going on in comparative literature and English departments. But what, apart from the idea of comparison, unites them? I say, right now, to the extent that they are united, they are united by two things: a common sense of the shape of debates about theory, and a model of attending to cultural artifacts which is rooted in the reading of literary texts. But if you are going to talk about TV *and* comics, hip-hop dance styles *and* signifyin' on the street, why should what is most interesting be what can be said in the languages developed to talk about romantic poetry and the novel?

I myself see no point in trying to do everything at once. I see no harm in a focus on the written texts of particular traditions, narrowly or broadly conceived. I also see no harm in attention to movies and music, dances and toasts, in relative isolation from the high literary canon. Interesting work in any of these areas *can* draw on work in any of the others. But if we give up the idea of distinctive trainings, what we are going to get is not interdisciplinarity—the disciplines will have disappeared—but an unstructured postmodern hodge-podge. The report addresses this worry in these words: "This field challenges the very notion of interdisciplinarity, to the extent that the disciplines were historically constructed to parcel up the field of knowledge into manageable territories of professional expertise." I don't think that this gets the issue right, however. "Comparative literature" is not really a "manageable territory of professional expertise" within the field of knowledge; nor are any of our recognized subfields: Romanticism or eighteenth-century English literature or the Scottish Enlightenment. Neither, conversely, are the connections of genres—the sonnet, the novel—nor literary movements—Romanticism, again—simply artifacts of professionalization and the contest of faculties. There is a complex dialectic between subject matters, human interests (them-selves shaped deeply by literary and other dimensions of culture), and profes-sional organization which goes into the historical process of the construction of a field of discourse. The old comparative literature responded to more than the taste for languages: it responded to the historical interconnectedness of a field of European texts that came to be central to Europe's high culture. I hope this study can go on in the university alongside the multiple comparisons and the scores of languages in which the study of literature and orature flourish; and the history that Wellek studied can be seen as one instance of that broad set of multilingual cultural histories which we call a civilization.

If the *Geist* is what bound Western civilization together, there are other spirits abroad in the world, and one kind of comparative study could indeed explore what can be learned by looking at them together.

5

COMPARATIVE LITERATURE
AND GLOBAL CITIZENSHIP

MARY LOUISE PRATT

As it happens, I grew up in a farm town about one hundred miles from Toronto in Perth County—some of you have probably passed through it on the way to Lake Huron. In Perth County, fencing is a big issue. You have to keep your cattle in, your neighbor's out, keep your chickens in and the foxes out, keep the bulls from the cows, the boars from the sows, and everybody out of the manure pile. Fences take a lot of monitoring and maintenance.

All this fencing is what came to mind, then, when I read the Reports on Standards issued by the ACLA in 1965 and 1975. The impression they give is that to be in the field of comparative literature is to be the farmer always walking the fences and patching them up to make sure nothing wild gets in, nothing valuable gets out, no unforeseen matings and crossbreedings occur. As the new 1993 report suggests, comparative literature in the United States seems to have been founded by a rhetoric of vigilance associated with the Cold War.

I'd like to propose another image. Let us imagine instead that we Comp-Lit types are the animals in the coops and pens. The farmer no longer exists. He has retired to Florida, and before he left, he opened all the doors and gates. What do we want to do? The foxes now have access to the henhouse; the hens, however, are free to go somewhere else. Animals will move from pasture to pasture and pen to pen; strange matings will occur and new creatures born. The manure pile will be invaded and its winter warmth enjoyed by all. It will be a while till new order and new leadership emerge. But the farmer won't be back.

Globalizing, Democratizing, Decolonizing

The current flux in comparative literature, attested by the 1993 report, can be attributed, I suggest, to three historical processes that are transforming the way literature and culture are conceived and studied in the academy: globalization, democratization, and decolonization, by which, briefly, I mean:

1. globalization. The increased integration of the planet, the increasingly rapid flows of people, information, money, commodities, and cultural productions, and the changes of consciousness which result.

2. democratization. Mainly, in this context, the opening up of higher education and the professoriate in the United States to groups traditionally excluded, especially women and people of color; the resultant diversification of both personnel and intellectual agendas; and the challenge to structures of exclusion formerly taken as natural.

3. decolonization. In this context, two related processes. First, the entry of the Third World into dialogue with the First, and the latter's recognition of itself as constituted by relations of contact beyond its borders; second, the decolonization of the United States' relationship to Europe in the domain of culture, and its concomitant redefinition of itself.

With respect to these processes, the question faced by the writers of this most recent report could be posed as: "Does comparative literature want to globalize, democratize, decolonize?" I confess I am unable to conceive what it would mean to say no to this question, though there are clearly colleagues who would do just that. The answers that come to my mind, rather, are (a) it is already happening and (b) why not? The 1993 ACLA report, produced under some controversy, can be characterized as a partial embrace of the changes being wrought by these three processes. The gesture could not be more welcome. The report includes a number of truly salutory proposals which, to return to my earlier metaphor, move some fences so they give people more room and move others to where the people actually are. Without in any way trivializing European high-cultural traditions that have been the established ground of the field, it sets aside their traditional monopoly, and their status as its center of gravity. One wholeheartedly applauds the insistence that knowledge of literary works "should extend beyond their value for the analysis of literary meaning to their value for understanding the role of a native tongue in creating subjectivity, in establishing epistemological patterns, in imagining communal structures, in forming notions of nationhood, and in articulating resistance and accommodation to political and cultural hegemony." The proposal that "the old hostilities toward translation should be mitigated" even while we continue to stress "the necessity and unique benefits of a deep knowledge of foreign languages" could not be more welcome, nor more sane. Proposals to expand comparativeness to include comparisons between media or within national cultures enhance the best traditions of the field, as does the proposal that undergraduate majors be required to take courses that "study relations between Western and non-Western cultures."

At the same time the report continues to include "fencing" statements that recall its predecessors and that seem to clash with the spirit of the above examples. "It *may be* better," we read, "to teach a work in translation, even if you don't have access to the original language, than to neglect marginal voices because of their mediated transmission. . . . We *would even condone* certain courses on minority literatures in which the majority of the works were read in translation" (emphasis mine). The tentativeness of these proposals surprises. Who argues that it might be better to neglect marginal voices than teach a work in translation? That one might *not* condone courses on minority literatures if most of the works would be read in translation? Equally curious is the assumed equation of translation with the minority and the marginal here. Would one accord that status, say, to a syllabus on contemporary Middle Eastern or eastern European fiction?

Not surprisingly, then, the new report seeks compromise between a renovative permissiveness and old-style fencing. Such compromises are the stuff of our institutional lives and livelihoods. Since I am not being asked here to compromise with anyone, however, I am perhaps free to welcome the renovation and object to some of the fencing. Consider, for instance, the proposal regarding the undergraduate major. Such majors, it is suggested, "should teach not just 'great books' but also how a book comes to be designated as 'great' in a particular culture." This sensible suggestion is followed by another: "More advanced courses might occasionally focus class discussion on current controversies about such matters as Eurocentrism, canon formation, essentialism, colonialism, and gender studies." I confess to finding this statement astonishing and cannot believe it represents the committee's actual views. Surely they do not think that matters of Eurocentrism, canon formation, essentialism, colonialism, and gender studies should be *withheld* from students till they have reached an advanced level, and then dispensed only sparingly? What reason could there be for protecting beginners from some of the most powerful explanatory insights of our time? Or does the statement imply that teachers who use these tools should teach comparative literature only occasionally and to advanced students? This is undoubtedly not what the committee *meant* to suggest, but then where does this wording come from? What surprises most perhaps is the statement's unreality. Maybe I live in a different world from that of my colleagues, but it's my impression that on the agenda of undergraduate literary studies matters such as these now have more than an occasional place. And, to repeat the earlier question, Why shouldn't they?

Priorities and Accountability

As comparative literature engages with the three processes of globalization, democratization, and decolonization, the effect is a broadening of subject matter which calls for shifts, among other things, in priorities and modes of accountability. For example, if one begins working beyond a handful of European languages, the issue of translation versus original language relates to a different set of priorities. There are things that can only be done via translation which are too valuable and important not to do. Consider, for instance, the Summer Institute on Southeast Asian Literatures, organized two years ago by the Social Science Research Council (SSRC), planned and taught by scholars in Thai, Malaysian, Vietnamese, and Philippine literatures, all of them comparatists of one kind or another. From the outset it was obvious that if this institute was to take place at all, the materials would be read and taught in English. The situation was hardly a comparatist's nightmare, however, even in traditional terms. The faculty teaching each literature had read the texts in the original language; everyone was bilingual, and many were multilingual; the project was collective and collaborative. Surely it would be tragic if comparative literature or its leadership were to refuse validity to a project such as this. I think the authors of the report would agree, yet it remains significant that this institute, though funded by the NEH, was begun and carried out by the SSRC.

Moreover, one does not see similar initiatives coming out of comparative literature today, despite the extraordinary richness of contemporary Asian, African, and Latin American literatures and the rapid globalization of scholarly networks. One continues to be haunted by a specter that surged forth at the height of the so-called Western culture debates—of a panicked professor backed into a corner screaming "No! I won't do it! Don't make me read any new books!" As I encounter, even in this new revitalizing document, language like "we should be wary," "we might even condone," I find myself wondering, where is our sense of purpose? Where is our excitement, our curiosity, our passion? What stands in the way of statements like "we welcome," "we rejoice," "we face the extraordinary possibility," "we can hardly wait"?

In the latter spirit, let me sketch an alternative view of the kind of leadership I think comparative literature can perform today, a view that sets aside reactive categories of wariness, fear, border patrolling. These days I like to advance a concept of comparative literature as a site for powerful intellectual renewal in the study of literature and culture. My list of particulars has six items on it, but the big picture is of comparative literature as an especially hospitable space for the cultivation of multilingualism, polyglossia, the arts of cultural mediation, deep intercultural understanding, and genuinely global consciousness. It can develop these things both as scholarly endeavors and as new forms of cultural citizenship in a globalized world. These are things I think comparative literature at its best has always done. We now face an opportunity to broaden and enrich the ways they are done. Many aspects of the 1993 report point in this direction. The six particularities, stated as proposals, are these:

1. Comparative literature should remain the home for polyglots; multilingualism and polyglossia should remain its calling card. But it might help to update our rhetoric on this issue. Instead of producing students who "know foreign languages," maybe we should start talking about producing *bilingual, bicultural* people (or multilingual, multicultural people). Maybe we should link our endeavors to the need for deeply informed, culturally competent individuals in a globalizing world. This seems a good moment to reverse the United States' blind commitment to monolingualism and the tendency to cede the terrain of "globalization" to English. To monolingual anglophones it may look like everyone in the world is learning English, but the more accurate statement, visible from where we stand, is that the world is becoming increasingly multilingual. Many people learn a kind of instrumental English as an international lingua franca. But anglophones place themselves at a great disadvantage if they rely solely on this medium to conduct their relations with the rest of the planet.

Comparative literature scholars are in a strong position to make the case that this is no time to be monolingual. This matter usually does have to be explained to people in this fiercely monolingual country, and especially to deans. For of course monolingualism saves money. This is a real issue and one that is truly worth fighting over. When we explain our commitment to languages, however, it might help to shift the emphasis from the issue of reading everything in the original to the question of global citizenship and the need for people who have deep familiarity with more than one language, literature, and culture. At both the graduate and the undergraduate level, comparative literature is likely to grow fruitfully along these lines.

2. We might want to consider adopting a term like *expressive culture* to describe the home terrain of comparative literature. Such a term would reflect the broadening out of the inquiry beyond the institution of elite literature, while distinguishing its domain from that of cultural studies. This broadening out is not just a mindless proliferation. It is necessary, for example, if we are to work "contrapuntally" in the sense Edward Said defines in *Culture and Imperialism*, studying literary and cultural formations relationally, reading "across the imperial divide," or studying the interplay of hegemonic and counter-hegemonic forms of expression, or the interaction of media. As we know, such expansions of scope deprivilege canonical literature in some ways, but they reprivilege it in others: after all, literature itself does not in the process lose its extraordinary expressive power. Nothing has enriched contemporary literary study more than the paradigm shifts of the past twenty years.

3. We need to address head-on the crises of accountability and expertise produced by the reconfiguration of objects and methodologies in connection with globalization, democratization, and decolonization. Here leadership is surely needed. Francine Masiello raised the issue in a forum at the 1992 MLA convention, where she spoke of contradictions that arose between her dual roles as a Latin American specialist and a comparatist. "From a conservative perspective," she notes, "one might ask for an accounting of academic credentials in leaping the frontiers of the disciplines, but from a progressive view, we might also ask what constitutes the basis of anyone's cultural authority if not the final coherence of that person's course or her sustained commitment to scholarly inquiry in the field defined." It is no coincidence that this concern is expressed by a Latin Americanist, for the issue of accountability is most acute at the points at which the metropolitan academy engages with texts from nonmetropolitan, nondominant traditions. It is vital that we be able to distinguish between decolonization and critical neocolonialism, for example. Facing the crises of accountability and expertise will have the overwhelmingly positive consequence, one hopes, of clarifying the need for *collaborative* work in literary studies. Developing global perspectives cannot mean that each person must try—or claim—to know the whole globe.

4. It is helpful to recognize that comparativism now includes both the familiar "horizontal" work of comparing case A with case B, and also "verti-

cal" work relating the global and the local. I find promising models of comparative literature degrees which require significant local expertise (and accountability) in a particular area and combine it with training in translational and global perspectives. It is important in this context not to equate the global/local dyad with either the theory/text or the universal/specific dichotomy. The so-called universal, for instance, has been a locally European discourse in metropolitan academies, though today non-European theorists have embarked on numerous local efforts to break the European monopoloy on the category of the universal. As Masiello points out in the essay quoted earlier, in nonhegemonic contexts, theorizing and theory themselves are often highly local in nature, formulated around specific sociohistorical conditions or crises.

5. I wish to suggest in the strongest possible terms that comparatists take the lead in expunging the term *foreign* to refer to languages other than English. Nothing is more repugnant to someone working in Spanish in this country than to hear it referred to as a "foreign language." Its history here, after all, predates that of English. "Foreignness" equally misapplies to French, Cantonese, Italian, or Japanese—to say nothing of Lakota, Navajo, or Cree. Following the tradition of the MLA, let us agree on the term *modern languages* and put an end to another lexical legacy of the Cold War.

6. This last point takes up the final "word of caution" found in the 1993 ACLA report. Here the authors respond to the current fiscal crisis of higher education in the United States. "Budgetary restrictions," they assert, "have caused literature departments to define their needs in conservative ways," and the wave of the future is being held back at many institutions. Students, it is suggested, should be prepared to present a more traditional profile if they want to get a job, and advisors should apprise them of that.

The report here echoes a widespread perception. Its seriousness began to dawn on me this year when CompLit students began showing up at office hours in confusion and distress: in order to get a job, they were told, they could not simply pursue the interests they had come to the program to pursue. So why were they there? We may need to explore further both the logic and implications of the report's final recommendation. There is no reason simply to assume that departments automatically respond to scarcity by conservatism. Indeed, this claim needs to be meticulously verified before it is used to guide and restrict students. One has no trouble, for example, finding departments which, faced with eroding resources, choose to invest in newly emerging forms of inquiry at the expense of traditional fields. Disciplines and departments simply don't stop evolving or renewing themselves intellectually during a budget crunch—there is no simple connection between these two things. Moreover, students themselves are part of the process of evolution and renovation; they have a real role in driving the job market, though they feel mainly driven by it. How many of us have seen our "cutting edge" students fail to find a job the first year they look, then succeed the next year—not just because they "packaged" themselves better but because the market moved in their direction? Perhaps we are leaving out of the equation the intellectual integrity of ourselves and our field—the ability to recognize fine work and intellectual promise, and the commitment to fostering them among us. Surely these will or should remain the priorities that will keep our intellectual agendas from being budget driven.

6

ON THE COMPLEMENTARITY OF COMPARATIVE LITERATURE AND CULTURAL STUDIES

MICHAEL RIFFATERRE

Three positions put forward in the Bernheimer report deserve special scrutiny, less because of the importance of their separate objects than because of their common motivation, the same ideological frame of mind all these reflect in their own separate ways. Ranging as they do from advocating a specific technical procedure to defining a basic interpretive postulate to mapping out a new domain for comparatism, they in fact respond to the growing importance of cultural studies, to its encroachments in the field of comparative literature, and to alternate approaches and standards that seem to call for revisionist solutions.

The technical position, reversing a longstanding policy of the discipline, adopts a practice of cultural studies and calls for generalizing the use of translations for comparative purposes. Again following the example of cultural studies, contextualization is offered as the postulate that must underpin the new comparatism. The third position downgrades a so-called high literature to the advantage of popular literatures. The report's solution is clearly to bring comparative literature closer to the field of cultural studies by annexing some of its territory and most of its methods. It goes so far as to distance itself from the literature that gives its name to the discipline.

I shall limit my remarks to these positions not just because all these are so revealing of a trend and of a perhaps premature eagerness to jump on that bandwagon but because all these admit just as well of a very different solution to the problems they raise.

Indeed, I should like to suggest that it is counterproductive to assume that a very real ideological conflict will perpetuate itself. Notwithstanding the fact that comparative literature has to some extent institutionalized a supercilious attitude toward cultural studies, these assumptions stem from a confusion between research and teaching, between the comparative approach and building a canonical aesthetics and a normative hermeneutic upon that approach. But the risk of such a confusion occurs only in the teaching of literature as a facet of a national or group identity, that is, in connection with a political agenda. There is no reason to fear such a confusion if comparative literature sticks to comparing, to defining general and constant rules, and cultural studies to focusing on identity and difference, the unique blend of a given social setup and the verbal forms expressing that difference.

I propose accordingly that the future of the discipline lies not in a partial or total merger with cultural studies but in a redistribution of their respective tasks and in defining the two approaches as complementary rather than as polar opposites.

The feasibility of this suggestion is immediately apparent at the technical level of research tools, in the specific instance of translation. Traditionally, it was held to be true that a comparatist should master two or more foreign languages, a belief or principle now suspected of elitism. While not forsaking this long uncontested standard, the report only pays lip service to it. Not only are we no longer told that studying literature in the original language is the only approach proven and true, but its pertinence is displaced from literary facts to their genesis: to be a polyglot enables one to understand intimately the culture from which a given text emanates. By contrast, the report praises translation both as useful and emblematic. Useful: translation is made necessary by the recent scholarly attention to a great many cultures that comparative literature has allegedly ignored in the past. As the report puts it, students should have the opportunity to go "beyond the European cultural matrix." Emblematic: "translation can well be seen as a paradigm for larger problems of understanding and interpretation across different discursive traditions. Comparative literature . . . aims to explain both what is lost and what is gained in translations between the distinct value systems of different cultures, media, disciplines, and institutions." Sounds good, but I doubt any literary translation can achieve that. As we know, however successful it may be, such a translation cannot reproduce stylistic features intrinsic to the original without wreaking havoc with the target language. Hence, we end up with gibberish if the original is translated verbatim, or erasure if the translation resorts to analogs. Erasure is the problem because it is invisible, and not even a comparatist could notice, let alone interpret, the gap between the two versions, unless he or she were versed in the original language—a vicious cycle if there ever was one.

At best, content alone is allowed to cross the divide, leaving us with the bare skeleton of the referential fallacy, surely not enough for the hapless reader to answer a basic question which, according to the report, should cast a light on cultural differences: "Where do I speak from, and from what tradition(s), and countertraditions?" The question is supposed to be asked in the voice of the translated text, if not quite in the voice of the author. This voice, it seems to me, must be analyzed in its two constituents, the author's style, and the sociolect against the background of which this style stands out in its difference (difference within difference therefore). Even if we were to assume that the translation succeeds in reflecting the first constituent, probably an impossible feat, analyses would still be stymied by the *intentional* fallacy, as they would if their object of study were in their own native tongue. Chances of success are higher in rebuilding the foreign sociolect, with its ideologemes and its stereotypes, but this can hardly be done from the translation itself: I submit that the solution would be a linear commentary that, first, points out the traits of the other tradition, for which the target language has no name and which the translation has therefore erased; and that, second, indicates the words on both sides of the border which are homonyms rather than synonyms. The commentary would also have to focus on cases where the plainest translation of such traits remains misleading. The translation may be plain and direct because the translated word and its correlation in the translation have the same referents. And yet it may fail, but invisibly so, because the referential identity does not extend to the connotations, associations, and symbolisms of the referents. The task of making these connotations accessible to the reader is left to the commentary. I propose, that is, not an interpretive or critical commentary but rather a compendium of allusions like the ones that used to be compiled for overcoded texts within our own code (consider, for instance, the case of *Finnegans Wake*) or like dictionaries of mythology for classical literatures. Happily, the fast-developing techniques of hypertextuality are multiplying much needed databases of the contextualizing type.

But how are we to distinguish pertinent from irrelevant associations? By shifting the burden from the translation to the commentary's glosses. Instead of transposing a crux in the original into a crux in the translation, which is the failure inherent in a *literary* translation, we can afford a minimal and therefore unfaithful translation, awkward though it may be, so long as we make up for its deficiencies by glossing them, through periphrasis or paraphrase.

I am not suggesting that literary translations should be ignored, since they constitute a genre, and as such an object for criticism and theory. But they are not a reliable index of cultural difference. By contrast, the nonliterary, dumbly literal transpositions I advocate are not a genre, not an object of criticism, but an analytical tool, the index of culture difference we need. They would not claim to translate verbal art but to re-create its original cultural conditions, or to put it otherwise, to contextualize it.

Here theory has much to say. It has already much advanced our understanding of literariness. I am thinking of deconstruction, the interpretive communities model, and the like. It is now high time to determine what it can do for comparatism.

What, then, must be our surprise when we find that the report has given short shrift to literary theory. To be sure, theory is mentioned several times but without any specifics, as if the committee had just gone through its check list and made sure it had not forgotten anything. Theoretical contributions to our understanding of translation, as a research and teaching tool, only concern the comparatist's techniques. But theory would be just as powerful in redefining the discipline itself.

Theory, for instance, is much quicker at identifying and categorizing those invariant features that any comparison presupposes. This approach is central to comparative literature, and theory shows that it need not threaten or ignore the multiplicity of cultures. The multiple variables are logically and semiotically inseparable from invariants. Furthermore, these invariants are not just a smaller group of features, thus easier to grasp; they form a finite set of types without which variation could not make sense, let alone be perceived. Each type spells out the kind of difference that might issue from it.

Until now, comparative literature has chosen to rely on literary history for a definition of the invariant features of change, with the result that invariance and variation have been contaminated with values attached to the *time* dimension, depending on whether the observers' interests or ethical perceptions make them favor tradition or evolution, or sublimate evolution into revolution, and so on. I am thinking, for instance, of the scale of diminishing range which goes from topoi to themes to motifs but whose objective gradation is upset when the lure of the quest for roots causes scholars to invent an *Ur* level of reference before everything so that an archetype may shine forth. Or, in a different vein, concepts of the genealogical type are employed to produce a factual or counterfactual narrative, reducing imitation, for instance, to a two-faceted syllepsis, to a symbolic bridge that allows only for building or burning. Now, theory has the signal advantage over history that it starts from abstract models. These models reflect only the logical, minimal constituents of any combination of classes of factors. They remain valid at the class level, irrespective of the endless welter of actual tokens within such classes; indeed, they approximate universals in the Aristotelian sense of the term. Needless to say, the *vernacular* sense of the term would sound a general alarm among the proponents of cultural studies. But this need not happen, since the first rule for a universal is that it should include all the variants of the invariant that justifies the theorist in hypothesizing a class.

I would even venture that theory renders the relationship between cultural studies and comparative literature more objective. The justified resentment against past hegemonies has left traces in the metalanguage of cultural studies. The distinction occasionally is blurred between ideological polarizations and legitimate semantic polarities basic to the definition of any sign. I am alluding to a rhetoric in presenting differences, a rhetoric left over from the struggles toward self-assertion. One senses the lingering petulance that transposes objective differences onto scales of value judgments. Thus we find that any departure from a norm interpreted as hegemonic becomes a positive marker. Yet this practice can be remedied through theory.

Contextualizing, for instance, is a positively valorized concept in cultural studies, and the report dutifully encourages comparatists to adopt it: a lack of emphasis on the concept would signal either an urge to secede from cultural studies or a poor understanding of the maxim that everything has a context and can be explained by it. And yet, if there is contextualizing, theory foresees that a *de*contextualizing must follow. The aptness of this concept can be verified easily in the case of literary texts, for a text can be said to be literary when it survives the extinction of the issues, the vanishing of the causes, and the memory of the circumstances to which that text responded.

A perfect example of *decontextualization* in the sense I am discussing can be found in the accession of nonliterary texts to literature. In its emphasis on demoting literary phenomena from their cultural importance, or, to put it more crudely, on expunging the very word *literature* from the name of the discipline, the report proposes that "the production of 'literature' as an object of study . . . be compared to the production of music, philosophy, history, or law as similar discursive systems." This list omits a most significant aspect of discursive production: the literary production that occurs when readers eventually recognize the literariness of a work of history, of philosophy, or perhaps even of law. When this happens, which is quite often, the kind of reception and interpretation which initially focused on the text's cognitive telos becomes irrelevant. The text undergoes a change that remains external to it: its reception is now motivated by a twofold denial of its contextuality. This denial consists first in refusing to privilege the author's intention, which is commonly evinced to validate an object of learning or to explain and/or exemplify an approach to that object. Second, denial manifests itself in a hermeneutic shift from a value judgment based on the text's efficacy as a cognitive argument to a value judgment based on the text's aesthetic features. The time comes when we no longer read Montesquieu, Macauley, and Michelet as historians but as poets of the past and as heirs to genres such as the epic or the moral essay. Their works are therefore decontextualized and will remain so except for specialists in the history of ideas. Such texts indeed will endure, despite the fact that their narratives about past civilizations, societies, and events are no longer found adequate as mimesis. We now read them as symbolic systems, on a par with drama or fiction.

Contextualization is inseparable from history (not history as a genre this time but as a discipline). I am not suggesting that history is not an appropriate approach to literature: I merely propose that it is pertinent only to the circumstances of literary production, that is, to the genesis of the work of art and to its reception. But literature proper must not be confused with its genesis, nor with its reception. Literature is the text, and once established, and once the author is gone and can no longer make alterations, the text is ahistorical and its significance lies above all contexts.

Hence the elitist aura about it, and a monumentality that makes it a symbol of authority. Hence, also, the behavior of the traditional teaching communities of yesteryear, namely the promulgation of a canon. I have no time to address the canon issue, but let me state briefly that the canon is a cultural outcrop of the text, a framework for a certain type of worship behavior in a given social context: the canon therefore should be the exclusive domain of cultural studies.

However, the committee's reactions or overreactions to pressure from the proponents of cultural studies seem due to an embarrassed awareness of this authority. They betray a willingness to forsake or trivialize the very concept of literature. Consider, for instance, the following statement: "Literary phenomena are no longer the exclusive focus of our discipline." As if this were not bad enough, an admonition follows to comparative literature departments to "moderate their focus on high-literary discourse." Even if the advice is well taken, I would like to know what is wrong with high literature or why it should be downgraded to make room for other forms. I am not reading too much into this, as becomes apparent when the report goes on to allude ironically to "such heights" as we have admired, and when it finally puts the word *literature,* whether high or low, in quotation marks.

I confess puzzlement, since we have plenty of evidence that high and low literature share in the complexity of conventional forms, the use of stereotypes, the artifice of verse, the network of genres, and the like. The structure of the fable is recognizable equally in popular tales and in Emily Dickinson. But puzzlement and concern must be worse when we see the very concept of literature threatened.

Nothing in this report is more revealing than an obsessive preoccupation with the word *literature*. Let me analyze some of the points lined up against keeping the word *literature* in the name of the *discipline* whose future we are planning. The first argument is that the *space of comparison* has expanded way beyond literary objects, or even beyond artistic objects other than the literary, beyond the arts, beyond Western cultures, across borders separating genders, sexual orientations, ethnic groups, and so on. This accumulation of *crossings* is obviously meant to suggest that literature is the only concept that could not adjust to, let alone benefit from, the proclaimed "porosity of one discipline's practices to another's." The rationale for so strange an exclusion is spelled out as follows: "These ways of contextualizing literature in the expanded fields of discourse, culture, ideology, race, and gender are so different from the old models of literary study according to authors, nations, periods, and genres that the term 'literature' may no longer adequately describe our object of study."

Of course, the ways are new and different, but I cannot see why the "old models" should be incompatible with them. Why should a consideration of the *author* be inadequate, since the writer embodies or symbolically personifies discourse, culture, ideology, race, and gender? I, for one, could line up a few arguments against the relevancy of the notion of *author* to literary studies, along such lines as intentional fallacy and affective fallacy (fallacies totally unaffected by the prevailing view that New Criticism is old hat). Along such lines, then, I am quite ready to do without the author, but then the *text* must replace this figurative agent with a literal reality, one that is the perfect testing ground for approaches based on discourse, culture, ideology, and so on. And the same is true of *nation*, an objectionable term here, since it is but another name for a form of ideology. There is perhaps no point in pursuing this refutation, for it is quite evident that only an unwillingness to grasp abstractions can explain this diatribe against the word *literature*. I would rather maintain that, if anything, literature per se (without even adding *comparative*, without specifying the discipline that might provide the best approach to it), literature as a sign system, as a semiotic network, is automatically pertinent to all the fields listed in that unfortunate statement, because of its essential function, because of its very nature. On one side, you have the universe, all its parts, all the viewpoints for looking at it. On the other side, facing the infinity of objects, you have literature, which alone is pure representation, which alone among all discourses can contain and emulate everything else, including the other discourse. The very complementarity of being and representing makes it quite urgent that *literature* remain central to discourse, culture, ideology, and so on because literature encompasses all of them and raises questions about all of them by merely shifting its vantage points, namely, its genres and its conventions, another set of terms we are told are passé.

PART THREE

Position Papers

7

THE FUNCTION OF CRITICISM
AT THE PRESENT TIME

The Promise of Comparative Literature

ED AHEARN AND ARNOLD WEINSTEIN

In looking at the various statements of purpose put forth by distinguished scholars over the past three decades, one is struck as much by sameness as by difference. To be sure, the progression from the Levin report to the
Greene report to the Bernheimer report (and the responses generated by it)
displays the elitism and language exigencies of an earlier day being shaken by
the impetus of theory and interdisciplinary work and, in our moment, the
compelling challenge of cultural studies along with the phenomenon of multiculturalism. Each of these reports is demonstrably of its time, and yet each
one is, in some ways, still viable today; our discipline does not easily change its
skin. Taken together, they manifest the ferment and vitality of literary studies,
and it would be surprising if any single model or definition of the field could
establish itself as doctrinal. But what they also share and make visible, doubtless unintentionally, is the marginal status of comparative literature within
the institutional landscape of the United States.

It is not hard to see why this should be the case. Mastery of several
different literary traditions in their original languages, conversance with the
methods and principles of what we might call the theory revolution of the
past decades, these twin goals are not easily achieved in the United States, at
any level, from the professoriate on down. Given the arduousness of our
training, the taint of elitism makes more than a little sense. What we need to
see, however—and to start talking about—is that comparative literature can
play a central and crucial role in literary studies in our society. And it can do so
by taking seriously its educational as well as its intellectual mission. The study
of literature in particular and the study of culture in general entail profound
social and educational responsibilities and dimensions that constitute the

living context and framework for our professional endeavors. We may indeed read, teach, and write about literature because we personally love it— although this is not always visible in professional discourse—but we have not always been very good at explaining our purposes or bringing our views to the larger public of students whom we teach. Our students are not merely our audience; they are that larger society whose modus operandi, as it is expressed in culture and the arts, is arguably our field of study, that larger society whose behavior and values we seek not only to describe but also to influence. We are not speaking of lobbying or drumbeating on our behalf; our point is that comparative literature, conflicted and multivocal though it may be, has some large indigenous virtues that are both unremarked and sorely missing in today's educational conversation. Nothing popularizing or reductive is meant here; we would also say that the keenest and most radical perceptions that fuel our scholarly research end up being sorely compromised if they never get beyond seminar rooms or even the papers and books we publish. Our issues are large, but our audience is small. Our gifts could be central, and that is why it is distressing when we are marginal.

What are these virtues, these gifts, that characterize comparative litera-ture even today when we agree about so little? The most obvious response is the globalism, the internationalism of the field. The current debates on na-tionhood as construct, on ethnonationalisms, on the nature of global eco-nomic systems with their colonialist legacies, on the impact of electronic delivery and retrieval systems that network the planet: all this underscores the importance of our aggressively multinational perspective. We do not mean that we are training students to work in multinational corporations, although this would be nothing to be ashamed of; rather, we are saying that the geopolitical activities, conflicts, and dilemmas of our time require a citizenry that has learned something about the history, aspirations, and complex reality of other peoples, and that the study of literature and other arts is a privileged entry into these matters. However, unlike English or the national language departments or even cultural studies programs, comparative literature is inherently pluralist, aware of but not defined by Difference in all its powerful forms: language, religion, race, class, and gender. *Pluralist* is doubtless not the best term for our composite venture, because it suggests inert groupings, whereas the deepest energies of our work—along grounds that are concep-tual, moral, and political—have to do with *encounter*, with parallels and contrasts and juxtapositions that are motivated, critical, and eye-opening. We are not, as is sometimes thought, the "collectors" of literary studies, the connoisseurs with multiple passports and dual citizenships, at home in several departments, central to none. On the contrary, our international perspective remakes the entire deck, reconceives not only the individual text but the national corpus, makes it possible to discern kinships and allegiances and patterns that are invisible to the national literature scholar, of whatever stripe he or she may be.

We are obviously referring to our second major indigenous virtue, indeed our defining disciplinary move: *comparison*. How strange that none of the documents about the profession dwells very much on this issue, as if it were axiomatic that comparatists compare. It behooves us today, more than ever, to reflect on the nature and meaning of *comparison*. A thick philosophical tome could be written on this concept, and there have been moments in the history of our field when much ink was spilled over proper (versus improper) comparisons. Our concern, however, is with recovering and highlighting the energies of comparison—rather than legislating how and when it can take place—because this particular intellectual operation is really the heart of the matter for us today. What is uniquely critical and what is uniquely creative in comparative criticism both stem from this fundamental procedure. The critical side of the ledger is self-evident: the comparatist brings to the study of single texts and cultures awareness of other texts and cultures, making it possible to illuminate artistic performances more richly, more variously, more contrastively than is possible in a single field. We have all become adept at seeing how very much that our culture gives as natural is in fact constructed; surely, from a certain point of view, nothing is more constructed than national literature departments, not only because "nationality" is something of a fiction, tuning out far more voices than it tunes in, but also because literature itself is irrepressibly mixed, stereophonic, porous, marked by exchanges and influences, international. The debate among classicists about the significance of Afrocentric scholarship might be thought of as emblematic rather than exceptional, and there is no period or place of artistic production which is not similarly mixed, cross-cultural, cross-pollinated. Virgin literatures, like the virgin land, are a myth. Comparatists are the people trained to bring us this critical news.

Less easy to articulate but no less crucial to our argument is the creativity, the freedom of comparison. In ways that are at once elemental and complex, the act of comparison is a liberating act, a shaping venture that ceaselessly reconfigures its materials and proffers pattern and gestalt where there had been discrete entities. This undertaking draws every bit as much on the fashioning powers of synthesis as the critical procedures of analysis, and its respect for particularity, indeed for Difference, is compatible with its commitment to field pictures and transnational groupings. The implicit binarisms and polarities of our discursive terms are ultimately misleading, however, because the premise that fuels our procedure is that these new constellations of materials shed indispensable new light on the single item. A new Dickens emerges when pirouetted in the light of Balzac and Dostoevsky; the filiation of Blake and Rimbaud illuminates the agenda of Burroughs; Saikaku's rendition of commodification shows us much about Defoe's practice which we might not otherwise see; more diachronically, the poetics of exile, as worked out in Ovid and Du Fu, affords a fresh perspective on some of our century's lyrical performances: Victor Serge, Nelly Sachs, Joseph Brodsky; the list could be continued.

These groupings are at once culture specific and cross-cultural, and they accommodate both the "lateral site-specific" findings of the new historicists and the more freewheeling contrasts and juxtapositions afforded by comparative and thematic criticism. Above all, they embody an intellectual orientation that has much to recommend itself to students in the United States at this moment of our history. For all our concern today with multiculturalism and opening the canon, it would be ironic indeed for us to ignore the central blind spots of American culture: its monolingualism, its unawareness of cultures that exist both close to and far beyond our borders, its implicitly hegemonic view of America's place in the world order. These issues and the mind-set behind them cry out for attention today, and comparative literature is arguably the sole humanistic discipline equipped to meet this educational and ideological challenge.

It should be stressed that this "engaged" model of comparative literature is hospitable to virtually all varieties of literary analysis. From the textual subtleties of New Criticism and intertextuality and even psychoanalysis, on the one hand, to the new vistas created by the insights and revisions proposed by Marxists, feminists, new historicists, students of ethnicity, race, sexual orientation, and so forth on the other hand, all of these approaches are compatible with the twin principles of internationalism and comparatism which give us our identity. Graduate offerings would thus continue to share many common features with English, cultural studies, and the national literature programs, but their programmatic reach into disparate cultures would ensure that issues of Eurocentrism, canon formation, East/West and North/South relations, colonialism, and the like would at once come to the fore and into focus.

It should follow, from all that has been said about the premises of our field, that the undergraduate program in comparative literature should be positioned at the hub of literary studies at the college or university. Joint appointments and shared assumptions about the common ground that underlies all cultural study are obviously crucial here, and the well-known politics of "turf protection," departmental rivalries, and administrative intervention will do much to bring about or prohibit our field's "centrality" within our various institutions. The point worth emphasizing here is our *logical claim* to be at this center. Not only does our composite reach intersect with all the particular literary programs, but our rosters should reflect this sense of common cause and common ground. Still more crucial, however, is the value of what we have to contribute to the education of today's college generation. We are effectively the humanities counterpart to international relations, in that our field testifies to a major fact of life: the world around us is increasingly interdependent, a mix of cultures and societies and nations that are linked together in business, trade, information, environment, and much else. Whereas international relations usually focuses on the documentable socio-economic and political connections and conflicts between countries, comparative literature illuminates the artistic and cultural patterns of sameness and difference which exist both within and between societies, and it thereby gives us a precious contrastive portrait of societies' values and beliefs, as well as their aesthetic and literary traditions. In some basic sense, studying comparative literature should confer a kind of civic and cultural literacy, not of the "recognition" type promoted by E. D. Hirsch, but of a more substantive and critical sort, entailing knowledge of various cultural traditions, ideally a knowledge that is nuanced, aware of contradictions, attuned to discourses both mainstream and marginal. It is worth repeating that the kind of knowledge envisioned here has little to do with so-called core reading lists but rather with a special kind of intellectual posture, a way of looking at the world and, thus, at oneself.

We think we have this kind of graduate and undergraduate program at Brown University. Given that our discipline appears threatened at so many institutions today, whereas it is thriving on our home campus, it seems useful to sketch out the lines of our operation; to do so will also allow us to move from theoretical rationales to empirical example, by showing that our ambitious view of comparative literature is firmly grounded in our own institutional practice.

Thus, while retaining strength in the predominant Western languages and literatures, we have long presented East Asian, Judaic, and Scandinavian fields and recently added Arabic (both standard and vernacular language as well as literature). Secondly, because of the interdisciplinary openness of the university's curriculum, we have for a decade or more had fruitful interactions with some of the forces active in cultural studies—through such programs as Literature and Society, Modern Culture and Media, the Pembroke Center for Teaching and Research on Women, Afro-American Studies, Latin American Studies, Portuguese-Brazilian Studies (not to speak of joint appointments in history and philosophy).

Thirdly—and it is important to note how this differs from the general practice of the discipline—comparative literature at Brown began as an undergraduate enterprise. While we have a small and highly competitive Ph.D. program, we now graduate forty to sixty undergraduates annually. Since we do not view the undergraduate concentration as essentially preprofessional, students may complete the degree with advanced work in one foreign language. Many have more than one; many spend a semester or year abroad; all complete requirements in periods, genres, and theory. Aside from the excellence of their individual work, the size of our program means that we play a central role in the university's undergraduate curriculum as a whole, enrolling twelve hundred students per year in our courses and exercising an influence reserved to departments of English and history at most other campuses. There is no reason to think that this model would not be equally successful at other institutions. It is not a question of "selling" our discipline but rather of practicing it, of bringing our perspective to an audience that has great need of it.

Perhaps most strikingly, we have developed and pursued an interest in secondary education which is unique for comparative literature programs in the country but which demonstrates the particular pertinence of the comparatist stance for today's educational needs. As more and more theorists in education posit a larger social view that would link together the years of high school and college, we are acting on our own deeply held belief that our discipline can offer concepts and skills that are vital to our nation's young people. Although this "outreach" effort may seem beyond the pale of most university programs in comparative literature, it is worth considering just how overdue and critical such a move actually is; conversations with leading scholars in the sciences and social sciences convince us that the moment is ripe for a kind of educational awakening on the part of many academic disciplines and enclaves, a recognition that their intellectual and scholarly mission needs to be brought back into contact with the educational needs of our society at large.

Originally, at Brown, this effort took the form of numerous institutes and seminars for high school teachers and students, but since 1988 the effort has been recognized as of national importance through consecutive institutional grants from the National Endowment for the Humanities. The provocatively titled "Great Books Then and Now," and the current "Texts and Teachers," involve the creation of team-taught and progressively more interdisciplinary courses. The first program generated "Rites of Passage" (Greek, Chinese, Western medieval and modern texts about contrastive models of growing up, with increasing emphasis on matters of class and gender); "Sacred and Secular Readings" (Paul, Pascal, Kierkegaard, Kafka, and questions of truth, the divine, rhetoric, and representation as treated in religion, philosophy, and literature at different historical moments); "Exile and the Conditions of Writing" (Ovid, Du Fu, modern Western poets, with special emphasis on the interplay between political and psychological dimensions of exile, as well as the pivotal role of "original" languages in the exilic text); "A Tale of Two Cities" (literary and painterly texts about Paris and London from the seventeenth to the nineteenth century, focusing on the manner in which urban development is reflected in, and produces, artistic performance); and "Desire and the Marketplace" (*Moll Flanders* and *Madame Bovary*, but also Saikaku's *Life of an Amorous Woman* and contemporary writing by African women, Bâ's *So Long a Letter* and Emecheta's *The Joys of Motherhood*, together with Hogarth's engravings and seventeenth-century Japanese woodcuts, completed by selections on money, value, commodities, and consumption from Adam Smith, Karl Marx, Thorstein Veblen, and contemporary feminist theorists).

The second phase involves team-taught courses of an overtly interdisciplinary nature: one on literature and medicine, involving artistic and clinical texts, and another on the modern urban experience from the perspectives of literature and political science. These two ventures are, in some ways, the most ambitious component of comparative literature's program of exploration here at Brown, in that the kinds of expertise, methodology, and working assumptions at play in these courses are of very distinct and different sorts, requiring considerable efforts at synthesis and integration. Once again it follows that comparatists are the people most able and interested in performing these kinds of intellectual operations and in passing on to students a view of art and culture which is open to, indeed inseparable from, parallel developments in science, technology, and the social arenas in which we live. It goes without saying that such interdisciplinary courses stretch the resources and the professional expertise of literature professors, and one would not want to minimize this "cost factor"; but the gains are commensurate with the risks, and among those gains is the discovery—on the part of students and even of professionals—that literary materials have a unique bearing on many of the most intransigent social issues of our day.

At Brown we have already established something of a track record with each of these sorts of comparative courses: those focusing on literary issues from disparate parts of the globe, thereby reconceiving what is meant by "great books," and those devoted to interdisciplinary investigations of major topics. And we have brought our vision to a widening series of audiences, crossing the borders between institutions and regions as well as disciplines. With the cooperation of Brown's Institute for Secondary Education and Professor Theodore Sizer's Coalition for Essential Schools, these offerings have been planned with vital input by local high school teachers and incorporated into the courses taken by numerous high school students in Rhode Island and Massachusetts. In some, but not all, cases, these are English advanced placement or honors courses. High school classes study the books from the Brown courses, attend a number of the sessions at the university, and are visited by members of our teaching teams—as many as four faculty, as well as graduate and undergraduate teaching assistants.

It will be noted that there are also possibilities here of exposing top undergraduates to teaching and of interesting graduate students from several departments in interdisciplinary methods and in the question of links between secondary and higher education. For the teachers and the students in the high schools, the payoff is in the reading of new and complex texts at a far richer level than normally "expected." Moreover—and this is one of the reasons the program was funded by the NEH—our international perspective enables us to challenge and to amplify the traditional high school curriculum. The resultant courses, fostering a "conversation" between carefully selected but disparate materials, offer a welcome alternative to the survey model still so prevalent in secondary (and higher) education.

"Texts and Teachers" is so called precisely to highlight this community of teaching and learning interests among students and faculty at several institutional levels. Accordingly the program also includes intensive summer seminars bringing together teams of college and high school teachers from various regions (in 1993 from Boston, Chicago, Saint Louis, and California; in 1994 from Baltimore, New Hampshire, and New York). Meeting for two weeks for a miniversion of one of the courses, the participants immerse themselves in the texts but also engage in wide-ranging discussion of pedagogical issues in high school–college–university settings, in preparation for offering a similar joint venture at their institutions during the following year. The goal is to disseminate the comparatist method, hence both a wider repertory and a richer reading of texts, and the high school–college collaboration, at a number of sites throughout the nation.

Nothing here implies a top-down direction; the rewards for college and university students, faculty, and curricula are as potentially valuable as for those in high schools. And nothing here excludes—rather the opposite—the importance of mastering the languages of several cultures and of absorbing the most penetrating insights of literary theory and interdisciplinary cultural studies. What *is* emphasized is the way in which comparative literature can live up to its full potential, as a sophisticated, flexible, and engaged discipline capable of producing new knowledge and new perspectives in the high school–college–university spectrum of education.

Each of the courses in these programs is, in some sense, a textbook example of the comparative principles that undergird the discipline, and while they may not be shockingly new at the college level, they are revolutionary when introduced in the high schools. Common to each of them is a major topic or theme around which a battery of selected texts from disparate cultures, disciplines, and moments in history can be assembled. The challenge of such courses is to maintain enough cogency via the common topic to launch an investigation of difference and particularity. Students often come to these ventures with universalist conceptions of growing up, love and marriage, exile, and the like, but they leave these courses with a heightened sense of historicity, of how these large themes are often driven by the facts and fictions of ideology, race, class, and gender. For the high school students, these courses are very often their first serious encounter with non-Western, perhaps even non–Anglo-American materials, and they thereby learn something basic about the comparative model and the makeup of the globe. But they also learn another skill—comparison—which instills in them the capacity to discern pattern and sameness in disparate materials, to recognize that the "givens" of one culture may look very strange from the optic of another culture, to see that their own lives are both like and unlike those of the past and of other parts of the world. Although such goals may seem simplistic from the perspective of publishing scholars, it is arguable that they are far from self-evident to our society at large, that they are arduous to learn, and that they constitute the bedrock—verbal, moral, epistemological, political—on which our discipline is founded. And when we consider how the "English curriculum" is constructed at most high schools—Eurocentric, Anglo-American, often removed from the keen debates about ideology and theory which bathe our profession—then we grasp the large stakes of these matters.

8

COMPARATIVE EXILE

Competing Margins in the History
of Comparative Literature

EMILY APTER

The discipline of comparative literature, as many have pointed out, is unthinkable without the historical circumstances of exile. My concern in this discussion is to show that the future of the discipline "in an age of multiculturalism" is bound up with the way in which past and future generations define and lay claim to the material and psychic legacy of dislocation. Despite drastic shifts in the politics of the humanities since the postwar period, exilic consciousness, redefined by successive generations and constituencies, seems to have remained a deeply ingrained constant of the field, shaping its critical paradigms and providing a kind of overarching historical paradigm for the ontology of the discipline.

I want to argue that many of the territorial skirmishes emerging within the field today have to do with the way in which postcolonial theory has, in a sense, usurped the disciplinary space that European literature and criticism had reserved for themselves. Translating the discursive maneuvers of unhappy consciousness characteristic of postwar criticism into a politicized, multicultural critical idiom, postcolonialism is in many respects truer to the foundational disposition of comparative literature than are other more traditional tendencies and approaches (including biography, influence study, national literary history, formalism, rhetorical analysis). With its interrogation of cultural subjectivity and attention to the tenuous bonds between identity and national language, postcolonialism quite naturally inherits the mantle of comparative literature's historical legacy.

Of course several generations of Europhilic, deconstructively trained, predominantly white comparative literature critics do not necessarily see the matter this way; many are predictably loath to cede the field to a newly minted

Third Worldist community of scholars. Once the pressure is on to move beyond tokenism (and the pressure is on), once the intention is carried out to recruit in the field of the world, what, many argue, will prevent comparative literature from becoming Asian, Near Eastern, African, or Latino studies with some French, German, Slavic, or Portuguese thrown in to provide a wider global or historical perspective? The answer, I think, is that nothing will prevent this from happening; it clearly *is* happening; and as it happens, the historical European center of the discipline decries the loss of disciplinary identity.

But when, I would ask, was this identity ever secure? A brief review of comparative literature's beginnings reveals the discipline's keen awareness of the fit between its intellectual edge and its heuristic and cultural marginality within the American academy. This sense of marginalization was passed along to each generation like a kind of flame, lending the field its consistency of character as a relentlessly distantiating mode of criticality. It therefore seems to be the ultimate act of bad faith on the part of traditional comparatists to resist Third World literature and postcolonial theory by pejoratively "othering" it as a "cultural studies" that pays no attention to literature in the original language. This construction of cultural studies as the bad object of comparative literature, that is to say, as the hypothetical antithesis of literariness, is more often than not a poorly masked strategy for marginalizing the latest arrival in town (there are obvious analogies to the anti-immigration stance of second- or third-generation immigrants, concerned to keep out recent arrivals). Perhaps by going back over some of the early history of the discipline, we can better understand the hypocrisies embedded in current caveats and admonitions addressed to the perceived encroachment of cultural studies on the hallowed terrain of comparative literature.[1]

The early history of comparative literature, though relatively well rehearsed, provides a record of the privileging of exile. The émigré founding fathers—Leo Spitzer, Erich Auerbach, René Wellek, Wolfgang Kayser—arrived at American universities already steeped in a turn-of-the-century culture obsessed with theorizing alienation and subjective estrangement. Marx, Freud, Durkheim, Lukacs, Kracauer, Simmel, Benjamin, and Adorno were among those who had profoundly contributed to the Continental ethos of exile before the fact. After the fact, the early comparatists, concerned to forget the ideology-riven past, developed pedagogies of a panhumanist, theoretical literacy for which, as Denis Hollier reminds us in an article entitled "On Literature Considered as a Dead Language," "no visa was necessary."[2]

The conditions under which this denationalized Lit. Crit. was hatched were often dictated by dire personal circumstances; fleeing Nazi Europe, fueled by adversity, many wrote criticism as a kind of message in a bottle dispatched to former interlocutors whose whereabouts were unknown, whose lives were uncertain. As Auerbach put it in his still poignant epilogue to *Mimesis,* "finding a reader" was the book's lonely call:

> I may also mention that the book was written during the war and at Istanbul, where the libraries are not well equipped for European studies. . . . On the other hand it is quite possible that the book owes its existence to just this lack of a rich and specialized library. If it had been possible for me to acquaint myself with all the work that has been done on so many subjects, I might never have reached the point of writing.
>
> With this I have said all that I thought the reader would wish me to explain. Nothing now remains but to find him—to find the reader, that is. I hope that my study will reach its readers—both my friends of former years, if they are still alive, as well as all the others for whom it was intended. And may it contribute to bringing together again those whose love for our western history has serenely persevered.[3]

Once settled on the shores of North America, the study of literature and literariness turned out to be relatively compatible with the nation-neutral textuality of American New Criticism. But if distaste for nationalism was a common denominator, the lingua franca of the burgeoning discipline—like that of sociology and art history at their founding in this country—was more often than not German. As Erwin Panofsky pointed out in his contribution on art history to a collection of essays published in 1953 under the title *The Cultural Migration,* German *Kultur* was crucial to the postwar transformation of the humanities:

> Though rooted in a tradition that can be traced back to the Italian Renaissance and, beyond that, to classical antiquity, the history of art—that is to say, the historical analysis and interpretation of man-made objects to which we assign a more than utilitarian value, as opposed to esthetics, criticism, connoisseurship and "appreciation" on the one hand, and to purely antiquarian studies on the other—is a comparatively recent addition to the family of academic disciplines. And it so happens that, as an American scholar expressed it, "its native tongue is German."[4]

What is striking here is not so much the paradoxical indebtedness of a young field to a national heritage that it had good reason to abjure, but rather the anomalous prospect of an American discipline whose native language was not

English. By raising the question of "how German is it?" Panofsky's American colleague revealed the combination of ressentiment and awe with which homegrown critics greeted the new arrivals from Europe.

John Freccero's portrait of Spitzer, his teacher at the Johns Hopkins University in the fifties, confirms the otherness of early comparative literature as it first appeared:

> We sometimes wondered if this filial piety toward the continental tradi-
> tion, contrasting so sharply with his generally polemical relationship to his
> colleagues, were not simply another way to distance himself from the rest
> of us, like the opera cape he wore when it rained, or the Homburg set
> rakishly on a mane of white hair. In those days of crew cuts and white
> bucks, the figure of the continental virtuoso challenged every canon of
> male decorum— . . .
>
> His aesthetics fit in with the prevailing mood much more readily than
> his style; he had a profound effect on American critics who were seeking to
> escape the prevailing orthodoxy of the English Department.[5]

Spitzer's opera cape and Homburg, focused on in the fifties as emblems of theory's "difference," metonymize the profound Euro-envy of American converts to the field. Critics who were not themselves "foreign" born (such as J. Hillis Miller, Fredric Jameson, Neil Hertz) mandatorily absorbed and projected the aura of non-Englishness in their practice of comparative litera-ture.[6] The premier prerequisite of the field seems to have been an ethic of linguistic estrangement, a secessionism from mainstream American culture, even when and if American culture became the object of comparative research.

The allegorical melancholy emphasized by Fredric Jameson in the writ-ings of Walter Benjamin—composed of "private depressions, professional discouragement, the dejection of the outsider, distress in the face of a political and historical nightmare"—has, it seems, haunted comparative literature from one decade to the next.[7] "I was cruelly banished from the world of pure and univalent aesthetic forms," wrote Leo Spitzer, reminiscing over his pro-pulsion into "linguistics and literary history" as a university student in Vienna under the tutelage of Wilhelm Meyer-Lübke (LS 426). The giving up of textual essentialism is clearly qualified as an exilic experience. And if here the person-al intellectual trajectory mimes the epic of banishment from a Paradise of unfallen first forms, for the next generation, the deconstructionists and critics affiliated with the "Yale School," the emergence of theory from the trauma of exodus was even richer, more complex. Harold Bloom, conjugating the Freud-ian concept of primal anxiety with the "dark cultural prospects of American

Jewry," would produce stunning critical turns: "the anxiety of influence," "poetic misprision," "agonism," a "purified Gnosis."[8] Another modality of Jewish epistemological placelessness resonates in Geoffrey Hartman's post-Arnoldian "criticism in the wilderness" (somewhere between the Sinai desert where critics perish and the Promised Land where "a new and vital literature would arise to redeem the work of the critic").[9]

The current generation of exilic critics is often, as might be expected, deeply antithetical to their Eurocentric counterparts: non-German-speaking, nonmetropolitan, nonwhite, antipatriarchal, and, in varying degrees, hostile to elitist literariness. And yet one could say that new-wave postcolonial literacy bears certain distinct resemblances to its European antecedents imbued as it often is with echoes of melancholia, *Heimlosigkeit*, cultural ambivalence, consciousness of linguistic loss, confusion induced by "worlding" or global transference, amnesia of origins, fractured subjectivity, border trauma, the desire to belong to "narration" as a substitute "nation," the experience of a politics of linguistic and cultural usurpation.

Part of the uneasiness in the relationship between present-day postcolonial theory and European comparativism may be traced to a desire on both sides to disavow marked resemblances in their postures of cultural ambivalence. Though postcolonialism wants to foreground the particular alienation effect produced by colonial mimicry while Continental comparativism favors Heideggerian subject erasure in the context of posthumanist, late capitalist technologies of modernity, both have, in a sense, "agreed" on the subject's cultural self-misrecognition. Postcolonialism might be said to strive teleologically for identity retrieval, agency, and the empowerment of people of color, while Continental comparativism seems willing to settle for a cynical reason dedicated to semiotic undecidability, performative identity, and a color blindness rhyming with white. There is nonetheless a shared propensity to produce the subject as complexified; pulled back from the stereotype or the positive image; deferred and postponed in transnational, translational, transsexual, and transtechnological space.

Finally, there is also a common tendency to deliteralize the language of border crossing, so as to emphasize the ultimate unreadability of cultural hermeneutics. Compare, for example, Derrida and the Moroccan critic/writer Abdelkebir Khatibi. In Derrida, border trauma informs the theorization of the intractable "problem" of aporia:

> The crossing of borders always announces itself according to the movement of a certain step [*pas*]—and of the step that crosses a line. An

indivisible line. And one always assumes the institution of such an indivisibility. Customs, police, visa or passport, passenger identification—all of that is established upon this institution of the indivisible. . . . There is a *problem* as soon as the edge-line is threatened. And it is threatened from its first tracing. This tracing can only institute the line by dividing it intrinsically into two sides. There is a *problem* as soon as this intrinsic division divides the relation to itself of the border and therefore divides the being-one-self of anything.[10]

The ontological exilicity visible in the hyphens that gerundize "being oneself," or separate being and one-ness from the self, may be seen as a graphic corollary to the postcolonial dyslexia of Khatibi. In *Love in Two Languages* (*Amour bilingue*, 1983), Khatibi makes the airport the site of a "disorientation" that he subsequently assesses in a nonfictional mode as "foreign figuration":[11]

> Permanent permutation. He understood this better thanks to a brief sense of disorientation he had experienced one day at Orly, waiting for a boarding call; he found himself unable to read the word South, seen backward, through a window. Turning it around, he realized he had read it from right to left, as if it were written in Arabic characters—his first written form. He could place the word only by going by way of his mother tongue.[12]

Here, for better or for worse, the metaphoricity of border passing and boarding calls is allowed to resonate textually, sanctioning the compelling move toward the textualization of a politics of positionality.

Khatibi and Derrida, each representing distinctly different critical tendencies, are nevertheless easy to align with each other by virtue of their commitment to capturing, as *écriture*, the vagrancy of the comparative subject.[13] This comparative subject is indeed the subject at stake in debates over comparative literature's "new internationalism," adduced by Homi Bhabha to be "in a profound process of redefinition." Bhabha seeks to establish grounds for a "critical comparativism" affixing the affective, supranational bonds of identity politics to Marxist categories of economic and class-defined political identity:

> The currency of critical comparativism, or aesthetic judgement, is no longer the sovereignty of the national culture conceived as Benedict Anderson proposes as an "imagined community" rooted in a "homogeneous empty time" of modernity and progress. The great connective narratives of capitalism and class drive the engines of social reproduction, but do not, in themselves, provide a foundational frame for those modes of cultural

identification and political affect that form around issues of sexuality, race, feminism, the lifeworld of refugees or migrants, or the deathly social destiny of AIDS.[14]

Unlike Mary Louise Pratt's "kinder, gentler" vision of comparative literature as "an especially hospitable space for the cultivation of multilingualism, polyglossia, the arts of cultural mediation, deep intercultural understanding, and genuinely global consciousness,"[15] Bhabha's "worlded" literary space is less inviting, less open to mediation, more fractious, concerned, he says, "with a form of cultural dissensus and alterity, where non-consensual terms of affiliation may be established on the grounds of historical trauma" (LC 12). Referring to Nadine Gordimer and Toni Morrison's "unhomely fictions," Bhabha sees the new internationalism in "the moment of aesthetic difference that provides the narrative with a double edge, which like the colored South African subject represents a hybridity, a difference 'within,' a subject that inhabits the rim of an 'in-between' reality" (LC 13).

It is not surprising that Bhabha turns away from specific methodological formulations of "dissensual," "traumatic" comparativism, to fictional evocations of hybridity and in-betweenness. The task of translating nuanced modalities of split, interiorized exilic ontology into a curricular mandate would appear reductive and caricatural at best. That said, Bhabha's textual turn is a kind of theory, for he treats fiction as a way of getting to new theoretical places, places to which theory alone would not take him. Bhabha endows the literature of exilic consciousness with a theoretical agency and political urgency that in some sense it has not possessed since the early postwar period of comparative literature. By way of illustrating the parallels between early comparative literature and postcolonialism, I would point to some of the unexpected similarities between Homi Bhabha's "signature" terms of postcolonial theory and Leo Spitzer's analysis of the "homeless," "ablative," "hybrid form" of the trademark word *Sunkist* in his 1949 solo foray into American popular culture. Spitzer turns the native citrus into a vagrant trope:

As for the particular expression *sunkist*, we are probably justified in assuming a "poetic" intention on the part of the creator of the coinage because of the poetic nature of the concept involved ("kissed by the sun"); at the same time, however, he must have been conscious of its commercial by-flavor; he has been able to play on two chess-boards, to appeal to two types of consumers: those who admire a brisk, efficient, businesslike style, and those who think that "the sun of Homer, it shineth still on us." Thus our hybrid word, which is without roots in normal speech, is doomed to a homeless existence: *sunkist* is possible only in that No Man's Land where the prosaic is shunned—but the poetic is taken not quite seriously. (LS 342)

Bhabha *avec* Spitzer may seem as superficially incongruous as "Kant avec Sade" (the postcolonial modernist maljuxtaposed to the conservative European nostalgic), but each, in his fashion, activates cultural difference and disinheritance as engines of literary, existential analysis. In both cases literary praxis, or the ritual of the *reading*, generates theoretical topoi of placelessness imbricated in the very essence of what comparative study is all about. In this sense the theorization of *Heimlosigkeit*, as mode of critique, emerges, paradoxically as the the country of comparative literature. A substitute homeland, a placeless place that is homely in its unhomeliness, comparative literature becomes the institutional and pedagogical space of not-being-there.

If comparative literature today remains haunted by a recurrent scenario of eviction and forced emigration, its very early history reveals a different kind of exile—the exile of the colonial civil servant valiantly representing an Occidental ideal of civilization somewhere in the outback, the comparatist as "evictor" of native culture. I mention this "darker" side of the discipline's history because, in hypothetically negotiating among parties of exilic comparatists, I am concerned not to paper over the discipline's colonial legacy, still manifest in the assertion of Europe-based internationalism over minority discourses in many institutions and departments. As Anthony Appiah notes in the present volume (with a "global" turn of phrase straddling Greek, Yiddish, and British English), looking back at comparative literature's early self-christening, it is hard to believe "the hubris, the chutzpa, the cheek" of a label subsuming "thousands of languages" in a Western frame.

Vauri Viswanathan's study of the invention of English literature as *cursus* and pedagogy in the context of the British Empire in India highlights the colonial origins of comparative literature insofar as the two fields were historically intertwined.[16] Like English literature, comparative literature derived its institutional identity from the bureaucratic apparatus of British education packaged for export. By René Wellek's own account the first book entitled *Comparative Literature* was published in 1886 by an Irish barrister turned professor of classics and English literature stationed in Auckland, New Zealand. The author, a critic of Tainian leanings named Hutcheson Macaulay Posnett, conceived comparative literature grandiosely, on the scale of the British Empire and the world. "Should the present application of historical science to Literature meet with general approval," he wrote, "the establishment of chairs in Comparative Literature at the leading Universities of Great Britain, America, and the Australian Colonies would do much to secure the steady progress of this vast study."[17] Posnett's outline of "world-lit," with its provision for contrasting the literatures of western Europe with those of India and China, discloses the ironic point of interface between world literature as instrument of colonial ideology and world literature as *post*colonial answer to the Eurocentric parochialism of comparative literature. It is as if we have now come full circle to Posnett's originary design, though with entirely re-fashioned political principles and interpretive stakes.

If comparative literature moves in the future to an international house within the university which would accommodate, at least in theory, "thousands of languages," it will continue to spawn the most interesting permutations of diasporic discourse and critique. One of the obvious imperatives of the future is to continue reinventing world literature with a concern not to warehouse theoretical culture. This theoretical culture—a "dissensual" confusion of First and Third World critical perspectives—is worth holding on to, not only because it gives cohesion to a field that risks dilution in a sea of cultural and linguistic particularisms, but, more important, because the exilic melancholy of theory is profoundly in sync with the narrative movement of comparative literature and comparative culture.

In rereading the "founding fathers" of comparative literature against their postcolonial successors—Homi K. Bhabha, Gayatri Chakravorty Spivak, Edward Said, Anthony Appiah, Sara Suleri, V. Y. Mudimbe, Rey Chow, and others—I have moved to consider comparative literature as comparative exile. From Spitzer to Bhabha (despite their being worlds apart) one discerns a recalcitrant homelessness of critical voice. This unhomely voice, together with the restless, migratory thought patterns of the discipline's theory and methods, highlights the extent to which comparative literature's very disciplinarity has been and continues to be grounded in exilic consciousness. What seems to be occurring now in the reactions to the 1993 Bernheimer report, "Comparative Literature at the Turn of the Century," is not just crude generational/cultural warfare over Eurocentrism but, more diffuse and more serious, a contest for the title of who lays claim to the exilic aura of comparative literature's distinguished past. Bernheimer is characterizing this phenomenon as "anxiogenic"; I would tend to frame the issue as a border war, an academic version of the legal battles and political disputes over the status of "undocumented workers," "illegal aliens," and "permanent residents." What everybody knows is that no amount of border patrolling is going to "keep out" the new arrivals; they will find a place to park themselves much like the previous tenants: deconstruction, feminist theory, gay and lesbian studies, film, popular culture. Postcolonialism will claim its place whether Continental comparatism likes it or not; but I think the field stands to become a great deal more interesting if it provides an international house rather than a hotel for the multicultural future.

Notes

1. Such caveats are evinced, for example, in the majority of essays included in the recent anthology *Building a Profession: Autobiographical Perspectives on the Beginnings of Comparative Literature in the United States*, ed. Lionel Gossman and Mihai I. Spariosu (Albany: State University of New York Press, 1994). My thanks to Françoise Lionnet for bringing this book to my attention.

2. Denis Hollier, "On Literature Considered as a Dead Language," *Modern Language Quarterly* 54, no. 1 (1993): 22.

3. Erich Auerbach, *Mimesis: The Representation of Reality in Western Literature*, trans. Willard R. Trask (Princeton: Princeton University Press, 1953), 557.

4. Erwin Panofsky, "The History of Art," in *The Cultural Migration: The European Scholar in America* (Philadelphia: University of Pennsylvania Press, 1953), 83–84. This essay was later republished under the title "Three Decades of Art History in the United States: Impressions of a Transplanted European" in *Meaning in the Visual Arts* (Chicago: University of Chicago Press, 1955), 321–46.

5. Foreword by John Freccero to Leo Spitzer, *Representative Essays*, ed. Alban K. Forcione, Herbert Lindenberger, and Madeline Sutherland (Stanford: Stanford University Press, 1988), xii. Further references to this work will appear in the text abbreviated LS.

6. Here I place the word *foreign* in quotation marks as a way of assenting to Mary Louise Pratt's problematization of the word in her essay for this volume.

7. Fredric Jameson, "Versions of a Marxist Hermeneutic: Walter Benjamin; or Nostalgia," in *Marxism and Form: Twentieth-Century Dialectical Theories of Literature* (Princeton: Princeton University Press, 1971), 60.

8. Harold Bloom, *Agon: Towards a Theory of Revisionism* (Oxford: Oxford University Press, 1982), ix.

9. Geoffrey Hartman, *Criticism in the Wilderness: The Study of Literature Today* (New Haven: Yale University Press, 1980), 15.

10. Jacques Derrida, *Aporias*, trans. Thomas Dutoit (Stanford: Stanford University Press, 1993), 11.

11. I am referring here to his book *Figures de l'étranger* (Paris: Denoel, 1987).

12. Abdelkebir Khatibi, *Love in Two Languages*, trans. Richard Howard (Minneapolis: University of Minnesota Press, 1990), 20.

13. Derrida and Khatibi are perhaps not as different as all that. Spivak calls Derrida an "assimilated post-colonial," an appellation perhaps equally applicable to Khatibi. See Gayatri Chakravorty Spivak, *Thinking Academic Freedom in Gendered Post-coloniality* (Cape Town: University of Cape Town Press, 1992), 13. This published address also offers

an important discussion of "gendered subalternity" within the modern culture of western Europe, on many levels relevant to the debate over multiculturalism in comparative literature.

14. Homi K. Bhabha, *The Location of Culture* (London: Routledge, 1994), 5–6. All further references to this work will appear in the text abbreviated LC.

15. Mary Louise Pratt, "Comparative Literature and Global Citizenship," in this volume.

16. Vauri Viswanathan, *Masks of Conquest: Literary Study and British Rule in India* (New York: Columbia University Press, 1989).

17. Hutcheson Macaulay Posnett, *Comparative Literature* (New York: Appleton and Co., 1892), vi–vii.

9

MUST WE APOLOGIZE?

PETER BROOKS

Although I hold a Ph.D. in comparative literature, I have never been sure I deserved it, since I've never been sure what the field, or the discipline, is and never sure that I could really claim to be teaching it or working in it. I was trained at a time when comparative literature was ceasing to be what the Sorbonne long believed it to be, the study of sources, influences, literary schools, and "movements"—the ideal Sorbonne CompLit thesis was easily parodied as *Madame de Staël en Roumanie*: the definitive study of a French writer's export to a definable foreign market, though of course it allowed of such as *Goethe en France* as well. Comparative literature in America in the 1960s knew it was no longer that but didn't know quite what it was, other than a place of greater literary cosmopolitanism than departments of English or French or American studies: a place where faculty and students aspired to a certain cultural self-alienation, a wider contextualization, a poetic Euro-chic.

A persistent piece of graduate student lore at Harvard in the early 1960s concerned the dream of a student in comparative literature on the eve of his oral exams. The doorbell rang, the student stumbled from bed, opened the door, and found himself faced with Harry Levin and Renato Poggioli (the two professors in the department) dressed as plumbers, carrying pipe wrenches and acetylene torches, who announced: "We've come to compare the literature." The dream became proverbial no doubt because of the anxiety associated with that notion of "comparing the literature" and the problem of what it could possibly mean. I imagine that many young comparatists were asked, as I was, by well-meaning laypersons: "Well, what do you compare?" The answer, I recall, began with a mumbled admission that you didn't really *compare* anything. You simply worked in more than one literature, studying literature without regard to national boundaries and definitions.[1]

I think I began to rid myself of some of my own anxieties about the undisciplined discipline I had stumbled into only when I managed to stop worrying about "comparing the literature," about that adjective *comparative*. The name of the game seemed to have been formed on the model of other nineteenth-century usages such as "comparative anatomy" or "comparative linguistics," in a kind of pseudoscientific claim that there was a comparative method that could be universally applied, to the production of acceptable results. Surely this was the wrong model. We weren't "comparing literature." But what, then, were we doing?

Cure from anxiety continued with the founding, in the early 1970s at Yale, of The Literature Major, an undergraduate program created independently of the graduate program in comparative literature (which had no interest in taking on undergraduate instruction), somewhat under the impact of European structuralism. In proudly claiming the chaste, adjectiveless title of "Literature," we were staking a claim to study and teach literariness and the literary phenomenon, broadly conceived. The introductory course to the major, entitled (in pre–gender-unbiased usage) "Man and His Fictions," took its stand on the etymological sense of *fiction*, from *fingere*, both "to make," as in the verbal artifact, and "to make up," as in "to feign." We were interested both in the making of texts—in the way that the Russian Formalists had brought to our attention—and in the intentionality of fictions of all sorts, from daydreaming through riddles, folk tales, detective stories, advertising, to poetry. We allied ourselves with the quasi-anthropological spirit of early French structuralism: while analyzing instances of fictions, from both high art and popular culture, we wanted to ask what human purposes they served, how they defined the place of the human maker of sense-bearing sign systems, indeed how fiction making was an essential characteristic of the human.[2]

Ridding oneself of the adjective *comparative* was liberating and permitted me largely to ignore what was going on in the comparative literature establishment (and I confess that my membership in the ACLA was only brief, since it seemed to me a relatively misguided and futile organization). Yet the liberation was only temporary, since eventually I was invited to join the graduate program in comparative literature, and later it and The Literature Major combined into one department, with both graduate and undergraduate programs, and since in any event comparative literature remains the rubric that identifies, to students and deans, and in course catalogues, that still only vaguely defined enterprise from which I earn a paycheck. I recall that when Paul de Man was chair of the Department of Comparative Literature, in the late 1970s and early 1980s, and feeling some exasperation with the opposition of some colleagues to the kind of redefinition of the curriculum he favored, he once suggested that we might start a breakaway department, labeled "Poetics, Rhetoric, and the History of Literature." The unifying center of literary study for de Man was of course "theory," though this notion was for him complex because of the difficult relations it entertained to "reading."[3] If the object of the discourse on literature was "literariness," this was by no means (as the Russian Formalists seemed to believe) inherent in the poetic "function" of language but rather something always to be defined in an act of reading which always both postulated and undid its subtending theory.

"Poetics, Rhetoric, and the History of Literature" seems about as good a characterization of what I think my own Department of Comparative Literature teaches as one is apt to come up with, though it leaves a number of questions in suspense. It does, though, provide some background to both my comfort and discomfort with the 1993 ACLA report, "Comparative Literature at the Turn of the Century." I welcome the report's call for opening up broader interpretive contexts for the study of literature, and for moving out from the traditional Eurocentric definition of the field. In fact, much of the recommended opening of the field has already occurred in many departments: languages other than European are welcomed; the crossings of borders into anthropology, social history, philosophy, psychoanalysis have become routine; feminism, film studies, queer theory have contested and broadened the canon. When I look at the dissertations currently under way in our department, it's clear that a broad eclecticism has taken the place of what at one point had become rather too narrow a commitment to rhetorical reading of the deconstructive variety.

Yet my unease with the report is real. I am distressed by its abjectly apologetic tone when discussing the teaching of literature. To be told that literature is only "one discursive practice among many others," that "comparative literature departments should moderate their focus on high-literary discourse and examine the entire discursive context in which texts are created and such heights are constructed," that the "production of 'literature' as an object of study could thus be compared to the production of music, philosophy, history, or law as similar discursive systems" creates the impression that the study of literature is an outmoded mandarin practice that had better catch up with the hip world of cultural studies. The impression is confirmed in the next paragraph of the report, where we are told that "textually precise readings should take account as well of the ideological, cultural, and institutional contexts in which their meanings are produced."[4]

One wonders, first of all, where all those "shoulds" come from (the report is full of them). In the name of what are we being asked to consider literature as "one discursive practice among many others" and to "moderate" our focus on "high" literature? Is it certain, on the one hand, that these recommendations are not already in effect—possibly excessively so in some programs— and, on the other hand, that one speaks from any convincing basis in making them? For what is above all lacking in the report is any theory of the practices recommended. If it wants comparative literature departments to give up whatever forms of the teaching of literature are currently practiced in favor of ideological and cultural contextualizations and the study of literary production, let us at least have some reference to how that can be done. The problem here may be that cultural studies has yet to produce a coherent body of theory. This may be why the report contents itself with tired clichés where we want energizing definitions. When we learn that we "should" engage in "reflection on the privileged strategies of meaning making in each discipline," that we "should be actively engaged in the comparative study of canon formation and in reconceiving the canon," that our departments "should play an active role in furthering the multicultural recontextualization of Anglo-American and European perspectives," all we've been given is a list of some of the common topics discussed at MLA conventions for the last decade. What does it all mean, in what construction of textuality, of the university, of the world *should* we be responding to these imperatives? What kind of imperatives are they: intellectual, pedagogical, institutional, ethical? And isn't the rhetoric of virtue implicit in such imperatives quite at odds with the cultural relativism, the situatedness of analytical perspective, preached in the report?

While the report eventually gets around to noting: "All of the above suggests the importance of theoretically informed thinking to comparative literature as a discipline," one senses that it really hasn't much use for theory, that it places its faith exclusively in a progressive ideology and in the cumulative outcomes of the practices it recommends. Now, to downgrade the study of literature and those forms of attention and knowledge which it has traditionally implicated—including rhetoric and poetics—in favor of something as undefined and unsupported as the cultural studies alluded to here strikes me as being borderline suicidal. It risks replacing the study of literature with amateur social history, amateur sociology, and personal ideology.

I have worked myself into the position of claiming that professors of (comparative) literature *do* have something to teach. Northrop Frye, in his "Polemical Introduction" to *Anatomy of Criticism*, argued that one should be able to write a primer of the elements of literary criticism and to demonstrate that the mental process involved in literary study "is as coherent and progressive as the study of science."[5] The claim is no doubt exaggerated and, thirty-five years later, the primer still unwritten. But the point has a general validity. As teachers of literature, we do call on a body of lore by which we apprentice our students to more competent reading of literature. The study of literature is not in itself the acquisition of information, but it involves that: the information implied by poetics, rhetoric, and literary history. Poetics, especially—the understanding of genres, of conventions, of the way a sonnet makes its argument, for instance, or of the "rules" of neoclassical tragedy—represents an indispensable kind of lore for understanding, not the meanings of specific texts, but the processes by which meaning is made, the grounds for interpretation.

"Learning literature" still works, I think, according to the ancient, un-scientific, time-consuming process of apprenticeship: learning one's trade at the bench of the master craftsman. But it is not merely learning to manufacture single items: there is a generalizability to the process, precisely in the lore of poetics. I have recently argued elsewhere that Anglo-American literary studies, from New Criticism to deconstruction, have perhaps been too exclusively concerned with exegesis, with the interpretation of individual texts.[6] While exegesis can be contextualized in many different ways, the most imperative context is that of poetics. Students need to consider, for instance, that while *Madame Bovary* may be illuminated by comparison to Briquet's and Brachet's medical treatises on hysteria, a novel proceeds according to certain conventions, certain low-level rules of meaning creation, and that *reading* a novel is not quite the same as reading a medical treatise. The point is obvious, but one is aware of academic studies that put the difference of genres and discourses at naught.

In the call for contextualizing literature by way of "ideological, cultural, and institutional contexts," it is helpful to remember that literature itself is an institution.[7] It has probably always been an institution; certainly it self-consciously became one in Renaissance Europe. And this means, among other things, that writers are always responding, not only to ideological and cultural contexts, but as well to the history and situation of the literature in which they want to claim to be participants. An aspiring poet becomes an aspiring poet because he or she has read some poetry by others, not simply because he or she wants to respond to the ideological and cultural *Zeitgeist*. I don't, in fact, see that anyone could become a poet without having read prior poetry: the case simply doesn't make sense. And while the formal constraints of novel or essay may be looser, one still can't imagine the aspiration to write in a genre without some absorption of its previous examples. The origin of Montaigne's *Essais* in a selection of citations from classical authors remains exemplary of literary apprenticeship—as does parody, and imitation of all sorts.

The institutional history of literature is a real context for literary creation and susceptible of creative revision, as the powerful work of Harold Bloom, from the *Anxiety of Influence* onward, has so well demonstrated. To neglect the literary institution as context in exclusive favor of other contexts—often more overtly ideological and political—is to fail to perform a necessary act of mediation, one that recognizes that if "literariness" is not, as Jakobson and others claimed, in the nature of the literary usage of language, it is nonetheless part of the stance of literature in the world, part of its project, part of its institutional claim. Even the Supreme Court of the United States has understood this, in its recent decision that literary parody is not the same thing as the infringement of copyright.[8]

My argument, then, is that teaching literature as literature and not as something else—not as "one discursive practice among many others"— remains necessary if we are to apprentice our students to "learning literature." And it remains what we, as a professional caste, know how to teach. This is not to say that we should not cross all the borders we find confining, into whatever domains we find potentially illuminating (in my own work with psychoanalysis, I have tried to do that). It is rather to say that studying literature, as a form of attention, as a reading competence, needs to remain in focus. Here, it is perhaps worth a polemical caveat against a bland "interdisciplinarity," of the type so often touted by deans. Real interdisciplinarity doesn't come from mixing together a bit of this and that, putting philosophy and penology and literature into a Cuisinart. It comes when thought processes reach the point where the disciplinary boundary one comes up against no longer makes sense—when the internal logic of thinking impels a transgression of borderlines. And to the extent that this is teachable at all, it requires considerable apprenticeship in the discipline that is to be transcended.

So far, what I have said seems to apply to the teaching of any form of literary studies, in a French or English department, for instance. What is specific to comparative literature—or is it condemned to be a space of the undefinable? I think the answer to this question is implicit in what I have said so far: comparative literature might best conceive of itself as that place that provides the most probing and self-conscious reflection on what it means to study literature. It could be—and it often is—the place where poetics, rhetoric, and the history of literature are most closely attended to. It could be—and often is—the department where "theory" receives the greatest attention. Theory is in this understanding both what comparative literature can do better than other departments because it is open to and competent in theoretical work produced in other languages and cultures, and what holds the diverse endeavors of comparatists together. Theory is the lingua franca of comparative literature departments, sometimes the only one as students pursue more and more diverse work in cultures that don't necessarily find their center of gravity in the Latin West. The argument for the centrality of theory is not an attempt to impose one central theory. It is rather an argument for self-consciousness and self-reflexivity about what literature may be and what it may mean to study it. The opportunity, and the burden, of comparative literature lies partly in the fact that it cannot take refuge in national traditions and their definitions of the features pertinent to construct literary theory and history, that it must always find them not good enough. The centrality of theory to comparative literature does not in itself argue against the "cultural studies" model implicitly favored in the ACLA report, and in fact the incorporation of the cultural studies impulse within comparative literature departments seems to be under way in many institutions. The question in some institutions at present appears to be whether comparative literature ingests cultural studies or rather gets swallowed by it. Devourment in either direction would seem to me a mistake. I would prefer to think of comparative literature as providing a viable interlocutor to cultural studies, one that insists that contextualizations of literature in ideological and cultural terms remain aware of literature's institutional definitions and of the uses of poetics and rhetoric in understanding the ways in which literature creates meanings that both resemble and differ from those produced in other discourses.

As Michael Riffaterre elegantly argues in his essay for this volume, if cultural studies urge us ever to contextualize, literary studies also of necessity include a moment of decontextualization, "for a text can be said to be literary when it survives the extinction of the issues, the vanishing of the causes, and the memory of the circumstances to which that text responded." To say this need not entail the isolation of "high art" on a pedestal. It argues rather that the study of literature always involves a special form of attention to the structure and texture of the text which is often elided in other forms of cultural analysis. I have yet to be convinced that most practitioners of cultural studies are *readers*, in the strong sense inculcated by all the viable movements in literary study of our time, from New Criticism to poststructuralism.

Far from believing with the ACLA report that "the term 'literature' may no longer adequately describe our object of study," I would hence urge that literature must very much remain our focus, while by no means restricting its dialogic interaction with other discourses and its various contexts. When one thinks about the institutional future of comparative literature as a field of study, one feel that its strength is allied to its vulnerability. The extent to which it refuses definition, the extent to which it conceives itself as the center of intersecting discourses about literature, and the place of the theory of these discourses, makes it tempting for many, both inside and outside the field, to conceive it as a kind of omnium-gatherum of those humanities subjects and practices that have no other home. Thus university administrators have often found comparative literature a flag of convenience for small and homeless subjects, from marginalized languages to odd bits of theory. Or else they've wanted to submerge comparative literature in some larger interdisciplinary entity. It is not to retreat to older definitions of comparative literature to argue that our field needs to maintain some sense of identity, not perhaps as a discipline, but as a place for the very conceptualization of discipline as it is pertinent to literary study.

In more concrete terms, I believe that comparative literature at the moment finds its specificity and its raison d'être in an ever-renewed and multifaceted address to the question, What is literature, and what does it mean to study literature? This question cannot always be explicit in our teaching, to be sure, but I am convinced it ought never to be far away, always ready to resurface. Two years ago, I took on the teaching of the required introductory seminar for first-year graduate students in comparative literature in our department. This was a course inaugurated by René Wellek in the late 1940s (Wellek was the first professor of comparative literature at Yale, appointed in 1947) and for many years the crucial initiation of some of the most notable comparatists produced on native ground. Recently, the course had fallen into decadence, no doubt for the lack of someone with Wellek's range of knowledge and capacity for encyclopaedic organization, but also because the proliferation of critical schools and isms had made it difficult to perform any sort of magisterial conspectus of criticism and theory. I decided to reorganize the seminar under the title "Education and Cultural Transmission," focusing especially on the place of literature and its teaching in cultural debates and cultural institutions, including, in the final weeks of the seminar, the recent history of literary studies at Yale. The value of the seminar, for all its—and my own—limitations, came from the opportunity it gave students to think and talk about the strange enterprise of teaching literature.

For it is a strange enterprise, one that is never wholly comfortable in the university. We teachers of literature have little hard information to impart, we're not even sure what we teach, and we have something of a bad conscience about the whole business, which in part explains why some among us find a relieved refuge in the rhetoric of virtue which sometimes comes with cultural studies, in the conviction that one is demasking pernicious dominant ideologies and promoting a brave new multiculturalist millennium. I am not opposed to virtue, but I am convinced that the pedagogical practice of it must begin with our insistence that students learn to read, that they apprentice themselves to the difficult task of encountering textuality, that they try to understand that whatever contexts may be used to "explain" literature, they never entirely explain. Literature needs to remain a challenge to other forms of discourse with which it is in dialogue. And the teaching of literature needs to insist that it is a different form of attention from that practiced in any other field in the university.

I think there is much truth in Terry Eagleton's recent assertion—in his inaugural address as Wharton Professor of English at Oxford—that literary and cultural studies have become a battleground, within the university and without, in part because they have taken up vital questions that other disciplines, in their professionalization, have for the moment abandoned. Writes Eagleton: "For the great speculative questions of truth and justice, of freedom and happiness, have to find a home somewhere; and if an aridly technical philosophy, or a drearily positivist sociology, are no hospitable media for such explorations, then they will be displaced onto a criticism which is simply not intellectually equipped to take this strain."[9] Ill equipped, to be sure, but as Eagleton also notes, great moments of literary criticism tend to be those when, speaking of literature, criticism is speaking of that and more, "mapping the deep structures and central directions of an entire culture." It is in my view a good thing that literary criticism be under strain, so long as it recognizes the limits of what it can do, so long as it continues to deal with that strain, those tensions, in strong acts of reading. The response to strain need not be the abandonment of its central enterprise but rather the affirmation of that centrality.

For the teacher of literature, I seem to have worked myself around to some form of the advice famously given by Benjamin Disraeli to aspiring statesmen: "Never apologize, never explain." This, of course, is not quite right. We need constantly to explain the strange fact that poetry gained a place in the academic republic (one it didn't always have, one that many still find unwarranted) and that studying literature is a fundamentally different experience from any other in the curriculum. It cannot be reduced to cultural studies because it is fundamentally other, resisting full contextualization in other discourses, demanding different forms of attention, even of knowing. But apologies are not in order.

Notes

1. Checking references for the notes to this essay, I discovered that the Dream of the Plumbers had been recorded by Harry Levin himself, in "Comparing the Literature," in *Grounds for Comparison* (Cambridge: Harvard University Press, 1972), 75–76. Levin's version attributes the dream to the wife of a graduate student, an interesting displacement of anxiety.

2. On the original conception of the program, see my article "Man and His Fictions: One Approach to the Teaching of Literature," *College English* 35, no. 1 (1973): 40–49.

3. See Paul de Man, "The Resistance to Theory," in *The Resistance to Theory* (Minneapolis: University of Minnesota Press, 1986), 3–20.

4. I cite from *A Report to the ACLA: Comparative Literature at the Turn of the Century* (1993).

5. Northrop Frye, *Anatomy of Criticism* (Princeton: Princeton University Press, 1957), 10–11.

6. See Peter Brooks, "Aesthetics and Ideology: What Happened to Poetics?" *Critical Inquiry* 20 (Spring 1994): 509–23.

7. As Harry Levin noted many years ago: see Levin, "Literature as an Institution," *Accent* 6, no. 3 (1946): 159–68; revised and reprinted in *The Gates of Horn* (Oxford: Oxford University Press, 1963).

8. See *Campell v. Acuff-Rose Music, Inc.* 62 LW 4169. Justice Souter delivered the opinion of the Court, which clearly recognizes (though it does not use the word) the importance of "intertextuality" in the creation of a work that cites but transforms the original.

9. Terry Eagleton, *The Crisis of Contemporary Culture* (Oxford: Clarendon Press, 1993), 16.

10

IN THE NAME OF
COMPARATIVE LITERATURE

REY CHOW

If "literature" alone constituted the discipline of comparative literature, then we would have to ask why there ought to be "comparative" literature at all—why don't we simply have national literature departments? It seems to me that the "comparative" in comparative literature is equally, if not more, crucial a factor in considering the future of comparative literature: exactly what constitutes "comparison"—what kinds of relations, critical formations, analytical perspectives are relevant? More than the word *literature*, it is the interest in "comparative" which has allowed the practitioners of comparative literature to distinguish their work from that done within strictly national and national-linguistic boundaries and to say, with some rigor, that comparative literature is not simply a matter of adding/juxtaposing one national literature to another so that its existence is simply—as many of comparative literature's hostile opponents in national literature departments would charge— redundant and superfluous.

I am entitling my response to the 1993 Report on Standards by the ACLA committee "In the Name of Comparative Literature" in order to highlight a couple of preliminary considerations. First is the fact that, in a manner beyond the control of those who have strong feelings about what comparative literature is and is not, all kinds of claims are being made and all kinds of practices flourish in its name. CompLit in this first instance signals prestige, cosmopolitanism, and power—besides having the respectability of a long-established discipline, it is also a kind of "classy" designer label, like Armani, Dior, Givenchy, St. Laurent, and so forth, which many want to display. Second, however, precisely because comparative literature is simply a name, it must be subject to change. As a name and as a discipline, comparative literature should insist on its own permanence only if that permanence is accompanied by continual self-criticism. The currently constitutive features of comparative literature can as easily be manipulated to consolidate repressive cultural interests as they can be used to open up new intellectual avenues. This fundamental ambivalence of the name and the discipline means that CompLit will always remain institutionally controversial, appealing to astute administrators as an opportunity for fostering quality intellectual leadership in their organizations, but threatening those who lack such bureaucratic insight and courage. The following remarks are made in the light of these preliminary considerations.

Comparative Literature and "Eurocentrism"

I fully agree with the report's recommendation that languages and literatures other than the ones traditionally sponsored by comparative literature departments and programs—namely, English, French, and German—be more widely and routinely taught. At the same time, to someone like myself who has worked with non-European languages and literatures, this suggested "othering" of the curriculum is precisely the problem, not because it is difficult to initiate the teaching of these "other" languages and literatures, but because the teaching of, say, Arabic, Hindi, Japanese, Chinese, and so forth already has an institutional history in this country which is fully mired in practices, habits, and biases and which is fully peopled with intentions. Instead of being a blank space ready to be adopted or assimilated by comparative literature, non-Western language and literature programs have been sites of production of knowledge which function alongside United States State Department policies vis-à-vis the particular nations and cultures concerned— such as the former Soviet Union, East Asia, South Asia, Southeast Asia, the Middle East, Eastern Europe, Africa. The problems that exist in these "other" programs, which are at times organized under the rubric of area studies, are familiar to most who understand the basic arguments of Edward Said's *Orientalism*, first published nearly twenty years ago.

Even though many pedagogues of non-Western languages and literatures tend to make, with good justification, strong objections to the Eurocentrism of comparative literature, as far as I can tell their own practices and beliefs often fall strictly within the parameters of the same Eurocentrism. It is simply that they practice Eurocentrism in the name of the other, the local, and the culturally exceptional.

The Nation-State

Of all the prominent features of Eurocentrism, the one that stands out in the context of the university is the conception of culture as based on the modern European notion of the nation-state. In this light, comparative literature has been rightly criticized for having concentrated on the literatures of a few strong nation-states in modern Europe. But the problem does not go away if we simply substitute India, China, and Japan for England, France, and Germany. To this day we still witness publications that bear titles such as "comparative approaches to masterpieces of Asian literature" which adopt precisely this Eurocentric, nation-oriented model of literature *in the name of the other*. In such instances, the concept of literature is strictly subordinated to a social Darwinian understanding of the nation: "masterpieces" correspond to "master" nations and "master" cultures. With India, China, and Japan being held as representative of Asia, cultures of lesser prominence in Western reception such as Korea, Taiwan, Vietnam, Tibet, and others simply fall by the wayside—as marginalized "others" to the "other" that is the "great" Asian civilizations.

The critique of Eurocentrism, if it is to be thorough and fundamental, cannot take place at the level of replacing one set of texts with another set of texts—not even if the former are European and the latter are Asian, African, or Latin American. Rather, it must question the very assumption that nation-states with national languages are the only possible cultural formations that produce "literature" that is worth examining. Otherwise we will simply see, as we have already been seeing, the old Eurocentric models of language and literature study being reproduced ad infinitum in non-European language and literature pedagogy. The active disabling of such reproduction of Eurocentrism-in-the-name-of-the-other should, I think, be one of comparative literature's foremost tasks in the future.

Multilingualism and Multiculturalism

I very much agree with the merit of enforcing a multilingual discipline and especially with Mary Louise Pratt's suggestion in "Comparative Literature and Global Citizenship" that we should desist from thinking of non-English languages as "foreign" languages. Once again, however, I do not think that the cultivation of multilingualism and multiculturalism alone would solve the problems faced by comparative literature simply because multilingualism and multiculturalism are already part of comparative literature's constitutive, disciplinary features.

To begin with, I am not particularly worried about the "monolingualism" of our future world simply because multilingualism is clearly already part of the life of the elite classes across the globe today—and where there is power and money, there will be continuity. The children of these elite classes, whether they happen to be living in Geneva, Tokyo, New Delhi, Hong Kong, or Palo Alto, are being brought up in at least two or three languages. In the case of those growing up in Asian metropolises, the combination would usually involve English, French, or German, plus the so-called mother tongue, whatever it happens to be. Almost all such children would eventually find their way to privileged institutions of higher education, such as those in the United States.

In itself, multilingualism has always been part of a humanistic view of intellectual culture which can as easily serve the agenda of reactionary politics as it can serve progressive ones. Think, for instance, of the Jesuit and the Mormon establishments, the intelligence networks, and the diplomatic circles of the world, which, well before enlightened comparatists, knew of the need to master non-Western as well as Western languages in order to indoctrinate, to police information, and to conduct political exchange. Alternatively, multilingualism can also serve as an ally and accomplice to white liberalism. As Armani, Dior, Givenchy, St. Laurent, and their like are incorporating exotic fabrics and styles from non-European cultures into their prestigious fashion inventories, so the liberalist sectors of the North American academy, too, are advocating the need for other languages and literatures to appear in our curricula, our journals, our professional meetings. But in the liberalist instance, multilingualism is ultimately simply an alibi: the charitable "openness" to other languages and cultures often goes hand in hand with an utter ignorance of and indifference to the historical and political distinctions among "ethnic cultures" and "peoples of color." If reactionary politics uses multilingualism for purposes of indoctrination and surveillance, then white liberalism, in a more benign guise, uses multilingualism for embellishment and amusement, for a mere change of décors.

My point is that we should not let the euphoria of oppositional thinking lure us into assuming that, by positing a multilingual, other-culture–oriented approach to comparative literature and by making the gesture of welcoming non-Western cultures and civilizations into our curricula, we are going to make real changes—when, already, in myriad forms for an extended period of time, the very disciplinary structures that we seek to challenge have been firmly established in the pedagogical practices related to non-Western languages and literatures, when "qualifications" and "expertise" in so-called other cultures have been used as the means to legitimate entirely conservative institutional practices in hiring, tenuring, promotion, reviewing, and publishing, as well as in teaching. We need to remember that there has been a complicated history in the West of the study of non-Western, non-European languages; our Eurocentric multilingual comparatists have always had their counterparts in the great Orientalists, Sinologists, Indologists, and so forth.

In brief, being multilingual does not necessarily free one from bigotry. A multilingualism that was "Eurocentric" before could easily incorporate within it the dimensions of non-European languages without coming to terms with the Eurocentrism of its notions of language and knowledge. Because of this, the sheer enforcement of multilingualism cannot ensure that we educate our students about the power structures, hierarchies, and discriminations that work as much in the "others" as in "us."

I belabor the rather obvious points about the nation-state and multilingualism/multiculturalism because I think they represent the most entrenched intersections between comparative literature and national literature programs. National language and literature programs represent "local" versions of the problems that are equally shared by comparative literature in the guise of internationalism and cosmopolitanism. The problems of comparative literature—its "Eurocentrism" and its false claim to "universalism"—can therefore not be solved simply by strengthening the local versions of the same problems, nor by simply adding emphases to the study of non-European languages and cultures as if such study did not already have a fully implicated and complicit role in the history of the teaching of the humanities in the West.

"Theory" and the Evolving Concept of "Media"

Comparative literature has traditionally been the place where "theory" is investigated. While the bashing of theory continues, it is certain that theory has won the battle even among those who malign it but who nonetheless use it to dress up their inquiries. It should be pointed out that when theory or "Western theory" is demonized and attacked, the real target (usually uncomprehended by those parroting theory-bashing banalities in order to be safely politically correct) is deconstruction and poststructuralist theory—namely, the kind of theory, officially dating from the France of the 1960s but traceable to elsewhere and earlier periods, which questions the logocentric bases of humanistic culture in the West—whereas the continual adoption of nineteenth-century European historiographic methods (in the form of intellectual histories, literary histories, or histories of ideas) or twentieth-century

Anglo-American New Criticism (in the form of close readings of prose and poetry) is usually assumed to be natural rather than "Western." Against deconstruction and poststructuralism as such, deeply ingrained humanistic and historiographic versions of culture, themselves equally Western, are often mounted in the name of the other.

This is not the place to launch yet another full-fledged debate about deconstruction and poststructuralism, but it is worth arguing that one of the strongest justifications for studying the non-West has to do precisely with the fundamental questioning of the limits of Western discourse which is characteristic of deconstruction and poststructuralist theory. The questioning of the sign as such leads logically to the opening up of the study of other signs and other systems of significations, other disciplines, other sexualities, other ethnicities, other cultures. Thus, against the arguments of many, I would say that deconstruction and poststructuralist theory have very close ties with cultural studies, gender studies, gay and lesbian studies, and ethnic studies, in that the investigations of disciplines, class, race, gender, ethnicity, and so forth, however empirical, must always already contain within them the implicit *theoretical* understanding of the need to critique hegemonic signs and sign systems from without as well as from within. This kind of theoretical direction is the one in which I would like to see comparative literature continue.

Several aspects of this theoretical direction could be specified briefly as follows:

1. How to approach the version of Eurocentrism that is the passion for the nation-state?

Instead of reconsolidating the boundaries of nations through the study of national languages and literatures, comparative literature should remain the place where theory is used to put the very concept of the nation in crisis, and with that, the concept of the nation as the origin of a particular literature. Let me cite here the recent work by Nancy Armstrong and Leonard Tennenhouse, *The Imaginary Puritan: Literature, Intellectual Labor, and the Origins of Personal Life* (Berkeley and Los Angeles: University of California Press, 1992), as an example of what I think an alternative kind of comparative literature might look like. Explicitly, Armstrong and Tennenhouse's book is about a particular European national literature—English—in its historical formation. The theoretically path-breaking achievement of the book, however, stems from the remarkable manner in which they demonstrate how the "origins" of this literature in fact lie outside the boundaries of the English nation, in the popular and debased literature produced about and in the North American colonies. English literary "classics" and "masterpieces" such as Samuel Richardson's *Pamela*, for instance, could now be said to have their "origins" in the captivity narratives such as that of Mary Rowlandson, a type of literary production which originated not in the fens but in the American "wilderness," among "savages."

Through a sophisticated use of poststructuralism's radical implications, Armstrong and Tennenhouse offer a kind of *comparative* reading between vastly different types of literature, a reading that (a) challenges the sacredness of nationhood by showing "nation" and "nationalism" to be products of imperialist, puritanicist fantasies, (b) overturns the elitist, Eurocentric assumption that (print) "culture" flows only from Europe to its colonies but not vice versa, and (c) problematizes at once the hierarchical models of national language, masterpiece, and cultural "original"/translation which are crucial to the study of comparative literature. Most important of all, while working strictly from the perspective of one European literary tradition and one "national language," Armstrong and Tennenhouse nonetheless succeed in reinscribing the differences of English "national literature" from within, supplementing its glorious image as the depository of England's treasured intellectual culture—an image that to this day continues to be pedagogically disseminated around the world—with one that reveals it to be a product of England's own imperialism.

As a theoretical model, *The Imaginary Puritan* thus makes it possible for comparative literature to form significant connections with postcolonial studies by asking an entirely different kind of question about national literature: not "how is national literature, like class and gender, linked to the formation of subjectivity?" but "how does national literature participate in the histories of colonialism and imperialism precisely as widely distributed *habits of writing and reading*?" This kind of question would imply that not only the classics of the European canons, in English, French, German, Spanish, Italian, Latin, and Greek, but also the "masterpieces" of China, Japan, India, Arabia, Persia, Russia, and so forth would have to be fundamentally rethought. Comparative literature would no longer be a mechanistic juxtaposition of different national literatures in the form of mutual admiration societies but would be actively engaged in the comparisons of imperialist designs, narratives, and print cultures.

2. How to approach the issue of multilingualism?

While the command of multiple languages should remain one of comparative literature's disciplinary concerns, it should also be possible for students who do not necessarily have a deep knowledge of languages other their native ones to be introduced to comparative literature through the study of poststructuralist theory, simply because one of the key pedagogical aims of poststructuralist theory is the scrutiny of language itself. In the case of North America, where many students have English as their first language, this is crucial because of the multiple languages and cultural enclaves that already exist *within* English—precisely owing to the "international" history of British and American imperialism. Instead of asking our students to learn Arabic or Chinese in place of the more traditionally revered French or German, what about asking them to study black English, English as used by writers in British India, or English as used by present-day Latin American and Asian American authors? The many different types of postcolonial writings which continue to be produced in the "single" language of English or French should require us to rethink comparative literature's traditional language requirements, so that, in principle at least, it should be possible for some students to do work in comparative literature using one language (even though I very much doubt that that would ever be the case). Similarly, the issues involved in women's literature, gay and lesbian literature, ethnic literature, and so forth so far exceed the boundaries of the nation and national language that they demand to be studied with newer conceptual methods.

In other words, just as multilingualism does not necessarily prevent one from becoming an intellectual bigot, so monolingualism does not have to mean that one's mind is closed. Instead of having students add on languages without ever questioning the premise of language-as-power, we could also, within comparative literature, teach students how to be comparative within "single" languages. To this may be added the point that, as Mary Louise Pratt writes, often, precisely in multicultural contexts, (English) translations are the only possible texts to use, simply because many languages, even when they are from the same geographical area, do not share common linguistic bases in the manner typical of European languages.

3. What about comparative literature's relation with "cultural studies"?

The increasing sense of annoyance, anxiety, and threat felt by some comparatists toward cultural studies is a sign that comparative literature's own identity is a shifting one. This is not at all a bad thing. As Wlad Godzich argues in his essay "Emergent Literature and the Field of Comparative Literature," the field of comparative literature—that is, what constitutes its "identity"—is the very problematic of "field" itself.[1] Rather than being the cause for worry, then, I think the at times blurry distinction between comparative literature and cultural studies offers a good opportunity for comparative literature to rethink and restrategize itself.

If one strong criticism of cultural studies from comparatists is that cultural studies tends to be empiricist and monolingual, then wouldn't it be in comparative literature's interest to confront this problem head on—not by denouncing cultural studies *tout court* but rather by seizing the opportunity and making the rich array of cultural objects currently investigated under the rubric of cultural studies part of comparative literature's theoretical and multilingual inquiry?

To do this, comparative literature would need to extend its traditional attention to the materiality of verbal language into an equally meticulous examination of the notion of the "medium." I use the word *medium* here in its basic sense of a means of storage, retrieval, and transmission (of cultural information) and not in the sense of "the media" as we find it in more contemporary popular usage. In the age of hypertext, when electronic virtuality and speed technologies mean that even rare, faraway inscriptions made in vastly different media can be made available at our fingertips, our notions of the medium (and consequently of research, knowledge, and knowledge dissemination) are undergoing such vast changes that it would be inconceivable simply to proceed with our study of word-based texts in a manner that is unengaged with such changes. At the same time, once we think in terms of the medium, we must ask anew the questions "what is literature?" and "what is writing?" As Friedrich Kittler argues in a recent essay, in the "postmodern Tower of Babel" where "ordinary" language encounters the programming languages of the microprocessor, "We simply do not know what our writing does."[2]

In taking into consideration the evolving concept of the medium, we would be returning the word *literature* to an openness that was there before it became disciplined into the particular "body" that it has had in the past few hundred years in the West—to an alternative space and time when "literature" simply referred to materials relying on the medium of the printed word. This earlier notion of "literature" offers, in the postmodern age, the advantage of challenging the chronologically recent and much more narrow notion of "literature" which persists in many's understanding of comparative literature today.

Instead of simply resisting or discrediting cultural studies, therefore, comparative literature could borrow from cultural studies by way of opening itself to the study of media other than the word-based literary or philosophical text. To bring literature into crisis through the concept of "media" does not mean, necessarily, literature's demise. Perhaps, precisely in the name of comparative literature, a new discipline would emerge in which the study of literature is relativized not along lines of nations and national languages but, more rigorously, along lines of aesthetic media, sign systems, and discourse networks? Perhaps that name itself would eventually transform into an other, such as comparative media?

Notes

1. In *The Comparative Perspective on Literature: Approaches to Theory and Practice*, ed. Clayton Koelb and Susan Noakes (Ithaca, N.Y.: Cornell University Press, 1988), 18–36.

2. Friedrich Kittler, "There Is No Software," *Stanford Literature Review* 9, no. 1 (1992): 81–90.

11

COMPARATIVE LITERATURE,
AT LAST!

JONATHAN CULLER

———

"Comparative Literature at the Turn of the Century" recommends two courses of action, each of which has a good deal to be said for it. On the one hand, the report urges comparative literature to abandon its traditional Eurocentrism and turn global, an injunction that seems entirely justified, both as a reflection of contemporary cultural realities and as a response to the growing conviction that Western cultures in the past were in fact determined in part by their relations to non-Western others. On the other hand, the report recommends that comparative literature turn from a concentration on literature to the study of cultural productions or discourses of all sorts. This too is a course for which a good case can be made. Scholars of literature have discovered that their analytical skills can shed light on the structures and the functioning of the wide range of discursive practices that form individuals and cultures; and their contributions to the study of philosophical, psychoanalytic, political, medical, and other discourses, not to mention conduct books, film, and popular culture, have been so valuable that no one could wish to restrict literature faculties to the study of literature alone. Treating literature as one discourse among others seems an effective and commendable strategy.

Each of these turns, then, can be justified with plausible, even convincing arguments, but the result of the two moves would be a discipline of overwhelming scope, charged with the study of discourses and cultural productions of all sorts throughout the entire world. If one had the resources to create a university from scratch, one could construct a large department of comparative literature devoted to global cultural studies, but this would doubtless provoke at least two questions: should such a department still be called "comparative literature"? And should there be any other humanities departments in this university? This second question is especially pertinent: if comparative literature did indeed cover global cultural studies, what other departments would be needed? what sort of studies would the new comparative literature exclude? Should we also have departments that study different sorts of cultural productions on their own, without relation to others—art history, music, film studies?—or is this sort of approach rendered obsolete by comparative literature in its new dispensation? And should different regions or even countries have departments devoted to their study, or should not American literature, for example, always be studied in the comparative perspective that the new comparative literature represents?

As soon as one begins to think about the place that the new comparative literature should in principle occupy, one confronts the fact that the vision the report offers seems less a recipe for a separate discipline or department—one among many—than a recommendation about how literary and cultural studies of all sorts should proceed.

Since existing universities are not likely to take kindly to an imperialism in which comparative literature departments lay claim to all existing humanities and social science faculty or at least to all new and replacement positions in these domains, the recommendations of "Comparative Literature at the Turn of the Century" call for a comprehensiveness which, in practice, departments cannot even begin to achieve. Departments of comparative literature concretely face such questions of direction when they decide what sort of faculty member to appoint and what students to admit; and since such appointments and admissions are likely to be severely limited these days, departments risk spreading themselves impossibly thin if they adopt this broad definition and try to do everything at once.

Such considerations might lead us to return to the fundamental fact that, like the linguistic sign, disciplines and departments have differential identities. As Ferdinand de Saussure put it—though not with comparative literature in mind—"their most precise characteristic is to be what the others are not" (*Cours de linguistique générale*, ed. Tullio de Mauro [Paris: Payot, 1972], 162). Once upon a time, when literary study was organized according to national literatures, comparative literature was defined differentially as the place where the study of literature was organized by other sorts of units: genres, periods, themes. And since the question of what sorts of units were most pertinent could not be avoided, as it could be in national literature departments, comparative literature soon became the site of literary theory, while the national literature departments frequently resisted—or at least resisted sorts of theory which did not emanate from their own cultural sphere.

But as the national literature departments opened themselves to theory and, through theoretical questions, to projects that crossed national boundaries, the identity of comparative literature became a problem. It is in this context, where English professors may be writing about the history of the body and German professors about modernist film, that the insistence on reading texts in the original has come to be the distinctive, perhaps the only differentiating feature of comparative literature. It is striking that previously, while most comparatists did work on texts in the original, this had not been made the defining feature of the enterprise, and books by leading comparatists, such as Harry Levin's *The Gates of Horn*, presented their material in translation. Only as comparative literature came to lack other differentiating features did the insistence on work in the original languages come to seem so crucial.

Today, when national literature departments have increasingly become sites where a wide range of cultural objects are studied—not just film and popular culture but discourses of sexuality, conduct books, and any discourse that contributes to the construction of cultures and individuals—the turn from literature to other cultural productions will not help to differentiate or define comparative literature. Indeed, to the contrary, the turn from literature to culture makes sense for these national literature departments in a way that it does not for comparative literature. While national or linguistic divisions were never a particularly cogent way of organizing the study of literature— literature has always been transnational—they make much sense as ways of organizing the study of cultures in general. Perhaps, finally, as German literature departments, for example, turn into German studies, taking on all the cultural products that appear in their domain, the names of fields will represent divisions that are intellectually cogent. And as the national literature departments turn to culture, they will leave comparative literature with a particular role. If it resists the rush into cultural studies, comparative literature will find itself with a new identity, as the site of literary study in its broadest dimensions—the study of literature as a transnational phenomenon. The devolution of other fields will have left it with a distinctive and valuable identity at last.

This does not mean, of course, that members of comparative literature departments should be discouraged from studying literature in relation to other discursive productions—far from it. As always, comparatists will participate in the most interesting methodological and theoretical developments in the humanities, wherever these take them. Since literature is not a natural kind but a historical construct, the study of literature in relation to other discourses is not only inevitable but necessary. But in contradistinction to the other departments that would now be defined by their area of focus—French studies, American studies, Indonesian studies, or Japanese studies—and now charged with the study of cultural productions of all sorts, comparative literature would have as its central responsibility the study of literature, which could be approached in the most diverse ways.

This definition of the field—comparative literature by contrast with nationally based cultural studies—would not attempt to predict what sorts of approaches are most likely to advance the study of literature. On the contrary, any lively field must be animated by conflicting projects and priorities; so studies in poetics should occur alongside and in tension with, say, the investigation of contemporary world fiction as a multinational commodity, or with the attempt to test psychoanalytic models of identification on the various cases of Greek tragedy, horror films, and popular romance. And even if the newly distinctive charge of studying literature were falsely thought to entail a preference for more formal approaches over the more interdisciplinary, the differential definition of a field does not, in any event, constrain the activities of its members. To resist the recommendation of the report that departments of comparative literature simultaneously attempt to go global and to take on cultural productions of all kinds is not to restrict the work of individual scholars but only to insist that the injunction to focus on cultural productions of all sorts would not define the field of comparative literature, as it might the new departments of area studies.

The committee appears to suggest that comparative literature should be redefined in order to include or make central the most interesting work being done by people in literature departments today, who might then identify with a newly defined comparative literature. This seems both excessively imperialistic and unnecessary. Why should we redefine comparative literature so that Charles Bernheimer's *Figures of Ill Repute*—to take the latest book by the chair of the ACLA committee—counts as a work in this field rather than in French studies, to which it manifestly belongs? (Its subtitle is *Representing Prostitution in Nineteenth-Century France*, and it studies the figure of the prostitute in literature, painting, and sociological and medical discourses of the period.) Let me stress that I do not want to deny Professor Bernheimer's credentials as a comparatist (his first book was on Flaubert and Kafka), which are at least as good as my own, but only to stress that there is no need to redefine comparative literature as comparative cultural studies so as to include works that have a perfectly logical place elsewhere in the academic scheme of things.

Speaking as chair of a comparative literature department which, like most such departments, is given few resources and must consider carefully what it wants to do with them, I think that there is much to be said for allowing the national literature departments to progress down the road toward cultural studies, which is eminently logical in their cases, and for accepting the distinctive identity and important function that this leaves us: studying literature comparatively and attempting to attend to its global manifestations. French literature is obviously a part of French culture, so let French departments become departments of French studies to examine it in this way; but it is also part of literature in general, and to study it as such, in all its ramifications, is the task—still daunting and requiring all the resources we can command—of comparative literature. The evolution of other departments will, perhaps, let us become comparative literature at last.

12

LITERARY STUDY IN AN ELLIPTICAL AGE

DAVID DAMROSCH

A year after the Greene Report on Standards appeared in 1975, Greene's colleague A. Bartlett Giamatti, then my director of graduate studies, threatened to defenestrate me when I asked permission to receive credit for the study of Nahuatl. He was joking, of course, though as his office was located on the seventh floor of Bingham Hall, I did experience a momentary sense of vertigo—soon relieved when, with a shake of his head, he approved my request. In another sense, though, Giamatti wasn't joking at all but was responding to the facts of academic life as they still existed in the mid-seventies: a graduate student seeking the upward mobility of progress into an assistant professorship was likely to go nowhere but down by devoting too much time to marginal—or submarginal—subjects like Aztec poetry, not even taught in a literature department at all but in anthropology, in a class whose enrollment doubled when I signed up. Two years later, as I began to develop my orals fields, Greene himself cast his eye with some dismay over a transcript that by then also featured Egyptian hieroglyphics and Old Norse. With characteristic tact, he suggested that I should increase my emphasis on canonical texts, lest when I entered the job market some people who read my application "might" feel that I had only "been doing arabesques around the literary tradition."

I mention these conversations because I wish to stress the necessary and intimate connection that exists between intellectual questions and the institutional settings within which they are played out. The explosion in the number and variety of texts that are now under discussion has been an exciting and salutary development in recent years, but we are only just beginning to consider how our pedagogy and even our departments must change if we are to accommodate this expansion in material. I hope that we can, in fact, find a better solution than the one I felt I should adopt, namely to downplay the "arabesques" for a decade and devote myself to doing Judaeo-Christianesques *within* "the" literary tradition, at least until the question of tenure was safely past.

In some ways, it was worth the wait. In the late seventies, the only venue in which I could reasonably expect to publish a study of Aztec poetry would have been a specialized journal like *Estudios de Cultura Náhuatl,* a journal that most libraries don't even order and much of whose small but loyal readership isn't interested in literature in any event. The growing interest during the eighties in methods of cultural critique, and in issues such as imperialism, means that for the first time it has become possible to interest a more general audience in such material.

This is a major improvement, but I would like to discuss two problems we face, one intellectual and one institutional. Institutionally, comparative study is still confronted with the awkward fact that the division of literary study by linguistic/national area has yet to wither away, and the new emphasis on cultural context even tends to increase the nationalism of much study. If they are really to take hold, our changing conceptions of literature must find hospitable ground in the structures we have in place on campus, even as we work to change those structures over time.

Intellectually, the problem is that with so much new material coming into view, we run the risk that something equally important may be jettisoned. I believe that we can already identify what is most in danger of being lost, and it is an ironic loss indeed, in view of our intensified attention to historical questions. For it is literary history itself that seems in danger of eclipse. This is less true within the national literature departments, just because of their institutional base with its relatively fixed and usually period-based fields. Comparative literature, however, is in a more fluid situation, floating as it largely does in an interstitial space between the more solid masses of the national literature departments. This is good insofar as it renders us more attentive to new ideas—hence the prominence of comparative literature programs in the spreading of literary theory during the seventies and eighties; it is dangerous insofar as we have less to anchor us amid the shifting winds of current fashion.

Already in 1965, the Levin Report on Standards raised this issue, emphasizing that "the attractions of the modern period should not obscure the importance of sound historical training; a truly comparative method, after all, finds many points of reference in the past as well as among contemporaries." One of the chief dangers against which the Greene report warns is that we may embrace the literature of the entire globe at the cost of "slackening our dedication to the best of our heritage." We may well want to move beyond the elitism of "the best" and the implicit Eurocentrism of "our" heritage, but as we do, we should not lose sight of the historical weight that the report gives to the term *heritage*. As it goes on to say, "Comparative Literature . . . rests unalterably on the knowledge of history. The student who wants to specialize in Twentieth Century literature needs to know just as much about the past as his fellow students, if he is truly to understand his chosen period. Arguably, he needs to know more, since the cultural inheritance of our century is in the nature of things richer than any earlier period's." The report goes so far as to urge that every comparative literature student be required to learn an ancient language.

The issue of history is elided by the Bernheimer report, which either means that the problem has been solved or else that it has gotten much worse since 1975. Indeed, the 1993 report actually misreads the Greene report's line about the discipline resting "unalterably on the knowledge of history," which is now cited simply as evidence for anxiety about the rise of literary theory, whereas the passage is chiefly concerned with the growing popularity of the twentieth century as the favored period of study. For its own part, the 1993 report notes in passing that "students of older fields" should study an ancient language, and some study of earlier material may be presumed when it urges attention to the process of canon formation. Yet the only explicit recommendation for historical study is that students should study the history of *literary criticism and theory*, and the general emphasis of the report is on matters such as postcolonialism and cultural studies, which usually focus on quite recent material.

With these matters in mind, I studied the conference program while attending the most recent annual meeting of the American Comparative Literature Association (March 1994). I was curious to see how the papers were distributed historically. Not all paper titles indicated any particular historical basis, and some discussed works that I couldn't identify, but I was able to place about three-quarters of the papers by period. The results were as follows: there were 13 papers based in the nineteenth century, 9 based in *any* period before the nineteenth century, and 121 papers on twentieth-century material. The history that has been occluded here is not only European: those 9 papers were the only ones given on pre-1800 material from any country in the world, and only 1 paper, on T'ang poetry, was principally devoted to any material written before the year 1200. No doubt the balance of topics was influenced by the conference theme, "Borders, Exile, and Diasporas," though it is itself a suggestive fact that the conference organizers would consider it natural to choose such a modern-sounding theme for a national asssociation's annual meeting. The 1993 meeting, with a more varied set of three themes, showed greater historical diversity, but the modern emphasis was still strong: of the papers I could place historically, 20 were based in any period before 1800, 12 were based in the nineteenth century, and 96 were devoted to the twentieth century.

The national literature departments can perhaps congratulate themselves that they haven't reached this point, but they too should take heed. It may well be that the classics of every literature will soon find themselves under a similar cloud even within the protected spheres of the national literature departments. The situation here may be parallel to the position of classics as a discipline at the end of the nineteenth century, when the Greek and Roman classics ceased to be the centerpiece of college education. The modern languages and their literatures took center stage in literary study, and this change happened with breathtaking speed; few classicists in 1870 could have had any idea of how reduced their institutional role would become during the ensuing forty years. The proportion of undergraduates studying classics has declined ever since, and the major presence of classical literature on many campuses today is in the form of a segment of the introductory world literature course, often taught by nonclassicists. Even when classics has an important place in such introductory courses, there is often little carryover into the upper undergraduate years. At my own institution, for example, Greek and Roman literature and thought figure prominently in our sequence of core courses, and yet the number of new classics majors is averaging around six per year.

The study of the modern literatures can easily suffer the same fate in the coming decades, beginning with the study of earlier periods within the "modern" literatures. In the early decades of this century, medieval literature had a major place in literary study, while what was then contemporary and near-contemporary literature had a very small role. This situation has been reversed for some time now. If we increasingly use twentieth-century literature as the privileged or even the only place to explore current issues, we will only reinforce our students' already pronounced inclination to do the same. Over time, student interest in turn exerts a slow but tremendous pressure on staffing, as the chronically depressed job market for medievalists already attests. As limited as was the nineteenth-century scholarly world-view, in which little literature after about A.D. 400 was worthy of serious study, there was a real loss when most people came to feel that they could more or less ignore anything written before 1100. Some time ago, the cutoff date advanced to 1500; as 1500 turns into 1800, then into 1900, or 1960, the loss becomes all the greater.

Yet the classicists must share the blame for the unbalanced nature of the turn-of-the-century shift. Confronted with rising interest in European literature and in literary analysis, they retreated into the methodological and ideological purity of the glory that was philology, and most classics departments have held to that ideal ever since. We should certainly not follow them in clinging to a defensive emphasis on standards per se, and the opening up of comparative study to current trends is a hopeful sign. On the other hand, a wholesale abandonment of literary history can hardly be the best way to stay in the thick of things; a foreshortening of our perspective is likely to flatten out what we have to say and thereby weaken our contribution to broader debates.

Largely modern areas like cultural and postcolonial studies can learn much from the wealth of examples, and the depth of perspective, offered by literary history. Whatever position one takes in the scholastic debate as to whether nationalism did or did not exist before the turn of the nineteenth century, it remains true that numerous imagined communities prior to that time left extensive records of their self-construction, and studying them can help us in understanding how communities work. Imperialism too, so often treated as a modern (or at best a Renaissance) phenomenon, was not exactly unknown in antiquity. There are gaps in our knowledge of earlier periods, of course, and modern empires are crucially different from their predecessors in some, though not in all, ways. But if we use the evidence well, we should be able to improve our discussion of imperialism by widening our database. And while the ancient examples have their limitations, they also enjoy certain advantages over the modern ones: we can actually see *how things turned out*, something that cannot yet be known in the case of the British or Soviet empires. Further, our lives are less immediately bound up with those ancient outcomes, so that we have certain opportunities for dispassionate analysis of a sort that may be difficult or even improper to attempt in a contemporary case.

This is not to say that the comparative study of early materials enables us to achieve an objectivity beyond history. Classic texts serve modern academic debate in much the way that ancestors serve their descendants in many traditional societies. According to Mary Douglas, in studying cults of ancestors "the focus should be not on how they symbolize the structure of society, but on how they intervene in it. One could say that sitting back and receiving worship is usually the least time-consuming part of an ancestor's duties. The full job description includes continual, active monitoring of daily affairs in response to public demand."[1] The field of classics itself illustrates this well: as we know, the very creation of modern classical studies served pressing cultural-political purposes in eighteenth- and nineteenth-century Germany. At the same time, two things can be affirmed. The first is that, in the process, the German classicists achieved a better understanding of antiquity than anyone had had in more than a thousand years. Second, the Greek classics did indeed serve the Germans' resistance to cultural domination by France better than modern literature alone could do.

Keeping in mind this activist understanding of the uses of the past, I would like to turn from the intellectual to the institutional sphere and ask how comparative study can expect to thrive in our present academic world. The renewed emphasis on cultural specificity, coupled with the long decline in language enrollments at both the secondary and college levels, means that fewer people than ever feel the need, or find themselves equipped, to pay much attention to materials written outside the one or two languages they grew up knowing. Most literary scholars remain squarely located within a single national or at least linguistic area, and they no longer even need to turn to comparative literature for literary theory, both because so much foreign theory has now been translated and because we have developed such a thriving homegrown theory industry of our own.

Competence in several languages has often been taken to be the essential defining characteristic of the true comparatist, but the value of this skill has been undermined not only by the return to cultural roots but also by the explosion of the canon. Fifteen years ago, if you wanted to study postmodernism outside the Anglo-American sphere, you could probably have surveyed the field by looking at a judicious selection of French, Italian, German, and Latin American writers. By the late eighties, however, you would find yourself wanting to talk about Polish, Hebrew, and Japanese writers as well. Look a little further today, and you may come upon the very interesting Tibetan postmodernist Zhaxi Dawa, along with other novelists writing in Arabic and in Kikuyu. Inevitably you will be reading much of this material in translation, and the results that a "true" comparatist can achieve may no longer look so different from those of a monolingual English professor using the same translations.

Linguistic competence is not, however, the defining characteristic of a comparatist. Egyptologists have always been expected to develop a competence in cuneiform texts in Sumerian and Akkadian, not to mention a good reading knowledge of German, French, and Italian; yet few Egyptologists have done serious comparative work, as they usually treat their other languages in a purely ancillary fashion. The defining characteristic of comparatists is *comparison*. The Egyptologist and the English professor alike characteristically have a single culture in view, at least in the center of their vision and often filling the entire field of vision, whereas at any given time the comparatist will ordinarily engage with two or more cultures on relatively equal terms.

We hear a great deal these days about decenterings, margins, and border crossings, and these decenterings are breaking up the unities that have long reigned not only across international entities like western Europe but also within given national traditions as well. The greatest challenge today is for comparatists and noncomparatists alike to make sense of these changes. Simply to replace "center" with "margin" may be only a cosmetic change, a renewed centering. New texts and new themes—exile, for example—may occupy the center, but if these new ideas are themselves treated monologically, we may be left with a Cyclopean vision that all too closely resembles the centristic univocality we wished to go beyond.

We need a new literary geometry, one that would move beyond the circle with its single focus without falling into the opposite extreme of a total blur. I propose the model of the ellipse, that geometric form generated from two foci, and I would suggest that the comparative perspective is inherently *elliptical* in nature. This geometric shift can perhaps best be illustrated by a concrete example. I will discuss the pedagogical question of how to construct an anthology of British literature, in order to show the practical value of an elliptical comparative perspective even for the introductory study of a single national literature.

For the past thirty years, the immensely popular *Norton Anthology of English Literature* has displayed a highly centristic outlook, both in terms of literary history and even in terms of British literary *space*. It constructs a sort of Ptolemaic universe: the British Isles are largely folded into Anglo-Saxon England; England in turn revolves around its center, London. This is well illustrated by the Norton's end papers, which give maps of "England" and of London—naturally enough, perhaps, except that their "England" reflects a rather limited idea of British culture. The map shows England, Wales, and Scotland but leaves Ireland off the map altogether, even though the anthology includes such figures as Yeats, Wilde, and Joyce. Conversely, Wales is on the map, but actual Welsh writers are nowhere to be found, apart from Dylan Thomas, apparently admitted as an honorary Englishman.

This exclusion limits the presentation as early as the medieval section. The Norton anthology essentially duplicates the selections already found in the 1936 Scott-Foresman *Literature of England.* The major Old English text is *Beowulf,* plus a few brief secondary selections. For Middle English, both anthologies go on to Chaucer, *Gawain,* the Pearl Poet, *Piers Plowman,* and *Everyman,* plus some lyrics. The only variations are relatively minor: a couple of pages, perhaps, from Bede, or a selection from Margery Kempe (a nice addition to recent Norton editions).

What more could they have done? Remarkably, neither anthology gives *any* of the medieval literature of Ireland, Wales, or Scotland. The unfortunate thing here is that much of the greatest medieval literature produced in the British Isles was written in Ireland and Wales, yet only the Anglo-Saxon and Middle English texts have reached the anthologies. Indeed, you would have had a better chance of finding your way into the Norton anthology if you were writing in Latin than if you were writing in any of the indigenous languages of Britain other than Anglo-Saxon—and this despite the fact that Anglo-Saxon was transformed beyond recognition after the Norman invasion, while Welsh and Gaelic are living languages to this day. From the very beginning, we have a dramatic interplay of cultures within the British Isles, and there are many gripping texts that could help us to show this to undergraduates—haunting Irish narratives like the *Tain* and the *Mabinogion,* and the brilliant lyrics of Welsh poets like the trenchantly witty Dafydd ap Gwilym.

Such materials can be brought in to give a better picture of the real cultural dynamics of the earlier periods, and at the same time these texts can intervene creatively in present debates, as the writers often show an acute awareness of issues of cultural struggle between dominant and resisting social and ethnic groups. Thus a broad cultural perspective is not just a matter of adding in some postcolonial writers but can infuse our discussions from the earliest periods onward. British literature from the beginning has been more capacious than Anglo-Saxon or English alone, and the interplay of cultures and subcultures can be well illustrated by major poets like ap Gwilym, who gives ironic portraits of the English and their views of the Welsh; his obscurity at the present time is itself a matter for cultural reflection.

To reconceive of Great Britain as a collection of interlocking cultures does not require us to deny the importance of London within England, or of the English language within the British Isles; rather, it means locating England within a Copernican universe of many centers of gravity. Instead of seeing London as the center of a circle—a circle that leaves much British literature beyond the pale—we can present the literary culture of London as one focus of an ellipse, or more precisely as one focus for many different, partially overlapping ellipses, each with a second focus elsewhere. One such ellipse would encompass the relations between London and the Continent; others, those between England and its inner colonies of Ireland, Scotland, and Wales; another, England and the wider waxing and waning Empire; another, England and the United States—birthplace of T. S. Eliot and several other great "modern British" writers.

A comparatist's elliptical perspective, then, can alter our picture of British literary geography, once we attend to the presence of British literature that our students must read in English translation. But the question of translation remains an awkward one, especially as most instructors will need to use the translations as well, and the awkwardness increases as we move to more advanced levels of work. If the true comparatist can do little better than the monolinguist in discussing Dafydd ap Gwilym or Zhaxi Dawa, perhaps this is because superficiality is the fate of any global discussion, whether of postmodernism or even of the full range of British literature.

From the age of philology to the age of the New Criticism, a dependence on translation was the mark of the dilettante, and this sense of things contributed powerfully to the Eurocentrism of comparative study. Comparatists who were sensitive to language tended naturally to confine themselves to what seemed humanly possible to do, and even an adventurous soul would rarely attempt to learn more than one or two non-European languages. From the linguistic point of view, Eurocentrism was less a matter of cultural imperialism than it was a melancholy acceptance of unbridgeable limits. This is an important distinction, for a double reason: to the extent that it is a real problem, an ideological shift away from Eurocentrism will not in itself solve it; on the other hand, if we can find a way to go beyond those linguistic limits, we may be able to do interesting work of a kind that has never been done before.

My own reading of the history of our discipline is that in the optimistic internationalism of the postwar years, many comparatists began to wish that they could find an intellectually satisfactory way to work from a global perspective. The problem of language, however, kept bringing them up short. A good example of this can be seen in an essay by Harry Levin. In 1968, three years after he drafted the ACLA's first Report on Standards, he delivered the Presidential Address to the association. In this programmatic statement, Levin could find no way out of an ethnocentrism that he regrets even as he reinforces it. "We cannot but agree with M. Etiemble," Levin says, "that it would be valuable for any European comparatist to become acquainted with a non-European language. But to insist upon this as a requirement is a counsel of perfection. . . . [T]hough I am pleased to learn that South Korea now has a Society for Comparative Literature, I do not feel culturally deprived because of my inability to read its transactions."[2] Rhetorically, this is odd: even as he acknowledges the justice of Etiemble's position, Levin protests that he does not regret his inability to put Etiemble's views into practice.

Two quite different motivations lie behind Levin's claim. First, he cannot *afford* to feel deprived, since he finally can't solve the problem. But why couldn't he simply learn Chinese as Etiemble and other comparatists had done before him? Here we see the second factor: lacking Etiemble's *Sino*centrism, Levin sees the problem in its true dimensions. Learning Chinese is not, finally, enough; beyond Chinese—that staple of Euro-American "East/West" comparison—he now sees Korea, a new player in the game professionally as well as poetically. And not only Korea: Levin has Africa and its languages in mind too. The impossible trade-offs that all these choices portend lead him to employ emotionally freighted religious language: "What shall it profit our students," he asks, "to gain Swahili and have no Latin?" (12).

It would be possible, of course, simply to chalk up this speech to the self-satisfied Eurocentrism we wish to leave behind us, but I read it somewhat differently. It is striking that half a dozen times in his address Levin gives some kind of affirmation to the global perspectives he ultimately rejects. He is worrying the issue, and it worries him; he simply can find no solution. In the end he falls back, interestingly, on Auerbach, asking his audience to recall "the epigraph from Marvell that the late Erich Auerbach placed on the title page of his *Mimesis*: 'Had we but world enough and time . . .' Let us make sure that we do justice to those parts of the world of letters which definitely lie within our range" (12).

This is hardly a satisfactory resolution of the problem, as Auerbach himself quotes the line in order to express his regret at his inability to encompass the full *European* tradition, even just considering only the major western European languages. Matters are even worse in light of contemporary perspectives, as it is becoming a linguistic marathon even to traverse the literary space of the medieval British Isles—and we haven't even spoken of the growing body of work now being written in Britain in such languages as Arabic and Hindi.

This is a real problem, even if we avoid all-or-nothing positions; we may allow that many questions can be satisfactorily explored through translation, but we should also acknowledge that many others cannot. Yet what is to be done? Here I return to the need to reconsider our institutional practices. I want to argue that the elliptical perspective of the comparatist needs to be more than an intellectual outlook: it should also extend to an elliptical mode of scholarly *work*. By this I mean a process by which two (or more) scholars serve as the focal points for a single project, generating discussion and analysis between them. Comparatists in the past, like scholars in the humanities generally, have usually confined themselves to the range of work which could be accomplished *by a single individual,* and this is the heart of Levin's problem. We are going to have to become much more serious than we have been to date about working with other people, in teaching and in research, whenever our topics take us beyond our own areas of competence. We will also need to modify our undergraduate and especially our graduate programs in order to build in substantial components of collaborative training for our students.

This is not a "counsel of perfection," like the utopian requirement that everyone learn one non-European language or the vanished requirement to learn one ancient Mediterranean language, requirements that by now look like counsels of *im*perfection in any event, given the vastly expanded linguistic field we must now contemplate. Rather, I believe that a stress on collaborative work is becoming a counsel of necessity. It is also one of genuine intellectual excitement: both the only and the best way to avoid either the melancholia of the single scholar's linguistic limits or the hyperventilation of the jet-setting literary ecotourist. By working together, we can do much to mitigate the severity of the trade-offs we will otherwise find ourselves forced to accept: sacrificing range in order to achieve historical and linguistic depth (the traditional compromise) or, more commonly today, achieving a broad cultural reach at the cost of historical and linguistic shallowness.

The older unities of "the" tradition now present themselves within a multipolar world, and they require more multiple modes of work. Interesting disjunctions and surprising continuities can emerge in the process, both in our subjects of study and in the subjects who do the studying. In 1990, as I prepared an article on the aesthetics of conquest in Aztec poetry for an interdisciplinary New Historicist journal, I thought of sending an offprint to A. Bartlett Giamatti—then commissioner of baseball—and asking him which of us had moved further from Spenser. He died while the article was in press, and so I never got to ask the question, but now, reading his essays on the "green world" of the ball park, I suspect that neither of us had fallen as far from the seventh floor of Bingham Hall as one might have thought. Plotting from more than one focal point, we may find new ways to trace our texts' trajectories, and our own.

Notes

1. Mary Douglas, *How Institutions Think* (Syracuse, N.Y.: Syracuse University Press, 1986), 50.

2. "Comparing the Literature," *Yearbook of Comparative and General Literature* 17 (1968): 5–16, 12.

13

BETWEEN ELITISM AND POPULISM

Whither Comparative Literature?

ELIZABETH FOX-GENOVESE

There is little or no disagreement about where comparative literature began, only about where it should go. Nor is there much disagreement about the challenges it faces in the American academy, only about how appropriately to respond to them. As the differences about the future of comparative literature in a postmodern, global environment take shape, they seem, like so many other disagreements about our difficult and contested world, to be falling into two principal camps which, for lack of more nuanced terms, might be called the elitists and the populists. For the former, comparative literature should remain true to its initial mission as a demanding discipline grounded in the mastery of high literatures in their original languages. For the latter, comparative literature should expand in the direction of cultural studies by steadily increasing the kinds of texts it considers and by relaxing the requirement that works be read in the original.

Obviously, this crude simplification does something less than justice to the complexities of the myriad overlapping positions that do not fall neatly into one or another camp. Yet elitists and populists do represent respectively the main tendencies in the discussion, and, like magnetic poles, they tend inexorably to draw the innumerable variations into their orbit. Thus do the discussions, sooner or later, tend to reduce to the implacable choice: Are you with us or against us? More's the pity. Not because the polarization is out of step with the times, but because it so perfectly mirrors them.

Like all wars, the culture wars that have erupted on our campuses tolerate neither neutrals nor independents. Thriving on polarization, the wars are increasingly classifying all of us as either reactionaries or revolutionaries no matter how strenuously we resist. And when you consider the stakes, the pressure to polarization makes a certain depressing sense. Yet as the case of comparative literature makes abundantly clear, polarization tends to obscure precisely the questions that really matter. Does it, for example, necessarily follow that recognition of the emergence of a global culture requires one to defend a focus on "popular" rather than "high" culture, or requires one to defend instruction in translation rather than in the original? And what about history? Does an appreciation of historical context sentence the scholar or instructor to defend "historicism"?

If nothing else, these invidious choices testify to a pervasive anxiety among comparatists about how our discipline should position itself on the shifting sands that the academic terrain has become. Having initially positioned itself as uncompromisingly elitist in the sense of intellectually demanding, comparative literature now faces daunting challenges, including the changing preparation of students, the pressures of administrations, the proliferation of theory in English and the modern languages, the emergence of cultural studies, and the general infatuation with multiculturalism, diversity, and identity politics. Each of these challenges merits a discrete response, yet the general tendency is to lump rather than separate them, thus conflating ends and means. At the heart of the matter lies one set of disagreements over what comparative literature is and should be and another over how best to defend what it is and should be.

Those who defend the legitimacy of instruction in translation justify their position on a variety of grounds, notably the acknowledged inability of most students to read texts in the original and the moral claims of literatures that few, if any, of us, much less our students, can read in the original. To begin with the moral claims, who are we to exclude Polish, Finnish, or Hungarian, much less Thai, literature from comparative literature just because we are too limited (read imperialist) to appreciate it in the original? And what about the claims of cultures that have produced little or no literate culture? Are we entitled to dismiss them as unworthy of our attention? But these moral claims are overdetermined by our unhappy knowledge that many of the students we should like to reach—or at least to enroll in our classes—probably could not read a play, novel, or poem in French or Spanish, much less Thai or Swahili, and some may even have an inadequate command of English. This overdetermination has tempted some to see the claims of ill-prepared students as morally analogous to the claims of neglected cultures. They are not. Moral claims the students may have, but they are those of remedying their defective preparation, not pretending that it has no significance.

I do not wish to slight the possible value of teaching some texts in translation. Most students, especially undergraduates but too frequently graduate students as well, cannot read enough languages to permit a broad comparative perspective on the basis of texts in the original. But to cast the matter as an all-or-nothing proposition is not the appropriate solution. We must ask ourselves whether professors should be teaching texts that they themselves cannot read in the original, even if they teach translations. And we must ask ourselves if we should try to make comparative literature accessible to students who can read no language other than their own well enough to appreciate a literary text in it. If we answer no to both questions, as I do, then we must develop new strategies. We might, for example, simply insist that professors teach only (or primarily) texts they can read in the original and that students in comparative literature classes be able to read one of the relevant languages in the original. Under these conditions, we would not have to insist that in a specific course all students be able to read all of the texts in the original, although presumably the professor would. One of the benefits of this strategy would be explicitly to open comparative literature to professors in various cultures that comparative literature has not always included, perhaps because professors who know Thai have not usually taught literature classes.

It is easy to imagine the objections, beginning with the insistence that a specialist in Southeast Asia more often than not knows nothing about the theories and methods upon which comparative literature draws. But these objections bear reconsideration. Ironically, those who might most vociferously object might well be those who favor comparative literature's move toward cultural studies and who doubt the ability of traditional specialists to grasp the theoretical innovation that they believe binds comparative literature and cultural studies. Yet those who favor comparative literature's move toward cultural studies tend to be those who are most suspicious of its claims to concern itself primarily with high culture. These discussions might, accordingly, expose the lurking tendency within comparative literature to associate the discipline's traditional European focus with its traditional high-literary focus—as if *The Tale of Genji* were not every bit as much an elite text as *Madame Bovary.*

Eurocentrism versus globalism and high versus popular culture are not the same discussion, and their conflation barely masks an agenda that is no less ideological than comparative literature's original agenda is charged with having been. The main obstacles to comparative literature's adopting a global perspective on high culture lie less in the elitism of the relevant texts (although popular literature did develop primarily as a European phenomenon, largely because Europe had the technology to produce and distribute it) than in their difficulty and, for some, unpalatability. Most non-European countries were long more socially stratified than European countries, and they were much more likely to reserve literate culture for a circumscribed elite. Not surprisingly, under these conditions, their literatures were more likely than not to celebrate inequality among social classes and between women and men, or at least take those inequalities for granted. It is hard, in other words, to turn to non-Western literatures for a "progressive" message.

The popular cultures of non-European cultures frequently contain messages of protest against the status quo, although even they may manifest a disconcerting conservatism. But the main problem in teaching them within the context of comparative literature lies in the likelihood that until the twentieth century, and sometimes well into it, they were as likely as not to have been oral. And it is in the nature of oral cultures constantly to revise themselves without ever admitting to the revisions. Thus each generation will pass on "traditional" accounts of how things have always been, but will alter those accounts to reflect contemporaneous concerns. Not for nothing have Terence Ranger and Eric Hobsbawm written of the "invention of tradition." Social historians and cultural anthropologists have methods for dealing with these problems, although even they remain imperfect. But the tendency of literary methods to focus on texts (oral as well as written) as texts is not ideally suited to solving them, even with the assistance of deconstruction.

Some, to be sure, would take these caveats as justification for broadening comparative literature to include the methods of history and anthropology on the grounds that all texts must be contextualized and that to treat written texts as in some way privileged is to perpetuate illegitimate social inequalities and cultural hierarchies. Such arguments woefully distort the appropriate—and valuable—place of history in comparative literature. Indeed, the more broadly comparative literature casts its cultural net, the more valuable history becomes, precisely as a means of contextualization. It is difficult not to dismiss as irresponsible the presumption that we may select texts from around the world and teach them as unmediated expressions of human experience, although at some point we must also teach them in this way. But in order to do so responsibly, we must understand something of the social, political, moral, and religious values out of which their authors were writing.

Tellingly, the globalization of comparative literature has proved most effective with respect to twentieth-century texts. The experience of two world wars, decolonization, and the electronic revolution has indeed transformed a vast world into a global village. Increasingly, peoples throughout the world share at least the rudiments of common values, notably freedom and economic prosperity. But they remain deeply divided by their histories and even by the referents they attach to the privileged signs of freedom and prosperity. And the writers who attempt to capture their experience and aspirations themselves remain torn between a particularist past and a universal present and future. Think of Franz Fanon's condemnation of the Martiniquais textbooks that offered the descendants of African slaves "our ancestors the Gauls." Yet Fanon wrote through the prism of the existentialism that had characterized his own European education. Countless twentieth-century African and Caribbean writers have shared the essentials of Fanon's experience. And we may readily assume that by the time they wrote for publication they were primarily writing for other literate people who shared enough of that bicultural experience to recognize European as well as indigenous themes and influences.

To contextualize such writing, comparatists themselves need to recognize both influences and to know enough about both cultures to recognize the themes, tropes, and conventions that the writers chose to emphasize. We may, in other words, safely assume that for the most accomplished African and Caribbean writers, writing invariably entailed a process of selection and emphasis. We are quick to grasp what Baudelaire, Dickens, or Tolstoy chose not to write—what they repressed or silenced. We need to be able to do the same with Ousmane Sembene or Buchi Emchetta. We especially need to be able to evaluate the significance of the former's falling within the French orbit and the latter's within the British. And, above all, we need to appreciate their properly literary aspirations. For we pay them scant respect if we treat them only as cries of protest or voices of liberation. And we treat them with still less respect if we uncritically assimilate their distinct protests to our own assumptions. I still recall with disquiet hearing a respected comparatist cheerfully avow that the many pleasures of teaching postcolonial literature included the sense of spontaneity she experienced at reading the book for the first time and at the same time as the students. Presumably, under those conditions, one does not normally have time to refresh one's memory about the salient differences between Martinique, Nigeria, and Senegal. But then what are we offering our students except perhaps the comfortable notion that people around the globe feel much as we do? And suppose they do not?

History has an important place in comparative literature, especially as it expands its scope. For history affords the inestimable value of helping us to appreciate the context within which, and the audience for which, various authors wrote. And even as it necessarily calls attention to the differences between various authors (and texts), it also advances the work of genuine comparison by permitting us to identify elements that seem to make apples apples and oranges oranges. Historical reading in this sense must necessarily begin with appreciation of the context of meaning. The historicism that indiscriminately exposes the purported classism, racism, or sexism of various texts will not serve. Yes, the warriors of the *Iliad* were more likely than not to treat women as the spoils of war. And then what? Do we read the *Iliad* to savor the objectification of women or refuse to read it because it objectifies women? Not if we are sane. But then we must think about why we do read it—about what makes it an enduring text neither because of nor in spite of many of the attitudes and assumptions it embodies. The willingness to appreciate the *Iliad*—our own and our students' openness to it—depends in part upon a fitting sense of history which sifts the ways in which the world of the *Iliad* is different from and similar to our own. More often than not, especially in the case of texts that were produced in societies radically different from our own, the differences will emerge as a complex of social and political values, the similarities as some fundamental sense of what it means to be human—the ways in which it is possible to be human.

That modern authors still draw upon ancient texts for models of human possibilities should make us thoughtful. How do Antigone, Persephone, and Medea continue to figure as sources of significant meaning for such authors as Jean Anouilh, Maya Angelou, and Toni Morrison? How may we appreciate the power that Sophocles' Oedipus held for Freud and simultaneously appreciate Giles Deleuze and Felix Guattari's insistence that Freud's use of the figure of Oedipus must also be understood as specific to the rise of capitalism? These questions and others like them remind us of the significance of theory for comparative literature. They should also remind us of the simultaneous significance of history and of myth, which itself is best understood as history's antithesis. Above all, they should remind us that comparisons, especially literary comparisons, are inherently difficult and demanding.

Much clattering of computer keyboards has been enlisted to attack and defend theory in general and specific theories in particular. Once again, we would seem to be falling into false dilemmas. It would, frankly, be difficult to imagine comparative literature without theory, not least since the mere posing of the comparative problem is inherently theoretical. What do we seek to compare and why? Thus to take up arms against the theoretical project must raise the possibility of bad faith—or at least lack of candor. The issue is not theory or no theory, but which theory and, above all, toward what end. The war over theory seems to have emerged from the implicit assumption, fed by both sides, that theory itself is at war with learning or at least attempts to substitute itself for it. The charge may not fairly be leveled at the leading theorists—a Deleuze, a Derrida, or a Bakhtin. It may more plausibly be leveled at their epigones, especially novices who grab on to theory as a panacea for the inherent difficulties of literary understanding. How comforting, especially when one is making one's way through the shoals of academic competition, to have a simple—or, even better, complex—formula that explains everything.

Those who most appreciate the challenges of theoretical work are understandably loath to concede its reductionist comforts and possibilities. But one need only scan a random sample of dissertations or first books to know they exist. The comparative study of literature is not mathematics, which is to say its stars are rarely to be found among the young. For better or worse, the comparative study of literature, like fine wine, improves with age. The reading of many texts is an advantage, even if the quantity of that reading does not itself substitute for the intelligence and sophistication with which the reading is practiced. But comparative study of literature rapidly becomes sterile and boring without learning, if only because it lacks the texture that evokes resonances and invites further (or other) comparisons.

The intertextuality that has emerged as essential to the thick understanding of comparative literature and to the texts it considers requires textual density and breadth. It is all very well to scan a group of heterogeneous texts for the sign of woman or the feminine. But in the measure that most texts contain such signs, the gesture becomes so abstract as rapidly to become meaningless. Refinement of the sign, as in woman as wife, mother, mistress, daughter, virgin, or whore, helps, but only modestly. Beyond that, the possibilities are endless. And this is where learning, history, myth, and theory all come into play. For the sign of woman acquires its meaning in relation to other signs, and the other signs in relation to which that of woman is taken to acquire meaning or salience vary according to text, culture, and historical context. They also vary in relation to the systems of signs—the texts—with which the author is familiar which have preceded them. They may especially and most complexly vary in the work of authors who draw simultaneously on oral and literate traditions or who write on the cusp of literacy.

In attending to this myriad of possibilities, comparative literature aspires to be comprehensive—to include within its purview the essence and summit of literary studies and perhaps the humanities as well. For comparative literature does aspire to elucidate and enrich the literary representation of the human condition in all its variations. In this respect, intertextuality lies at the center of its sense of itself, even when that sense is most contested as it is today. But intertextuality poses its own problems, beginning with the relation between the intertextuality of texts which, however separated in origin and purpose, resemble one another and texts that explicitly converse with one another. Differentiation between the two groups requires knowledge of the cultures or societies from which they emerged as well as knowledge of their authors' literary universe. In instances in which there are no grounds for assuming that specific authors had any familiarity with texts the themes of which they appear to be echoing, we may begin to argue for universal or archetypal patterns in human experience and imagination or for recurring narratives of what it means to be human. In instances in which it is reasonably clear that specific authors from different societies and cultures had access to the texts of others whose situation differed decisively from their own, we may be dealing with a literary history that transcends specific social, economic, and political influences. Once again, the point is the difficulty and complexity of the analysis—and the importance of learning and experience to it.

Such questions have given rise to a growing concern with the relation between popular and high culture. For intertextuality almost always sinks its deepest roots into the everyday conversations and attitudes that shape any author's earliest experience and continue to impinge upon the experience of the adult. Thus, some would argue that popular books of piety, folk songs, television shows, or rap music may influence a writer's imagination more powerfully than anything Homer, Shakespeare, or Joyce ever wrote. Perhaps. Perhaps not. Most likely every writer uniquely combines influences from disparate sources. But the recognition of the significance of popular culture in the imagination of writers does not logically justify a repudiation of the discrete claims of self-conscious literary craft. Rather, it justifies broadening our understanding of the popular influences upon discrete writers or the role of popular culture in the high-cultural imagination, on the firm understanding that the uses of popular influences will be eminently idiosyncratic.

Cultural studies aims to erase the boundaries between elite and popular culture in the name of democratization. On what grounds may we justify holding "The Love Song of J. Alfred Prufrock" or the *Iliad* in higher regard than the latest release of Ice Cube or 2 Live Crew? The impulse to democratization has been fueled by the legitimate claims that high-literary studies have notoriously tended to exclude women, Afro-American, and non-Western writers, thus promoting the impression that the only human experiences or literary expressions considered worthy of serious study are those of elite white men. Forget, for the moment, that surprisingly few of the male writers who have traditionally commanded the greatest prestige were themselves born into the elite of their respective societies. The truth remains that the academic study of literature was unpardonably delinquent in its recognition of literary merit in unfamiliar guise. Elite academics did not normally take female or Afro-American writers seriously and probably had not heard of the most accomplished non-Western writers. Rectification of that unpardonable neglect does not justify the substitution of popular for high culture.

We know that the boundaries between high and popular culture are notoriously and unmanageably permeable, and it would be foolhardy to pretend to draw them rigidly. We also know that some works of literature better justify and repay sustained attention and rereading than others. Sexism alone cannot explain why *The Scarlet Letter* fared better in literary studies than *The Wide, Wide World*, even though the latter outsold the former in time and place. However imperfect, the criteria of complexity and depth which help to justify the literary reputation of *The Scarlet Letter* are the same as those that would accord Toni Morrison's *Beloved* greater literary prestige than Frances Ellen Watkins Harper's *Iola Leroy*, even though *Iola Leroy* is a better novel than its longstanding neglect would suggest. Indeed, one of the most important missions of comparative literature is precisely to delineate those imperfect boundaries without regard to sex, race, class, or place of national origin.

Comparative literature is and should remain an intellectually elitist enterprise, on the proud conviction that intellectual elitism may not be taken as a proxy for social elitism. Make no mistake: the "democratization" of comparative literature through an expansion into cultural studies will not ensure one iota of social democratization. Social democratization occurs when we ensure the openness of our self-consciously difficult and demanding discipline to practitioners of all backgrounds. If we aspire to secure our own position in the academy by easing our intellectual requirements so as to attract ever larger numbers of students, we will get what we deserve: first and foremost the dubious blessing of teaching students who have little interest in what we do and less ability to do it.

14

THEIR GENERATION

ROLAND GREENE

─────────

I belong to the generation of scholars educated in departments of comparative literature—or, as in my case, in other departments but largely under the tutelage of comparatists–between the late 1970s and the mid-1980s. This generation goes almost unrepresented in the report to the American Comparative Literature Association on the state of the discipline in 1993, nearly all the authors of which are more or less the age of my teachers in graduate school, and with two exceptions the most recent Ph.D.'s were junior professors at that time. In reading the report of Charles Bernheimer's committee and its antecedents by Thomas M. Greene and Harry Levin, one cannot help noticing the differences between these several conceptions of comparative literature and how they display a certain generational mutability. According to this essay's provisional, heuristic way of reading the field, each of the documents produced under the auspices of the ACLA is a snapshot of a generation of scholars rendered in a particular instant. Having their own identities, academic generations can be evaluated as such, sometimes in a light apart from their individual members. How they respond to circumstances—by articulating values, investing in change, and predicting the future—speaks to the ethical dimension of scholarship. We will be—we are—judged by our tact and imagination in coping with the future that we have brought about ourselves. We are all the proprietors of the field, and perhaps the first approach we make to it is through our academic generations.

When I speak of comparative literature, most of what I say is what my generation has learned from our peculiar experience. Comparative literature is, or ought to be, the practice of a vanguard among the literatures. It is the laboratory or workshop of literary studies, and through them, of the humanities. Comparative literature compares literatures, not only as accumulations of primary works, but as the languages, cultures, histories, traditions, theories, and practices with which those works come. A comparatist who works with English and Spanish, for instance, counterposes not only particular texts in their own linguistic and historical situations but their poetics and pragmatics, the continuing discussions around them, the canons in which they are implicated, and finally Anglo-American scholarship and Hispanism as academic and social constructions. Hence comparative literature compares not only texts but contexts; not literary works so much as ways of reading, writing, and thinking about such works—that is, literatures in the most catholic sense of the term. Moreover, the discipline works best where it can be intensely committed to the practices that enable literary studies but do not contain them, such as philology, historicism and historiography, critical and literary theory, and cultural studies. If one field can be responsible for moving freely among these practices and maintaining their relevance to one another, that field is comparative literature.[1] No matter how many languages may be sampled in a specimen of literary scholarship, no matter what superficial definition of comparative literature it may satisfy, where this paradisciplinary work is not under way, comparative literature is not happening.

Even in its most traditional formulations, comparative literature recognizes the necessity of moving among the disciplines of the humanities, and even beyond those, in intellectually provocative ways. Harry Levin saw it clearly in many essays and lectures, early and late, which describe the fluid borders of the field: in 1954 he spoke of the interconnectedness of comparative literature and the other disciplines, including anthropology and psychology, within a "science of the imagination,"[2] and in 1965, in the report to the ACLA, he allows "the relevance [to comparative literature] of other than literary disciplines: notably linguistics, folklore, art, music, history, philosophy, and possibly psychology, sociology, and anthropology." Following this impulse, comparative literature is necessarily the most unsettled, the most difficult, the most mercurial of all the literary fields, because unlike the national ones it is undergoing reinvention at least every generation or so, perhaps every few years, and in principle every time a scholar begins to negotiate a new project out of this rich array of models. Moreover, comparatists who are pressing against different boundaries will often seem to have little in common with each other: a literary historiographer of the Middle Ages as against a scholar of contemporary cultural studies, a philologist of Arabic and Spanish versus a literary theorist who works with French and German. In principle this problem of identity within the discipline becomes a greater challenge with every generation, as the pertinent borders of the field are redefined and enlarged and the practitioners—if they really are practitioners of comparative literature—find themselves further from one another than ever. As a discipline with no common body of knowledge other than literary studies, and without a central purpose except to carry out its astringent or stimulant motions, comparative literature appears to invite misunderstanding even from its own family of scholars.

Perhaps because its work as a discipline is hard to describe and keep in mind, comparative literature tends to harbor a noisy antivanguardist faction of those who profess to see its job as routine or programmatic. The purpose of the discipline, this argument goes, is to compare literary works between languages, and therefore the capacity to work in several languages becomes the defining fact of participation in comparative literature. It matters little to this view what sorts of questions are being asked under the rubric of comparative literature, whether literature in the broadest sense is being interrogated or whether the intellectual status quo of the national fields is under test in any fashion. The criterion here is additive: comparatists know works and literatures in the same ways as other literary scholars, but they know more—more languages, more traditions, more critical apparatuses—which are not collated inquisitively into a paradisciplinary context but assimilated to one another and to an idealist conception of literature. In truth, what I am describing as a reactionary faction in the field, as though it were embodied only in a group of people, is probably better understood as a conservative impulse that runs through every aspect of comparative literature. We are all this sort of adductor and idealist. This notion serves most of us when we wish to make convenient distinctions between ourselves and others, and it does much of the disagreeable work of explanation and justification to administrative authorities. In the end, however, it betrays comparative literature because it caricatures, or even renders unrecognizable, the central feature of negotiation between theories, practices, and disciplines on which everything in the field depends. One might say that when comparatists ask the sorts of questions they usually do, the ability to move among different languages and literatures will almost always be visible in their work as a condition. Where that ability becomes instead an end, the necessary, continual process of writing out a new compact between the disciplines, with literary studies as the amanuensis, has collapsed into shorthand, and we stand to lose our identity—though, paradoxically, some of us may seem surer of it than ever.

By contrast, for comparatists like me who tend to see comparative literature as a paradiscipline, linguistic ability is a necessary, not a sufficient, qualification for the field. And as comparative literature inexorably expands and its practitioners grow apart from one another, it will become—it is now becoming—more thinkable that our disciplinary relations with languages will change, that they will be understood not simply as a credential but as a mode of engagement with our objects which can be examined critically, as we now examine the construction of national identity and the practice of translation. What does it mean to "know" a language? When can one be said to know English or Spanish, if these languages are so multifarious in themselves? How does a comparatist, with his or her paradisciplinary investments, need to know French differently than a scholar of the nineteenth-century French novel? How does knowing languages in the academic sense dispose us toward reproducing the conventional studies of the national literatures? In the meantime, with these questions on the horizon, we tend to cling to the additive notion of languages in the discipline—and with it, the sense of language as a neutral fact—when our certainties are most at risk. When, as most of us discover, the work of moving among both literatures and disciplines becomes too demanding, when it cannot be properly explained or carried out, this is the default.

If comparative literature has often had the unacknowledged role of provocateur and catalyst within literary studies, that role has entailed different commitments at particular times. The founding generation of modern comparatists who were at the height of their powers during and after World War II, such as Erich Auerbach (1892–1957), Leo Spitzer (1887–1960), and Ernst Robert Curtius (1886–1956), were largely philologists whose work in literary history and interpretation was founded on a wealth of textual and bibliographical knowledge. They invented a discipline that was inseparably historicist and philological, in which the two approaches validate each other in a continuous exchange of authority.[3]

Modeled on such work but hardly limited to it, the scholarship of Harry Levin's generation represents an adjustment of the emerging comparative literature in specifically American terms: this was the "American hour," as Claudio Guillén puts it in a recent book on the field.[4]

Levin's cohort, some twenty years younger than Auerbach's, displays a professional ethos that comes to be definitive of comparative literature in an American setting. This outlook tends to put ideas ahead of sheer knowledge, though the learning it entails would seem simply unattainable to most present-day scholars. Where a pull is felt between the two imperatives—an elegant interpretive formation versus an accumulation of literary and historical fact—the scholars of the Levin generation typically choose the former, and as a consequence their work is more varied, more occasional, more limber than that of their forerunners. Their criticism starts from many more points of entry—not only historicism and philology, not only strictly literary phenomena, but philosophy, sociology, the plastic arts, science—and ends having accomplished a greater number of discrete intellectual projects, and claimed more academic territory, in the name of comparative literature.

Moreover, those of Levin's generation had the opportunity and the inclination to think openly about the discipline of comparative literature—to give it a charter and an institutional identity in this country—which their forerunners, many of them elderly exiles after the war, seldom experienced. Levin and his group inaugurate the function of comparative literature as not only the most bravely synthetic of the humanities but the one that lives, for better or worse, by the highest degree of reflectivity, acuteness, and conscience directed toward the field itself.

Levin and company drew on the best of their immediate elders, domesticated it for an American academic setting, and built a field.[5] If the Auerbach cohort is responsible for the founding or "heroic" phase of American comparative literature, Levin, Wellek, and the rest preside over an entrepreneurial era—though this phase has its heroic moments as well, such as Wellek's manifesto "The Crisis of Comparative Literature," delivered at the International Comparative Literature Association in 1958.[6] The report of the Levin committee attempts to bring some order to an enterprise that has already succeeded beyond the expectations of its agents, now grown comfortable or even oracular; it is articulated from behind a thick screen of shared assumptions. "Members of the ACLA profess," Levin writes, "broadly speaking, a set of common objectives." It is not considered necessary in 1965 to say what those might be.

The disciplinary values of Levin's era persisted without serious challenge through a third generation of scholars who found their professional voices between the mid-1950s and the mid-1960s. This is the cohort that produced the Report on Standards of 1975. The members of Levin's group had shared with their forerunners a sensibility for personal and political upheaval, a feeling for contingency which can be read out of their work even today, but added to that a shrewd understanding of how to work within American institutions. Those scholars who followed, however, came up within the horizon of prosperity which had been established at great cost by the two preceding generations. The scholars of the 1975 committee, it must be said, had never been provocateurs or impresarios but were largely the former students of the Levin generation, whom they had encountered fairly late in

147

their teachers' careers. All but two of the Greene committee are Americans, and none can claim to have established a beachhead for the discipline as several of their teachers did.

Only ten years after Levin's report, a great deal had already happened. In the Greene committee's report, amusing in its efforts to make anxiety sound genteel, one sees immediately the loss of the consensus they had inherited and an effort to get it back. But although they were then the custodians of the institutional authority they had received from their mentors, the Greene committee were not the builders of consensus about the field—neither latter-day Auerbachs or Spitzers who would personify a new discipline, nor Levins or Welleks who would confront an outmoded orthodoxy with a fresh agenda. Instead, they were the legatees of such an orthodoxy, received at second hand. Their accounts of the field—of what they were doing and why they did it— are strikingly complacent; even now, in retrospective essays about the making of the field such as those collected by Lionel Gossman and Mihai Spariosu, some of the prominent members of that generation can scarcely bring themselves to address the nature of comparative literature in an explicit, analytical way.

Moreover, the Greene report catches the discipline on the cusp of a major reorientation: away from philology and literary history and toward literary theory, which in the years around 1975 became the product that kept the franchise intact. The dramatic entrance of the theory industry into comparative literature, and literary studies generally, was made possible in large part by the superannuated vision with which it competed and which it quickly overwhelmed. More or less exactly when the postwar consensus around comparative literature had expired, the discipline found a renewed purpose in disseminating theoretical models, largely European and almost entirely concerned with literature rather than society or culture, across the literary fields. Even where socially oriented approaches came into its hands—feminist theory, for instance, or Marxism—the comparative enterprise of the seventies and eighties insisted, with some success, on stripping these of their extraliterary dimensions and treating them as alternatives to literary formalism, literary structuralism, and so forth. The work of reducing "theory" to manageable dimensions for disciplinary purposes was often thoughtless. The typical proseminar on the discipline of comparative literature became, in this era, a survey of theory: no philology, no historicism, no real crossing of disciplines, only a strangely reified theory, handled in exaggeratedly evenhanded fashion. In the early eighties I sat through several graduate seminars in which we took up structuralism, Marxism, feminism, and so on as though we were trying on hats. It seemed not to occur to our teachers that some of these things were strategies for reading literary texts, some were multidisciplinary systems of knowledge, some were world-views. No matter. They would all be processed by a comparative literature determined to keep its identity intact. What an urbane philology was after the war, an even more urbane, denatured theory became in the sixties and seventies—the official product of comparative literature as a discipline, its reason for maintaining its uneven foothold between the literary fields.

Perhaps my own story is relevant here, since I came of age intellectually at the time in question. In the mid-seventies I was a public high school student from Los Angeles, half Mexican American and half Anglo, determined to study literature without seeing my experience reflected there in an unmediated way. I wanted to study something relevant to myself without studying myself. With a generous scholarship I went to college at Brown University, where I majored in English but took many courses in comparative literature, Spanish, film, religion, and history—in effect, making myself a comparatist the hard way, instead of majoring directly in the field itself. Having had an undergraduate experience that exposed me to a great deal of literary theory, I went off to graduate school at Princeton, thinking that, in that stronghold of a traditional historicism, among professors whose work I admired but had little feeling for, I would become (I am embarrassed now by my naiveté) the complete scholar.

To my surprise, I encountered a historicism in retreat from its own principles. With the exception of D. W. Robertson, Jr., and one or two others, the Princeton Departments of English and Comparative Literature were having an acute intellectual crisis. The sweep of structuralism and especially poststructuralism into the humanities had seemingly undermined everything of value, and for a few moments in the late seventies and early eighties, it appeared to many of these distinguished scholars that their world was about to dissolve at the hands of literary theory, that the historical and aesthetic constructions in which they had invested would be theorized out of existence by an intellectual model whose agent was a newly militant comparative literature. In the face of this hegemonic theory, the responses of these scholars ranged, in my experience, from reasonless resistance to panicked acquiescence. I remember one term in which, a couple of weeks after the start of classes and on orders from the departmental powers, most of our seminars abruptly shifted gears and became in effect surveys of literary theory. Shakespeare and literary theory, *Hudibras* and literary theory, Romanticism and literary theory, modernism and literary theory—the improbability and redundancy of this retooling bothered the authorities not at all. Nor did they hesitate over what already seemed to me then the antitheoretical basis of such a pedagogy, assuming as it did that theory was a factor that could be injected into any setting with equal, predictable results. Only literary theory's worst enemies, in fact, could be capable of such an expedient, and as it turned out, many of its most ardent converts in the eighties were such enemies. They believed in it without understanding it and without comprehending that there were alternatives for renewal. That was the climate in which I and my generation learned our discipline and our profession.

At the same time that I studied at Princeton, I was traveling regularly to Texas to visit a girlfriend and sat in several times on Gayatri Chakravorty Spivak's seminars in Austin. Spivak's courses and writings of that era—she had already enacted the turn from sheer deconstruction to the more politically oriented work of her middle career—were far more complex than what the consensus of the field considered theory. Here was perhaps the most appalling omission of the theory industry, in which both genuine theorists and opportunists were complicit: in the industry's rush to package its product and dispense a program for others to follow, the actual, nuanced work of the most inventive theorists of that moment was left out of the picture. Though she prospered from it, Spivak was far ahead of the consensus in favor of a hegemonic, undifferentiated theory. She was not the only one. I remember standing on Broadway and Ninety-eighth Street in Manhattan in about 1983 and hearing a graduate student at Columbia tell me emphatically that there were two scholars named Barbara Johnson: the well-known deconstructionist at Yale, and another one who was publishing essays on African American women's literature. I suppose there are several possible interpretations of this episode. What struck me at the time, though, was that the field's view of itself simply could not contain the possibility that one of its paragons might already be restless with the theory that was being sold to everyone else, the awareness that a Spivak or a Johnson was successfully negotiating between deconstruction, historicism, feminism, and interpretation. The rhetoric of crisis and panacea, of one-stop disciplinary renewal, would not allow it.

What I was cultivating without quite knowing it at the time, and what most of my generation shares, is a post-theoretical view of the discipline: a sense of comfort with theoretical scholarship which many of our teachers never attained, an understanding that literary (and now cultural and other) theory is indispensable to the enterprise of comparative literature, and a conviction that, while it must not be neglected, it cannot become the single focus of the field.[7] In fact, there is no central activity of the field. We learned through experience, I think, that consensus in comparative literature is far from a desirable condition—is, rather, a sign that genuine disagreements are being ignored and values overridden, that something is being repressed to break out later. While many of the polemics against the theory boom were uninformed and irrational, they correctly understood that comparative literature is—ought to be—a pluralistic discipline. Every department of comparative literature includes people who scarcely recognize themselves as belonging to a single enterprise, and this is as it must be. It is the honest condition of our discipline.

Moreover, each generation has the obligation to rethink comparative literature from its own standpoints. The deferral of that project in the 1960s and 1970s is understandable in some ways, given the continuing influence even then of Levin, Wellek, and their cohort. When one generation passes on its responsibility, however, its successors receive an outsized task, and the rhythm of reconception turns abrupt. The ACLA report of 1993 is a good example of this problem. Having inherited a stagnant field, Bernheimer and his committee propose thirty or forty years of change in one motion; having witnessed pluralism under threat, they aim to be aggressively impartial at the expense of the recent past. This unusually alert clutch of scholars has seen its field shift significantly two or three times during its career and is determined to get ahead of the next cycle of change. Michael Riffaterre's protests in this connection would be poignant if they were not ironic: "The report has given short shrift to literary theory," he writes. "To be sure, theory is mentioned several times but without any specifics, as if the committee had just gone through its check list and made sure it had not forgotten anything." But in moving ahead without looking back—in arguing for the widest possible borders of the field—the Bernheimer committee displays a curious impatience with the study of literature itself, which is finally the center of comparative literature for historicists, theorists, philologists, and cultural critics alike. What is missing at the center of the document is a recognition of the open questions with which literary studies can still be engaged in the 1990s and beyond—the issues and problems that give meaning to our forays into other disciplines, other cultures, other media. If literature is "no longer the exclusive focus of our discipline," as the committee writes in 1993 and with which I emphatically agree, it is still our intellectual basis, the type of discourse by which we measure all others, the object of our most successful practices.

Today comparative literature has an opportunity to renew the encounter between its practical and theoretical elements—to insist that historicism, literary and cultural theory, and the rest confront each other productively.

Comparatists who are involved with several of these elements will find them-selves increasingly at the center of this decentered field. Moreover, compara-tive literature is well prepared to build contexts around the drift toward ethnic and minority studies now evident in many national literatures, not only North American but Latin American, German, French, and others, and this task will implicate scholars of the earlier periods as well as the present. When I committed myself primarily to Renaissance Europe as a field, it was probably because I saw there the early modern origins of a great many aesthetic and ideological constructions that are treated too often in a more or less presentist fashion; the early modern period seemed the likeliest place to gratify my impulse to study a version of my own experience after a refraction by histori-cism or literary theory. The same goes for poetry, the genre I have been and will be most involved with over the years. I believe that lyric discourse in all its forms is the most sensitive register of social and cultural change available to us and that comparatists can make that case with historical, theoretical, and cross-cultural authority. We can argue, for instance, that a chapter in the early modern development of the economics and politics of race can be seen in the lyrics of the sixteenth century, where poets such as Wyatt, Shakespeare, and Sidney install shifting constructions of color, *mestizaje*, and slavery at the centers of their amatory projects; or that the poetry of Whitman and his trans-American contemporaries makes seminal interventions in political and cultural change during their period of *criollo* awareness and national inde-pendence. Where comparative literature builds such conditions around eth-nic and minority writing of the present, out of periods and genres that would not be readily evoked by the scholars who work with such texts every day and tend to see them against the horizon of the present, the discipline lives up to its charge of knowing not simply more but differently.

Comparative literature holds out the prospect of exposing Chicano and Latino literatures, for instance, to a multicultural and paradisciplinary inter-rogation they stand little chance of finding in their usual departmental sites. When I teach Chicano literature in a comparative context, its texts come into contact with historical antecedents starting from the sixteenth-century Peru-vian mestizo historian the Inca Garcilaso de le Vega, as well as contemporary countermodels of a specifically New World writing such as the avant-garde poetry of Mexico, Chile, and Brazil. The work of a Chicana writer such as Gloria Anzaldúa can be set in specific contexts that make different kinds of sense out of her work: not only the received canons of Spanish American and Anglo-American literatures, where her exoticism will go unquestioned and her speculations will seem entirely new, nor the self-authorizing circle of recent Chicano writing, but a freshly elaborated setting that includes Whitman, José Vasconcelos, Vallejo, Mário de Andrade, Toomer, Nicolás Guillén, Alfonsina Storni, and Ginsberg as well as Anzaldúa's Mexican American antecedents and contemporaries. Such an itinerary draws us off the easy route and makes it likelier that when we examine a paradigm such as Anzaldúa's "borderlands," it will be with consciousness—even a surplus of consciousness—of what the term evokes in history and theory, in international and multicultural usage.[8] Comparative literature takes the investments of the literatures and gives them a fourth dimension—a further degree of self-awareness, of inquiry, of exactitude.

Another lesson learned between the eighties and today is more oblique: that no one is a comparatist once and for all, but comparative literature comes into and out of scholarship and careers according to the questions being addressed and the pressures on literary studies at a given time. Academic institutions dissemble when they designate some of us comparatists for life and shut others out; no one is always doing paradisciplinary work, but many of us do it at one time or another. We should resist the question of who is a comparatist, as though that were a stable identity, and remember that the work of comparative literature emerges from departments of English, German, Chinese, philosophy, anthropology—in short, anywhere that humanistically oriented scholars engage literary and other texts of cultural import with an emphatic measure of disciplinary awareness. Whether the academy allows for this fact or not, we should acknowledge it ourselves. In fact, it answers the stratification I remarked earlier. Instead of small groups of official comparatists who harbor very different conceptions of the field and eye one another suspiciously, the discipline should be populated—at least in spirit— by everyone in the literatures with an interest in the programmatic questions that keep scholarship in motion, and no one else no matter how many languages they happen to read.

One of the opportunities of the next several years will be to install a renewed conception of the field without the headlong growth that tended to accompany such shifts in the past, and that we will surely experience if we decide that comparative literature "is" world literature, literature in translation, or cultural studies, to invoke three misnomers. The Greene report demonstrates the perils of a discipline that is both elitist and unclear as to its reason for being: the latter condition produces an unchecked expansion of programs and departments while elitism denies this recognition, and the field is at odds with itself. We should be explicit about our values and assumptions rather than elitist, renovative rather than conservative, discriminating rather than indecisive. Further, the paradiscipline in which we work ought to question our own generational and institutional standpoints as critically as it does language, nation, canon, and other constructions—including, of course, literature. An approach to the discipline along the lines I have sketched here might begin to break down the impediments that divide some comparatists from others and from the history of their own field, and to live up to the identity we have received from the past and are transforming for the future.

Notes

1. This is perhaps another way of saying what Wlad Godzich insists in a convincing dictum: "The 'field' of Comparative Literature is field [or "the enabling condition of cultural elaboration"]. . . . Within the prevalent organization of knowledge, it is incumbent upon comparatists to inquire into the relationship of culture to givenness, to its other." See his essay "Emergent Literature and the Field of Comparative Literature" in *The Comparative Perspective on Literature: Approaches to Theory and Practice*, ed. Clayton Koelb and Susan Noakes (Ithaca, N.Y.: Cornell University Press, 1988), 28.

2. Harry Levin, "New Frontiers in the Humanities," *Contexts of Criticism*, Harvard Studies in Comparative Literature 22 (Cambridge: Harvard University Press, 1957), 9.

3. Or reinvented a discipline, to speak precisely. Comparative literature had existed in several forms for many years; those of Auerbach's generation redirected it in the direction of their particular interests and experiences. On this prehistory, see René Wellek, "The Name and Nature of Comparative Literature," in *Discriminations: Further Concepts of Criticism* (New Haven: Yale University Press, 1970), 1–36.

4. Claudio Guillén, *The Challenge of Comparative Literature*, trans. Cola Franzen, Harvard Studies in Comparative Literature 42 (Cambridge: Harvard University Press, 1993), 60–62.

5. On this collective achievement, see Wellek's "Memories of the Profession," Levin's "Comparative Literature at Harvard," and Victor Lange's "Experiences and Experiments," all commissioned for *Building a Profession: Autobiographical Perspectives on the Beginnings of Comparative Literature in the United States*, ed. Lionel Gossman and Mihai I. Spariosu (Albany: State University of New York Press, 1994), 1–11, 13–23, and 25–35, respectively. An informative piece on Levin's early years is "A Personal Retrospect," *Grounds for Comparison* (Cambridge: Harvard University Press, 1972), 1–16.

6. "The Crisis of Comparative Literature," *Proceedings of the Second International Congress of Comparative Literature*, ed. W. P. Friedrich, 2 vols. (Chapel Hill: University of North Carolina Press, 1959), 1:149–59. Rpt. in *Concepts of Criticism*, ed. Stephen G. Nichols, Jr. (New Haven: Yale University Press, 1963), 282–95.

7. Compare Spivak's recent arguments against the American academic construction called "theory" as a "shorthand" for a much larger and more complex body of thought, and her view that it requires no space of its own in the literature curriculum: *Outside in the Teaching Machine* (New York: Routledge, 1993), 274–76.

8. Gloria Anzaldúa, *Borderlands/La Frontera: The New Mestiza* (San Francisco: Spinsters/Aunt Lute Books, 1987).

15

COMPARATIVE LITERATURE
ON THE FEMINIST EDGE

MARGARET R. HIGONNET

Humanity, Jean Paul Richter once suggested, is "the great dash in the book of nature."[1] Comparatists in turn play the role of a hyphen in the world of humanities. Shuttling between languages, cultures, arts, or discourses marks the condition of a comparatist. As indispensable as a suture in an operation, the comparatist works at the edge of the matter. The edge I want to address here is that where comparative literature meets feminist criticism.

Like comparatists, feminist critics have stressed the reexamination of critical boundaries. To be sure, feminists tend to focus on the cultural construction of gender, whereas comparatists traditionally have focused on genre or period conventions and on the transnational movement of forms. While comparatists have identified fences that organize national literary study in order to leap over them, feminists have danced in the minefields of the margins.[2]

Gender, feminist critics point out, is one of the categories that organize literary production and reception. This social variable draws lines within literary institutions; it encodes voices as masculine or feminine and separates generic spheres such as the male and female bildungsroman or diverging currents within modernism. At the same time, like racial or class demarcations, gender divisions cross national boundaries and assume new definition and value in each culture. Gender studies, in short, should be comparative. The affiliations and telling distances between the two modes of analysis seemed to me so rich that I undertook several years ago to edit a volume, *Borderwork*, which would explore the space of the hyphen in comparative-feminist, while acknowledging the contested identities of both modes.[3]

Of course, every analytical discipline engages some type of comparison.

Just what kind of comparison is the question. Without a category of inclusion, we cannot begin to locate historical change or cultural specificity. Each category of inclusion, however, implies the exclusions that characterize a discipline's strengths and weaknesses. There are many ways to slice a cake, but if you make a horizontal cut near the top, one person will get all the icing. Feminists have often focused exclusively on differences of gender, while comparatists have focused on national or linguistic identity as a primary locus of difference. As Diana Fuss argues, a problem arises at the point "when the central category of difference under consideration blinds us to other modes of difference and implicitly delegitimates them."[4]

The issue of locating the defining categories of comparative literature has triggered much of the debate over the Bernheimer report. When we try to delimit our field, we run into difficulty because the kinds of tasks which comparatists set themselves involve precisely the testing of conceptual boundaries. In the context of genre theory, Derrida has argued that the particular member of a set always undoes the set: "With the inevitable dividing of the trait that marks membership, the boundary of the set comes to form, by invagination, an internal pocket larger than the whole."[5] Theory, insofar as it seeks out the border case, tends to undo its own generalizing goals. Further, because comparative literature crosses the boundaries set by other disciplines, skeptics outside the field find that a degree in comparative literature widens, as Veblen put it, "the candidate's field of ignorance."[6]

Part of the condition of a comparatist is productive anxiety, or what Ulrich Weisstein once suggested is the "permanent" sense of crisis in the field.[7] The problem of self-definition has become all the more troubling in the nineties, as the construction of englobing theories has come under attack. The ideal of a universalist schema to encompass variations in periodization, maps of genres, and the definition of national literatures has come to seem a will-o'-the-wisp. A wide spectrum of comparatists, as the Bernheimer report points out, now use methods borrowed from cultural studies, new historicism, feminism, or subaltern studies as they gravitate to localized and historicized models of cultural production.

In recent years many feminist critics have likewise sought to move beyond theoretical and historical claims whose universalism masked particularist assumptions, whether national, class bound, or tacitly racial. The stimulus for self-criticism came from various quarters: from African American "womanist" work, from subaltern studies, and from Marxist-feminist critiques. These critiques have pushed feminists, first, from women's studies toward cross-cultural gender studies, and second, from a generalizing but basically national literary study toward historically anchored comparative analyses.

The new directions in feminist criticism are by no means identical with the study of marginalized literatures or of the contact zones within multicultural societies. But these subjects have held a special place within feminist criticism as points of comparison and contrast in the development of theory. Thus the subversive strategies of American women's humor are in some ways analogous to those in the African American literary tradition; a juxtaposition of the two foregrounds elements that are specific to women's cross-class culture or specific to the African diaspora.

One of the primary tasks of feminist criticism has been to interrogate the problematic assumption of a "female" identity in literary representations. The construction of feminist theories on the inscription of the body, whether through paradigmatic scenes of rape, slavery, or excision, needs to be brought into perspective through cross-cultural analysis. Since language constructs the categories of sex, as Judith Butler argues, a comparative analysis of linguistically inscribed sexuality is in order.[8]

Covertly essentialist thinking infects even feminist critiques of essentialism, including attempts to acknowledge cultural differences. Trinh T. Minh-ha eloquently questions the postulate that difference is "uniqueness or special identity." Rather, she suggests, such "limiting and deceiving" concepts lead at best to a romantic exoticism, an ethnographic projection of a coherent cultural subject. Feminist theory, she proposes, should dismantle the very notion of identity.[9] Similarly, Rey Chow has challenged the well-intentioned exoticizing of the voice of the other, the projection of a monolithically different Third World Woman. "To my mind, it is when the West's 'other women' are prescribed their 'own' national and ethnic identity in this way that they are most excluded from having a claim to the reality of their existence."[10] To presume the primary import of national or ethnic difference both denies today's world economy in its cultural manifestations and shapes a reductive politics of identity. The import of these questions for comparative work is undeniable.

Nonetheless, we cannot yet celebrate a happy marriage between comparative literature as a discipline and feminist forms of critical practice. Historically, comparative literature took institutional shape in an age of formalist criticism; feminist theory flourished in the heat and politics of the civil rights movement. While feminist criticism has fused disciplines such as history, epistemology, linguistics, and anthropology, comparatists continue to debate the merits of interdisciplinary study as against "intrinsic" literary study. Linguistic skills have been considered the sine qua non of comparative literature. By contrast, many feminists are either monolingual or make little use of their linguistic skills in their critical analyses.

Not only does their interdisciplinary work make many feminist critics today difficult to locate within comparative literature as an academic discipline, but earlier feminist writers who explicitly located themselves at the intersection of literary traditions have also failed to attract comparative study. We have devoted a body of inquiry to Goethe and not to Mme de Staël, even though her *De la littérature* and *De l'Allemagne* are among the founding texts of comparative literature. Similarly, comparatists have been drawn to mediators among cultures, such as Kafka or Rilke, rather than to Isabelle de Charrière, an eighteenth-century Dutchwoman who lived in Switzerland, wrote in French, translated from English (like Jane Austen she gave a distinctively feminist twist to narrative conventions), and published not only fiction but operas.

The omission of broad ranges of literature from comparative consideration was a clear symptom that something was wrong with comparative paradigms. Already in 1975, the Greene report acknowledged that the older "comfortable European perspectives" were "parochial." What once seemed a blessing—the fact that readings and courses focused on recognized peaks of the literary landscape—has long since come to seem problematic. Whereas Wellek and Warren earlier argued on behalf of "intrinsically" literary rather than political norms of periodization, historians and critics alike are reexamining the politics of ostensibly neutral literary norms. They ask whether women indeed had a renaissance, a romantic movement, or a modernism of their own. Did they live the moment to another pulse and record it in a counterlanguage not taught in the schools of men?[11]

Yet where national literature departments have been redrawing their reading lists in order to incorporate Charrière, George Sand, Aphra Behn, Fanny Burney, Harriet Jacobs, Hedwig Dohm, or Emilia Pardo Bazan, disciplinary requirements and professional journals in the comparative field have been driven by the goal of coverage toward the continuing mapping of "masterpieces."

In this context of misrecognitions and omissions, the Bernheimer report, with its endorsement of gender analysis, feminist and postcolonial theory, and cross-cultural topics, has found a warm welcome from many of my colleagues, especially those who have collaborated with me on *Borderwork*. One reaction was: "At last I recognized myself."

But what kind of self can one attribute to a comparative-feminist? Not surprisingly, the problem of the critic's identity has generated vigorous feminist debate. Some have laid claim to the territory of gynocriticism, or the study of women's writing, on the basis of lived experience as women and have contested the intrusions of cross-dressing Tootsies. Others, today I think the majority, reject the imposition of a female ghetto defined by identity politics in the realm of critical imagination. They likewise reject the automatic assumption (latent in job advertisements) that a critic who comes from an ethnic minority would prefer to focus on the literature of that minority rather than other topics. They ask how the several hats worn by the critic as feminist, and at the same time as Arabist, deconstructionist, bisexual, or new historicist, can be turned to profit: how might self-conscious labeling, especially the splitting or multiplication of labels, serve critical analysis?

This affirmation of the multiple ideologically colored positions a critic occupies stands in sharp contrast to the goal of neutral formalism which once defined comparative literature. Gayatri Spivak, for example, writes about herself in the third person using a hyphenated label, Marxist-feminist-deconstructionist, and wittily subverts the reader's expectations as well as her own apparent argument by changing her implied position in mid-essay.[12] Her strategy of interruption opens a gap to force the reader into the metacritical work of comparative interpretation.

Like Spivak, one can script a critical role that plays feminist concerns against comparative ones in order to observe their mutual contest and shifting boundaries. Here, then, I would like to pick up a few of the renovations in the house of comparative literature proposed by the Bernheimer report and to ask how they look when viewed by one feminist. Nation, translation, and language are the most important of these changing concepts; indeed, all three concepts cast up questions of language for our consideration.

The report addresses the foundational concept of national identity indirectly, through questions of language and multiculturalism. Thus, it proposes shifting attention from international differences to differences within national cultures which are determined by factors such as gender, ethnicity, or political status which might be reflected in differences of language. It also proposes that we acknowledge the interest of many comparatists in interdisciplinary area studies.

Certainly, I would agree that the concept of nationality within comparative practice needs to be pressed for deeper insights about the intersection of nationalisms and sexualities. Homogenizing visions of national identity construct "horizontal" imagined communities that elide or ghettoize sexual, ethnic, and racial difference.[13] While the nation and especially the land are often symbolized by a female figure, citizenship has typically been represented as masculine. The "foundational fictions" that emerged in Latin American literature at the moment of independence, Doris Sommer has argued, marry these two figures of the representative citizen and the land. By eroticizing the traversal of racial lines, these fictions seek to symbolically transcend racial and regional conflicts over citizenship and political power which broke out at independence. The resulting romance plots allegorize the possibility of nation building by wedding the protagonist as a leader to a figurative representative of the land and its indigenous peoples.[14]

Such literary patterns demand ironic and contestatory responses from minority writers. In their efforts to represent World War I, for example, minority women writers confront a conception of national identity which excludes them, both by gender and by race, from national service. To write patriotically, then, can become a politically subversive act. The countertraditions that emerge within the frame of a national tradition call for comparative treatment.[15]

Some of the most innovative work by feminist critics today, however, lies not in national but in area studies. This type of department has been viewed with suspicion by comparatists because it takes political or social science as its center of gravity, apparently minimizing linguistic training. Yet language is the common thread in some of the best work of this kind. Gloria Anzaldúa and the contributors to *Criticism in the Borderlands* stress the importance of linguistic play in Chicana and Chicano literature. Debra Castillo wittily foregrounds women's kitchen talk in her study of Latin American women's writing. And Regina Harrison's prizewinning study of Quechua women's oral poetry brilliantly crosses disciplines as well as national boundaries to explicate connections between agriculture, spirituality, and verbal arts.[16]

The importance of language to comparatists' self-definition seems clear from the controversy elicited by the Bernheimer report's pragmatic comments on the utility of translation in the classroom. The limitations of our own linguistic training and the accidents of our students' diverse linguistic abilities push us toward work in translation; even a graduate seminar must often order books both in the original languages and in English.

Nonetheless, we should note that reliance upon translations ironically can have a conservative impact, since only translations of texts believed to have world rank and a wide audience remain in print. Genres directed to a male audience are sometimes assumed to have a broader readership than those directed to a female audience. Furthermore, patterns of translation which overlook the forms of intertextuality typical of women's culture flatten out texts by women. Until this year, the only available translation of Charrière omitted her opening ironic commentary on Samuel de Constant's *Mari senti-mental* and failed to exploit her echoes of Rousseau's *Emile*. Like bicultural texts, women's texts at times play with forms of humor and linguistic hybridization. Predictably, the force of much women's writing gets lost in translation.

Given the importance of linguistic difference as a founding concept of comparative literature, we must rethink the gender-neutral understanding of language which governs the field.[17] Although Deborah Cameron argues that "there is little warrant for notions of a separate women's language, or even what used to be called a 'genderlect' (i.e., a distinctive dialect used by one gender)," she also argues that women historically in most cultures have suffered from social disadvantages that produce specific linguistic behaviors. Men have controlled literacy and certain elite linguistic registers.[18] The latent preference in much comparative study for "high" and "resonant" literary forms that incorporate verbal allusions to extended written traditions, especially in dead classical languages, devalues not only dialectal forms but also the resonance of oral and demotic patterns of allusion in writings by women and minorities barred from education in elite literary traditions.

The usual organization of comparative study around national *Sprach-literaturen* privileges the linguistic purity of a "standard" language defined by dominant groups. The comparatist too often overlooks the linguistic riches to be found in the shared tropes and codes of a gay sociolect, the resistant hyphenated or parenthetical orthographic inventions of a feminist philosopher like Mary Daly, or the literary specificities of a local or racial dialect.

Where men and women have lived in highly segregated spheres, separate linguistic usages emerge which inflect literary production. Limit cases may be useful here, such as that of Elisabeth Martinengou, an Ionian writer of the mid-nineteenth century, an autodidact who taught herself Italian and French in order to read the literature of the Enlightenment at a time when most other women in her society were unlettered. Forging a demotic vocabulary in part borrowed from her literary readings and richly informed by oral culture, she created a clear, stripped, yet spontaneous and poetic style that made her one of the first important writers in modern Greek.[19]

Or one could adduce Nu Shu, an ancient Chinese women's language rediscovered by an anthropologist studying minorities in Hunan province.[20] Painted in a style called "mosquito-ant" onto fans and handmade books or embroidered onto silk, this language has been passed down for at least a thousand years from mothers to daughters. Nu Shu is thought to have originated in the Sung dynasty (about A.D. 900–1279) when a young woman from this province was sent to the imperial palace; she wrote home about her misery in her own local script, which was unknown at the court and had been abandoned by men at home, as they became involved in commerce and adopted the official Han script. Historically, the language was used to permit women to communicate with one another in secret; they used it to inscribe female friendship pacts, to record rituals of divination, and to express the loneliness and laments that only a mother or close friend might be permitted to know. Sung aloud by one woman to another, the poems use a local dialect known as "sitting singing" in a custom that is unique to women's language.

Encoded verbal practices can serve to shield and unite groups in the face of repression by dominant political, racial, or sexual cultures. These verbal strategies can be woven together in complex forms of *métissage*.[21] Recent work on Chicana literature stresses the importance of linguistic hybridity and code switching to the formulation of ethnic and sexual identity at the border. A writer like Gloria Anzaldúa in fact firmly locates herself at the space of the slash, mixing languages in defiance of state-imposed monolingualism even in the title of her book *Borderlands/La Frontera: The New Mestiza*.

Code switching enables Anzaldúa to suggest the multiplicity of identities which she carries, like a turtle, on her back. As a lesbian poet, she is "half and half—both woman and man, neither—a new gender." For her as mestiza and cultural critic, "*es difícil* differentiating between *lo heredado, lo adquirido, lo impuesto*. She puts history through a sieve." "To live in the borderlands," she writes, "means you are neither *hispana india negra española ni gabacha, eres mestiza, mulata*, half-breed caught in the crossfire between camps."[22]

The solution Anzaldúa offers is one we can embrace here:

> To survive the Borderlands
> you must live *sin fronteras*
> be a crossroads. (*Borderlands* 195)

Notes

1. "Der Mensch ist der große Gedankenstrich im Buche der Natur." Jean Paul Richter, *Die unsichtbare Loge*, in *Sämtliche Werke*, ed. Eduard Berend (Weimar: Hermann Böhlaus, 1927), 2: 2.

2. I borrow the phrase from Annette Kolodny, "Dancing through the Minefield: Some Observations on the Theory, Practice, and Politics of a Feminist Literary Criticism," *Feminist Studies* 6, no. 1 (1980): 1–25. One should distinguish feminist activists

who work to dismantle discriminatory social barriers from feminist theorists and critics who focus primarily on the social meanings conveyed by such boundaries and the literary forms that they shape.

3. Margaret R. Higonnet, ed., *Borderwork: Feminist Engagements with Comparative Literature* (Ithaca, N.Y.: Cornell University Press, 1994), in press.

4. Diana Fuss, *Essentially Speaking: Feminism, Nature, and Difference* (New York: Routledge, 1989), 116.

5. Jacques Derrida, "The Law of Genre," *Critical Inquiry* 7, no. 1 (1980): 59.

6. Thorstein Veblen, *The Higher Learning in America* (Stanford: Academic Reprints, 1954), 207.

7. Ulrich Weisstein, "Lasciate Ogni Speranza: Comparative Literature in Search of Lost Definitions," *Yearbook of Comparative and General Literature* 37 (1989): 99–100.

8. Judith Butler, *Gender Trouble: Feminism and the Subversion of Identity* (New York: Routledge, 1990).

9. Trinh T. Minh-ha, *Woman, Native, Other: Writing Postcoloniality and Feminism* (Bloomington: Indiana University Press, 1989), 95–96.

10. Rey Chow, *Women and Chinese Modernity: The Politics of Reading between West and East* (Minneapolis: University of Minnesota Press, 1991), 163.

11. René Wellek and Austin Warren, *Theory of Literature* (New York: Harcourt, Brace, 1949). See Margaret Ferguson, Maureen Quilligan, and Nancy Vickers, eds., *Rewriting the Renaissance* (Chicago: University of Chicago Press, 1986); Anne K. Mellor, *Romanticism and Gender* (New York: Routledge, 1993); Bonnie Kime Scott, ed., *The Gender of Modernism: A Critical Anthology* (Bloomington: Indiana University Press, 1990).

12. Gayatri Chakravorty Spivak, *In Other Worlds: Essays in Cultural Politics* (New York: Routledge, 1988).

13. Andrew Parker, Mary Russo, Doris Sommer, and Patricia Yaeger, introduction to *Nationalisms and Sexualities* (New York: Routledge, 1992), 1–18.

14. Doris Sommer, *Foundational Fictions: The National Romances of Latin America* (Berkeley and Los Angeles: University of California Press, 1991).

15. Hortense J. Spillers, ed., *Comparative American Identities: Race, Sex, and Nationality in the Modern Text* (Routledge: New York, 1991); Joyce W. Warren, ed., *The (Other) American Traditions: Nineteenth-Century Women Writers* (New Brunswick, N.J.: Rutgers University Press, 1993).

16. Gloria Anzaldúa, *Borderlands/La Frontera: The New Mestiza* (San Francisco: Spinsters/Aunt Lute Books, 1987); Héctor Calderon and José David Saldívar, eds., *Criticism in the Borderlands: Studies in Chicano Literature, Culture, and Ideology* (Durham: Duke University Press, 1991); Debra A. Castillo, *Talking Back: Toward a Latin American Feminist Literary Criticism* (Ithaca, N.Y.: Cornell University Press, 1992); and Regina Harrison, *Signs, Songs, and Memory in the Andes: Translating Quechua Language and Culture* (Austin: University of Texas Press, 1989). See also Mary Louise Pratt's provocative reflections on the many-faceted operations of cultural imperialism and the emergence of multicultural forms in what she calls the "contact zone." Pratt, *Imperial Eyes: Travel Writing and Transculturation* (New York: Routledge, 1992).

17. Ulrich Weisstein, for example, proposes *Sprachliteratur* as the "most suitable" term to describe "the entities we use as counter in our comparatist game." "Linguistic

criteria," he writes, "govern our foremost activities" such as translation. Weisstein, "Lasciate Ogni Speranza," 103.

18. Deborah Cameron, "Introduction: Why Is Language a Feminist Issue?" in *The Feminist Critique of Language, A Reader*, ed. Deborah Cameron (London: Routledge, 1990), 24.

19. I am indebted here to Eleni Varikas, "Ecrire derrière les jalousies: Le journal intime d'une recluse," unpublished paper.

20. Carolyn Lau, "Nu Shu: An Ancient, Secret, Women's Language," *Belles Lettres* 6 (1990): 32–34.

21. See Françoise Lionnet, *Autobiographical Voices: Race, Gender, Self-Portraiture* (Ithaca, N.Y.: Cornell University Press, 1989).

22. Anzaldúa, *Borderlands*, 82, 194.

16

SPACES OF COMPARISON

FRANÇOISE LIONNET

One could perhaps say that certain ideological conflicts animating present-day polemics oppose the pious descendants of time to the determined inhabitants of space. . . . Our epoch is one in which space takes for us the form of relations among sites.
—Michel Foucault, "Of Other Spaces"

Growing up on a small island, you become intensely aware of the rest of the world. When it is an island in the Indian Ocean whose history is completely contained within that of colonialism, your awareness of that world is the only canvas that you have, the only mirror into which you can look. To make sense of your insularity, you try to understand what this small place represents and how it has figured in the European languages that you speak. You know that your identity is marked by these languages; yet you do not feel circumscribed by them. Your sense of place is relational: you can understand who and where you are only when you begin to see that this place, the island on which you were born, played a role in Europe's construction of its own identity just as much as it helped shape the lives of the islanders.

In Mauritius, two European countries competed in different ways for the privilege of educating and civilizing us: France and England. This allowed for a healthy skepticism vis-à-vis the claims of universality which each culture made in its own way. France had the upper hand culturally, England politically. We learned both French and English perfectly. But the African and Indian bases of our Creole vernacular grounded us in a very different epistemology. Our identities, it seems now, were always "in process" before we knew the word and the concept. We were all "comparatists." Our location at the intersection of several systems of knowledge provided a certain kind of productive discomfort: Mauritius has a two-hundred-year literary history, more daily and weekly newspapers per capita than most countries, and several small publishing houses. But the school curriculum exposed us only to the classics of English and French literature—Shakespeare and *ancien régime* authors. The education was first-rate, and the schools attempted to make us into those "pious descendants of time" evoked by Foucault, to fold us into teleological History. The outcome, for those of us who loved learning, would normally be departure from the island in search of more learning—the prototypical colonial intellectual odyssey.

During my last years of high school, I moved to the neighboring island of Reunion, still a French *département d'outre-mer* (overseas department), or DOM, fourteen thousand miles away from Paris. There, I accidentally discovered Faulkner in a French *Livre de Poche* edition. It was in Faulkner's pages that I first began to see a reflection of my own colonial society: no other books that I knew (the year was 1966) evoked its racial, cultural, and gender dynamics and exposed its flaws without apology. Aimé Césaire had published his *Cahier d'un retour au pays natal* (*Notebook of a Return to the Native Land*) in 1939, but it was not available in the DOM, nor was African or Caribbean literature taught in the schools. In the mid-sixties, the closest I came to hearing echoes of my colonial background in literary texts was to pay imaginative visits to Faulkner's Yoknapatawpha. In the mid-seventies, living in Toronto, I discovered similar echoes in Margaret Laurence's Manawaka. These fictional worlds offered a historical geography that made some sense of my experiences and wove together the legacies of long, shared colonial histories.

Faulkner's protagonists express themselves in a vernacular that seemed like an echo of our own Creole. The novels of Edouard Glissant, Maryse Condé, Marie-Thérèse Humbert, and Toni Morrison would later give me access to the same kind of *imaginaire*. In 1966, however, the only other writer I knew who had written about heat, about barefoot women such as Lena in *Light in August,* and about the kind of natural world with which I was familiar was Baudelaire. Our very French and newly arrived *professeur de lettres* insisted that we were lucky to be from this part of the world which so inspired Baudelaire's sensual and exotic poetry, "À une dame créole" or "La belle Dorothée." This *prof* had clearly come to the Indian Ocean in search of the Baudelairian myth of the tropics. She went on pilgrimages to those parts of both islands where Baudelaire is known to have spent several months in late 1841, waiting for the sailing ship *L'Alcide* that was to take him back to Bordeaux. I appreciated Baudelaire—I loved poetry, and he was after all rather *osé* material for a Catholic high school—but I also knew, as did my classmates, that our *prof* was living a mystified life: the poetry and exoticism of the tropics, as she saw it in Baudelaire, was for us just "literature," a myth that had very little to do with the colonial reality of this outpost of the recently crumbled French empire. Besides, we perceived this newly arrived, pale-faced, and somewhat overfed teacher as a *métropolitaine* whose access to sensuality was at best limited—we spent the better part of our weekends on the beach, whereas she seemed never willing to expose herself to ultraviolet rays. It seemed very odd indeed to be introduced to Baudelaire's poetry by such a teacher. She did teach us to love *Les fleurs du mal* (*Flowers of Evil*), but what I remember from those days is a profound sense of disjuncture—between Baudelaire's poetry and this seemingly asexual teacher on the one hand, between the poetry of exoticism and the politically and economically repressive reality of the DOM on the other. Somehow, the first disjuncture reflected the second, and modern literature became a locus of the historical and geographical paradoxes that were woven into our lives. This experience inaugurated my personal "era of suspicion."

In my high school *classe de philo*, we read Plato, Aristotle, and Descartes, but also Freud, Marx, Bergson, Merleau-Ponty, and Sartre. I remember Sartre's and Beauvoir's early texts on America. They reinforced my growing interests in contemporary American literature as "the" literature of our time. I wrote a paper on *Light in August* and existentialism. American literature had become the canvas and the mirror. In it, questions were raised, lives would unfold, and the past was articulated in ways that were not available in the standard historical narratives of colonialism. At least, not yet. Foucault had recently published his *Histoire de la folie* (*Madness and Civilization*), but the question of madness and colonialism was still a marginal one, despite Fanon's eloquent contributions in *Les damnés de la terre* (*The Wretched of the Earth*). At the university in Aix-en-Provence, I gravitated to courses in philosophy, literature, and American studies. When I obtained an exchange fellowship to Ann Arbor in 1969, I did not hesitate. From the "New World" of the Southern Hemisphere to what has recently been termed the "Extrême-Occident," the leap now seemed inevitable. Space was beginning to take for me "the form of relations among sites."

I became another statistic in the brain drain that takes Third World intellectuals to Western research centers. The development in the seventies of Afro-American studies and women's studies opened intellectual avenues that did not exist at home. I could have gone back, to get involved in some practical political issues that interested me: Mauritius had become independent in 1968. But being female, I had fewer choices than my male relatives, one of whom actually became the leader of an important neo-Marxist political party. I chose literature instead, and after a master's degree in English, transferred to comparative literature, where my knowledge of French and German was an asset. I am pretty sure that I was not aware of the existence of the 1965 and the 1975 Reports on Standards, but graduate courses in theory had familiarized me with Wellek and Warren, E. D. Hirsch and Croce. Suddenly I was focused again on the canonical European traditions, and I experienced a renewed sense of disjuncture and discontent. I had also taken courses on Afro-American literature, structuralist poetics, and Russian formalism. Somehow, the sum total of this education did not add up then to the kind of comparative work I wanted to do. I am not black, and no one would recommend that I specialize in Afro-American literature in this country. I could have gone back to France and worked with Americanists such as Michel Fabre or Jean Guiguet. My personal life took me in a different direction.

I lived and taught in Canada for a few years. Quebec literature offered another "site" in which issues of language (English, French, and Joual) were often raised, echoing the preoccupations of writers from many other colonial contexts. I put Marie-Claire Blais and Claire Martin, Hubert Aquin and Michel Tremblay, along with other Francophone authors from Africa and the Caribbean, on the syllabi of the French classes I was teaching. The most common formal denominator of these texts is the first-person narrative: the genre of autobiography provided a productive way of thinking about issues of identity and subjectivity, race, class, and gender. I came back to the United States in 1980, audited classes at the New School, Columbia, and New York University: Susan Sontag's course on autobiography, Todorov's on the conquest of America, and Michel Beaujour's on Montaigne and self-portraiture. Ross Chambers had moved from Australia to the comparative literature program at the University of Michigan, and his intellectual rigor, generosity, and openness gave me the final nudge.

I wrote my dissertation on autobiography and tried to expand the theoretical boundaries of women's autobiographical practice by privileging the writings of cultural métis from a wide chronological and linguistic range. This dissertation quickly became a book, but not without initially raising many eyebrows: "Augustine and Nietzsche? Along with black women writers? Are you serious?" There was no apparent coherence to such a grouping: the individual writers belonged to such disparate traditions, I was told. I am sure that for some it seemed like "an unstructured postmodern hodgepodge," to use a phrase from Appiah's response in this volume. In fact, my book uses poststructuralist theories to make a deconstructive argument, the aim of which was to clear a cultural space where the reconstruction of alternative genealogies might be possible. I tried to derive my interpretive strategies from the texts themselves. I showed that deconstruction as a practice has accompanied decolonization as a historical event and that several contemporary African American and Francophone women's narratives actually *perform* the kind of cultural critique which some contemporary philosophers later set out to theorize. In 1990, Cornell University Press nominated *Autobiographical Voices* for the ACLA's Wellek Prize. I did not win, nor did I expect to. But it was gratifying.

Had I "arrived"? That is, had I won some points in what José Piedra has called the "game of critical arrival"?[1] Does it matter? Only to the extent that such recognition contributes to opening up a field that has been resistant to both feminisms and noncanonical literatures and has denied agency and creativity to the peoples of "lesser" traditions.

Had I followed a more traditional path to the degree, I am sure I would never have found the tools that allowed me to interrelate a set of literary texts in a way that would be productive, for me, of new insights about writing and culture, shared histories and related geographies. The areas in which I work clearly do not coincide with the field as mapped in both the 1965 and the 1975 Reports on Standards, although both positively emphasize "interdisciplinarity." But interdisciplinarity is not multi- or interculturalism: two sentences in the Levin report are a good index of the misunderstandings and blindspots that have plagued academic debates about pluralism:

> Since there has been some talk about an American school of Comparative Literature, we should like to reaffirm our belief in the internationalism of our field . . . . It is largely because of America's cultural pluralism, above all its receptivity to Europeans and European ideas, that we have been enabled to develop centers for the study of Comparative Literature since the last war.

Strangely enough, this "American school of Comparative Literature" that advocates "internationalism" and admits having benefited from America's cultural pluralism is totally indifferent to the literature and expressive culture of *this* country. Surely Sartre's discussion of American writers in the chapter "Situation of the Writer in 1947" in his essay *What Is Literature?* qualifies as "European ideas." Yet the displaced European intellectuals who built the profession in the postwar era seemed to equate America's pluralism with the opportunities that come with virgin territory. America had no "history" as understood by the Levin report. On the face of it, American literature could not constitute a proper field of study.

The 1965 report stresses that "for historic reasons which must be respected, certain countries have figured prominently in [the field's] pioneering investigations, as indeed have certain periods and types of relationships." Let us be generous and suppose that this sentence did leave its authors open to the possibility that a reexamination of the history on which claims of cultural superiority are made could call for new kinds of comparative endeavors linking new "spaces of comparison" according to shared experiences based in, say, European colonialism. It seems logical to suggest this much. If we "post/colonials" are "the determined inhabitants of space," then some understanding of the material conditions and appropriative gestures that produce a disciplinary space is required. This understanding is necessarily historical, but it changes the "types of relationships" which would now constitute the field.

I recently had occasion to look into the history of the late-seventeenth-century French *Querelle des anciens et des modernes*. It was instructive to discover that women had been the principal target of Boileau's *Satire X* because they questioned the authority of the past and supported the moderns against the claims of those, like Boileau, who upheld the traditions of classicism. Among the moderns: Corneille, Molière, Pascal, La Fontaine, and Charles Perrault. *Plus ça change . . .*

What is surprising, then, as I read the three responses to the 1993 report that Charles Bernheimer has included in this volume, is to find a distant echo of the 1965 formulation in Anthony Appiah's paper:

> There is a complex dialectic between subject matters, human interests (themselves shaped deeply by literary and other dimensions of culture), and professional organization which goes into the historical process of the construction of a field of discourse. The old comparative literature responded to more than the taste for languages: it responded to the historical interconnectedness of a field of European texts that came to be central to Europe's high culture. I hope this study can go on in the university alongside the multiple comparisons and the scores of languages in which the study of literature and orature flourish; and the history that Wellek studied can be seen as one instance of that broad set of multilingual cultural histories which we call a civilization.

Of course the study of Europe's high culture will go on. How can it not, given the importance of that *Weltanschauung* to the self-understanding of contemporary peoples? The point, as I see it, is not to replace the old with the new but to make room for those ancient civilizations that had been marginalized *and* for those subcultures and countercultures that question the authority of the past (as seventeenth-century literary French women did). These deserve representation in all the senses of the word: not because of academic altruism but because we all contribute, in different ways, to the advancement of knowledge.

The construction of the field à la Levin, Wellek, and Greene left out elements (e.g., contemporary American literatures, women's histories, African literatures) which are an integral part of the "complex dialectic between subject matters, human interests," and cultural production and reception. This is especially true if the arena of reception is the American academy with its diverse population. But it is also increasingly true of Europe. Study of its high culture is enriched by the perspectives and intertextual references of bilingual writers such as Abdelkebir Khatibi in *Amour bilingue* (*Love in Two Languages*) or Assia Djebar in *L'Amour, la fantasia* (*Fantasia, An Algerian Cavalcade*). Knowledge of nineteenth-century European literature and painting is just as important as familiarity with Arabic to appreciate Djebar's works. And reading Djebar brings the European tradition of Orientalist paintings into renewed focus.

That is why the study of the classics cannot just go on "alongside" that of more recent texts. It is no longer possible (if it ever was) to consider Europe's traditions in isolation, as though the Enlightenment philosophers' elaboration of the sovereign subject did not rest on the simultaneous othering of cannibals and Persians, Africans and Orientals, whether in narrative or in museum displays. I should think that it is precisely the interweavings of traditions, languages, and perspectives which offer the richest avenues for the archeological work that old and new "fields of discourse" offer together. It seems to me that once you understand knowledge as a field of interrelated practices, the fear that something so central as European cultures (whether we like it or not) would no longer be taught in the American academy becomes ludicrous. More important, knowledge thus understood makes it anachronistic to write, as the Greene report does, that "it goes without saying that we cannot begin to absorb the wealth of exotic literatures before firmly possessing our own." No literature should be seen as "exotic" if "our" purpose is to gain a better understanding of the networks of influence and power, lure and seduction, freedom and liberation, not to mention containment and subversion, which link the local to the global, the former colonies to their metropoles, and last but not least, various local manifestations of interrelated cultures. The symbolic understanding of cultural forms in a global framework provides the basis for what Edouard Glissant has called "une poétique de la Relation" (a poetics of relationality): one that takes into account the indigenous productions of non-Europeans as well as their respective relationships to the sites of Western modernity. Geographical connections are becoming as important as historical ones, and the current convergence on spatial thinking in many disciplines highlights the search for alternative ways of knowing.

According to a U.N. report, more than 50 percent of the world's population will be urban by the year 2005.[2] Visual and musical urban popular culture is already that of the majority, and we need to take this into account. That is why I do not think that it would be giving up "the idea of distinctive trainings" (Appiah) to include popular culture (however defined) within the purview of comparatists. Shakespeare's plays were "popular culture" in his time, as were the troubadours, François Villon, and Rabelais in theirs: they used the vernacular, not Latin, as their chosen mode of expression. Critical languages developed by semioticians and formalist critics have been been useful to the study of myths, folktales, Russian *skaz*, and orature. Specialists of visual culture use them as well. Mineke Schipper's *Beyond the Boundaries: Text and Context in African Literature* shows how formal critical tools can illuminate the intercultural and comparative study of African texts and of the written orality that Russian and African literatures share (albeit from vastly different contexts).

Jocelyne Guilbault's *World Music* talks about the hybridization or *métissage* of Caribbean *zouk*, of its French-Creole lyrics and West African beat. If the old comparative literature could see the relevance of Wagner to the study of Nietzsche, there is no reason why world music cannot belong in the comparative study of Caribbean and African oral and literary cultures. James Baldwin wrote his books while listening to Bessie Smith. Understanding the highly structured elements of what is wrongly called "improvisation" in jazz or blues helps us to see the similarly structured and complex patterns of African American literature.

I do happen to think, along with Michael Riffaterre, that the category "literature" has a valuable specificity. The writers that I read and work on do indeed claim the field as their very own. They value writing as an intransitive activity that cannot always be subsumed under larger political agendas, and they strongly resist the attempt to reduce their efforts to the simple manifestation of cultural determinants. As Glissant's 1993 book *Tout-Monde* suggests, he for one is engaged in an enterprise of invention and liberation aimed at freeing consciousness from false and abstract universals, from tired and sterile hierarchies. Salman Rushdie and the numerous Algerian writers whose lives are threatened because they exercise the right to freely "do literature" assert the same need for creative expression in a medium that is not constrained by readily identifiable codes. V. Y. Mudimbe's essays and novels similarly expose the contradictions and dislocations that are those of the African intellectual caught between knowledge systems and revolutionary praxis. Hence, I am as uncomfortable as Riffaterre (but for different reasons) with the 1993 report's suggestion that "'literature' may no longer adequately describe our object of study." I think there is a confusion here between "belles-lettres" and how that category is produced over time, and the activity of writing the kind of texts that escape or transform rigid cultural conventions. Some literary critics may have focused on a disembodied and decontextualized study of the text. Surely this does not mean that *literary* criticism is synonymous with decontextualized readings. Insisting on the literary aspect of an analysis simply asserts an object's status as "literature"—according to an author's intention and publishing opportunities. It does not mean that the critic subscribes to a binary evaluative episteme (high/low; aesthetics/politics).

In our desire to embrace "cultural studies," I would hate to see us reduce the contemporary non-Western writer to a mere epiphenomenon of identity politics and, worse still, privilege Western *mass* culture and the theoretical tools applicable to it as the most interesting site for innovative investigations. The danger here is that under the guise of antiethnocentrism, once again cultural relativism and American liberalism will join in encouraging a "hands off" attitude toward the non-English-speaking world beyond the U.S. borders. There is a risk that more and more students will focus exclusively on U.S. cultures, ignoring in the process the voices of less visible peoples who have much to contribute to our current debates and who often pose questions or offer imaginative solutions directly relevant to the dynamics of multiculturalism in this country. One of the limitations of Anglo-American cultural studies has been this somewhat parochial focus at the expense of broader, international, and multilingual approaches. This is therefore a moment of great opportunity for comparatists, and it behooves us to seize the occasion and to "globalize" and "democratize," as Mary Louise Pratt puts it. The decolonization process has already been under way for quite some time now. But what we seem to fear, as a profession, is the messiness of globalization and the risk of contamination that might result from the democratization of the idea of literature as an intersubjective practice.

I have nothing against television, hypertext, and virtual realities, but access to the necessary resources and technology is not democratic. Where I come from, pen and paper continue to be the cheapest means of self-expression, after music and storytelling. And this is the only means that is not communal and ephemeral. Hence, literature as "pure representation" of impure phenomena will continue to challenge, and fascinate, to open doors and to provide points of entry into the *impensé*, the still necessarily opaque and unspoken dimensions of a chaotic contemporary world in which a multiplicity of histories have left their traces. Writers and artists offer us powerful insights into the processes of negotiation which intercultural contact demands: we would be doing a disservice to our students if we did not encourage them to learn from these global transformations and to contribute to the latter in a theoretically and culturally informed manner.

Of course, this does not mean that there should exist a disciplinary hierarchy between different kinds of comparative studies, depending on the forms of discourses which occupy the "space of comparison": " 'literature' . . . music, philosophy, history, or law as similar discursive systems" (1993 report), but also medical and scientific constructions of race, health, normalcy, and gender identity. That is why I also agree with Mary Louise Pratt's call for greater inclusiveness, for an expanded definition of the field, and thus even for going beyond the occasionally tentative formulations of the 1993 report. We should encourage students to devise programs of study which correspond to what compels them most, to the landscapes they most desire to understand or to inhabit. And we should teach them that patience is indeed a virtue: sooner or later, the discipline will catch up with you. I know, I've been there.

As Toni Morrison puts it, "All of us, readers and writers, are bereft when criticism remains too polite or too fearful to notice a disrupting darkness before its eyes."[3]

Notes

1. José Piedra, "The Game of Critical Arrival," *Diacritics* 19 (Spring 1989): 34–61.
2. "The World Urbanization Prospect," Population Division, U.N. Secretariat (Summer 1993).
3. Toni Morrison, *Playing in the Dark: Whiteness and the Literary Imagination* (Cambridge: Harvard University Press, 1992), 91.

17

"LITERATURE" IN THE
EXPANDED FIELD

MARJORIE PERLOFF

Ask any student in the United States why he or she decided to study comparative, rather than English (or indeed any single national) literature, and that student will tell you that the appeal of comparative literature is its *more than* status. René Wellek said it back in 1956 in *Theory of Literature*: "The great argument for 'comparative' or 'general' literature or just 'literature,' is the obvious falsity of the ideal of a self-enclosed national literature."[1] "Self-enclosed" is the key term here: how, comparatists have always asked, can one study, say, English Romantic poetry without some knowledge of its German precursors—Goethe, Heine, Hölderlin, to mention just the most obvious ones. How study Joyce without any knowledge of Flaubert? Aimé Césaire without a familiarity of French surrealism? And so on.

Then, too, comparative literature has always had a special appeal for those of us who want to work synchronically rather than diachronically. Let me confess that as a specialist in modern and postmodern literature, I have always resented the time (a whole semester!) I spent in graduate school making my way through *Piers Plowman*, when I might have been learning more about Dante or Gérard de Nerval or the amazing Whitmanian poet from Brazil, Joachim de Sousândrade. A synchronic model would have also made it possible for me to do more work in philosophy: for a variety of reasons, a course in Kant and Hegel would have been more personally valuable to me than was the course I had to take in *Beowulf*. And, as it happens, since I work in both literature and the visual arts, I am profoundly grateful that at Oberlin College, where I did my undergraduate work, I took six courses in art history—courses I still draw upon in doing my own brand of "comparative" study.

At the same time, the problem of comparative literature has always been that its terrain is amorphous. Again Wellek was one of the first to recognize this: "The most serious sign of the precarious state of our study," he complained in 1958, "is the fact that it has not been able to establish a distinct subject matter and a specific methodology."[2] This is the malaise that has haunted comparative literature from its inception and that continues to bedevil it in the "age of multiculturalism." American literature is, well, American literature: it can incorporate all the newer literatures and cultures—African American, Chicano, Asian American, Native American, Filipino, gay American, and so on—but its boundaries are precisely the boundaries of the United States. But what in the world is *comparative* literature? If, as the Bernheimer report insists, we move *beyond* the Eurocentric, if, as Mary Louise Pratt tells us we must, we now take on our role as "global citizens," just what is it we are going to study? And whom will that study benefit?

The "apparent internationalism" of the "old" comparative literature, the Bernheimer report tells us, was just a smokescreen that "sustained a restrictive Eurocentrism." More important: "the term 'literature' may no longer adequately describe our object of study"; "literary phenomena are no longer the exclusive focus of our discipline. Rather, literary texts are now being approached as one discursive practice among many others in a complex, shifting, and often contradictory field of cultural production." This Foucaultian assertion sounds sensible enough until we stop to think about it. For, if any and all discursive practices will be the object of our "discipline," what makes it a discipline at all? *Discipline,* let us recall, comes from the same Latin root as the word *disciple.* "Etymologically," according to the *OED,* "*discipline,* as pertaining to the disciple or scholar, is antithetical to *doctrine,* of the doctor or teacher; hence, in the history of the words, *doctrine* is more concerned with abstract theory, and *discipline* with practice or exercise." *Discipline* thus means "instruction imparted to disciples or scholars"; the first instance the *OED* gives comes from John Wyclif (1382): "Thou shalt finde grace and good discipline." During the Reformation, the "Discipline of the Secret" referred to the procedure of "gradually teaching the mysteries of the Christian faith to neophytes, and in concealing them from the uninitiated." The success of discipline is judged by its effect: as early as 1434, *discipline* is defined as "instruction having for its aim to form the pupil to proper conduct and action; the training of scholars or subordinates to proper and orderly action by instructing and exercising them in the same." "The notion of Discipline and Interference," said Ruskin in 1857, "lies at the root of all human progress or power."

"Proper and orderly action," "interference"—the downside of the concept of discipline, already evident in its earliest definitions, is that it involves *control*. In characterizing comparative literature as a discipline, then, the Bernheimer report evidently supports the notion that our role as comparatists is to bring our students to some form of "proper conduct and action." But if "literary phenomena are no longer the exclusive focus of our discipline," as the Bernheimer report tells us, what is its focus? What will the discipline in question consist of? For common sense tells us that no one can in fact learn all there is to know (or even a smattering) about "global" literature and culture; no one can study high and low, First World and Third World, anthropology and sociology, political economy and feminist theory, as well as specific literary texts. "More than" X means, in practice, less than Y.

What, then, would the new global, non-Eurocentric, nonpatriarchal, nonelitist comparative literature look like? According to Mary Louise Pratt, it would represent, first of all, a removal of those irritating "fences" of the "old" comparative literature, which seems to have been "founded by a rhetoric of vigilance associated with the Cold War." It is high time, she posits, for the "farmer" who has been busy "walking the fences and patching them up to make sure nothing wild gets in, nothing valuable gets out," to retire to Florida leaving all the doors and gates open so that the "animals will move from pasture to pasture and pen to pen [and] strange matings will occur." Indeed, the new "openness" is inevitable, Pratt argues, because of the increasing "globalization, democratization, and decolonization" of the planet. The big question as to the new "expanded field" that our "discipline" will presumably study can only be, in Pratt's words, "*why not*"?

But that "why not?" goes against some troubling facts of life in the academy of the late twentieth century. First, even as Pratt and others exult about the increasing globalization and democratization of the planet, we are witnessing, at this writing, the following phenomena: (1) "ethnic cleansing" by the Serbs in Bosnia of a sort unimaginable even a few decades ago—an ethnic cleansing not really different in nature from the Nazi terror of the 1930s; (2) the massacre at Hebron and the resulting seemingly irreconcilable conflict between Israelis and Palestinians; (3) an increasing display of violence in Mexico, beginning with the conflict in Chiappas and culminating in the March 1994 murder of Luis Donaldo Colosio, the leading presidential candidate; (4) the nuclear buildup in North Korea; (5) the dangerous stalemate between a United States that wants to impose its own human rights policy on an increasingly powerful Fascist China and Chinese resistance to the same. I could go on and on.

Some of us, then, are not as sanguine about globalization as is Mary Pratt. A second hesitation I have about her "why not?" is its dependence on the hegemony of English as the lingua franca. She herself reports enthusiastically on the Summer Institute on Southeast Asian Literatures she attended a few years back, "planned and taught by scholars in Thai, Malaysian, Vietnamese, and Philippine literatures, all of them comparatists of one kind or another." "From the outset," says Pratt, "it was obvious that if this institute was to take place at all, the materials would be read and taught in English." Obvious, I would ask, to whom? Not obvious to someone who is German or Russian or Italian. What is obvious, rather, is that because the United States is currently the only superpower in the world, it gets to call the shots when it comes to a lingua franca. Such essentializing of English, I would posit, perpetuates the old notion of centers and margins which the new comparative literature model is supposedly countering.

But the most serious response to "why not?" has to do with the current economy of academe. It is true that U.S. universities increasingly want to hire, in their literature departments, persons of color, minorities, and, to some extent, women—although white women are already suffering the fate of their male counterparts so far as academic entropy is concerned. What, we may well ask, is the role of a discipline that trains people for a jobless future? At this writing, the most promising white male Ph.D. candidates in the Stanford English Department have failed to get jobs for next year. Not failed to get *good jobs*, but *any jobs*. And the white women in the department have not fared much better. And this has happened no matter how much the Ph.D.'s in question have focused on Third World literature, postcolonialism, post-imperialism, gay and lesbian studies, and so on. We are, in other words, rapidly producing a two-tier system that works as follows. If you are already a professor with tenure, you will have opportunities to go around the world lecturing on queer theory or nationalism, or popular culture, and so on. But if you don't yet have a position, you won't get one by entering the so-called expanded field of the discipline.

Is this only a temporary situation, a situation brought on by the recession of the past few years, the decline of baby boomers, and the new retirement laws that allow the hardy professor to stay on after the age of sixty-five? Studies indicate that the opposite is the case, that the study of literature, however defined, is a shrinking field, that when billets become available, they are transferred to other departments, specifically to the sciences and social sciences. Even as the modern language departments at universities like Stanford are in crisis, the economics department seems to be in a very healthy state.

Why and how has this happened? Here I come back to the question of *discipline*. In his groundbreaking book *Cultural Capital*, a book that should be required reading for anyone currently working in the humanities, John Guillory traces the process that has taken us from the New Criticism of the fifties (a criticism posited on a distinction between "high" and "low" culture, between an elite difficult literature that demanded the mediation of the professor to make it understandable to the pupil and the "ordinary" literature, absorbable by the masses) to the theory phase of the 1970s and beyond. The ascendancy of theory, Guillory argues, occurred when it did because the breakdown of the "great divide" between high and low meant that the rigor once applied to the actual analysis of literary texts passed over to the master teacher (Paul de Man is Guillory's example), whose "deep" technical vocabulary and specialized theoretical understanding were meant to rival those of the technocrats on the other side of the campus.[3] The moment of theory, Guillory explains, was also the moment in America when the old cultured bourgeoisie was finally displaced by what he calls the new managerial-technocratic class, a class that does quite nicely, thank you, without knowing anything about literature or the other arts, indeed without knowing anything much about cultural history. We currently have a president and first lady who exemplify this new class perfectly. Bill and Hillary Clinton are astonishingly smart; they went to the best colleges and the top law school, and Clinton was a Rhodes scholar; from all appearances, their "success" was achieved without knowing anything much about Homer or Plato, Picasso or Gertrude Stein, Franz Fanon or Walter Benjamin, Richard Wright or Zora Neale Hurston.

Who, in other words, "needs" literature today and for what purpose? Guillory details the depressing fortunes of theory in the wake of the Paul de Man debacle. Discipline, he reminds us, depends upon an institutional discipleship; the charisma of the master teacher (like Paul de Man) is entirely linked to the enthusiasm of the discipleship, an enthusiasm that has, as Barbara Johnson has put it, been killed by its own success. "As soon as any radically innovative thought becomes an *ism*," Johnson argued, "its specific ground-breaking force diminishes, its historical notoriety increases, and its disciples tend to become more simplistic, more dogmatic, and ultimately more conservative, at which point its power becomes institutional rather than analytical."[4] The institutional embodiment of such rationalized and "official" critical study, Guillory observes, is the hardening of charisma into bureaucracy (CC 248). In the 1980s, the immediate consequence was the series of bidding wars held at Duke and other institutions to see who could hire Fred Jameson or Stanley Fish or Eve Sedgwick or Barbara Herrnstein Smith. The long-range effect, on the other hand, has been the increasing dissociation between the Star Trek theory displays performed in the graduate schools and an increasingly alienated undergraduate population.

And here I turn to the "new" or not-so-new cultural studies, which is supposed to redeem comparative literature, given that "literary texts are now being approached as one discursive practice among many" and that "the space of comparison today involves comparisons between various cultural constructions." The difficulty here is that cultural studies is, by definition, culture specific: one cannot, after all, even with the best will in the world study a sizable number of cultures any more than one can study a sizable number of languages and literatures. At its most successful, as, for example, in the Stuart Hall model at Birmingham, cultural studies has confined itself to very specific British class and race problems; the same holds true for American studies, which again has investigated specific problems of immigration and nationhood, as well as minority cultures. But when cultural studies enters the comparative literature arena, it becomes *cultural theory.* And cultural theory, which discusses not the specific cultural formations of a given nation but *the* nation, and not the anthropology of specific postcolonial entities but *the* postcolonial condition (on the model of Lyotard "*the* postmodern condition), falls into one of two traps. Either the term *cultural theory* is a code word for Marxist theory, a difficult, complex, arena that is certainly worth studying, although not at the exclusion of rival explanatory models, or cultural theory becomes so amorphous that it does nothing but perpetuate the celebrity game Guillory describes so well when he talks of deconstruction. Indeed, little has changed since the heady days of Paul de Man except that de Man or Derrida himself may now be replaced by Gayatri Spivak, who began, after all, as Derrida's translator and explicator. To supplement Derrida with Spivak, Jameson with Homi K. Bhabha, Kristeva with Trinh T. Minh-ha, Lionel Trilling with Mike Davis—these are, so far as the education of comparatists is concerned, little more than doctrinal maneuvers, doctrine, you recall, being the abstract and authoritative counterpart of discipline. The real question remains unaddressed—the question of what sort of training the "discipline" of comparative literture, if indeed it is a discipline, is going to provide, for whom, and why.

"The big picture of comparative literature," says Mary Louise Pratt, is that of "an especially hospitable space for the cultivation of multilingualism, polyglossia, the arts of cultural mediation, deep intercultural understanding, and genuinely global consciousness." It's an impressive list, although these are values I have always tended to associate with joining the Foreign Service (where you do have to learn many languages) or Peace Corps, or getting a job at the United Nations or with UNICEF. Even the army or navy might do. But when we get down to cases, how many languages can we expect our students, even our best graduate students, to learn—two? three? English-speaking students who learn, say, Japanese in college and go on to do Asian studies have told me that it's all they can do to master Japanese history, culture, and literature—much less Chinese or Korean or Vietnamese. Michelle Yeh, a professor of comparative literature at the University of California–Davis and a former student of mine, who was born and raised in Taiwan, has worked on English, French, and Chinese poetry and theory, writing, for example, on the relationship of Taoism to Derridean versions of metaphor. Could she also have worked German philosophy into the picture? I doubt it. And, even if so, even if she read Hegel and Habermas well in translation, what about Bakhtin's contribution to the new "deep intercultural understanding"? More to the point: what about earlier literatures and cultures? Is the polyglot student of, say, modern Egyptian literature in translation supposed to know anything about medieval Islam?

The new global consciousness, I'm afraid, is too often a code term for a syllabus at least as restrictive as any of those old fences Pratt so deplores. In practice, it means mastering a very specific list of texts from Nietzsche and Freud, Marx and Engels, to Althusser and Foucault, the Frankfurt school and Collège de Sociologie, down to Lacan and Derrida, Cixous, Iragaray, Donna Haraway, Judith Butler, Henry Louis Gates, Jr., and so on. Having discarded "mere" literature, especially "mere" Eurocentric literature written by dead white males, what remains for our students to take away and what sort of career will this new "global" discipline produce? What, to put it concretely, will all those experts on postcolonialism and imperialism, racism and sexism, now do, given a shrinking, indeed all but stagnant, job market for university professors?

Here an anecdote seems apposite. In January 1994, the Lannan Foundation, whose endowment is in excess of $110 million, announced that it was ending its multimillion-dollar program in collecting contemporary art. For two generations, Lannan philanthropy had played a central role in the art world: J. Patrick Lannan, its financier-founder, had, by the time of his death in 1983, acquired several thousand contemporary paintings, including work by Robert Motherwell, Clyfford Still, Agnes Martin, Frank Stella, and an early Mike Kelley. In Los Angeles, where Lannan is based, they have also sponsored poetry readings, art exhibitions, prizes for art criticism, and so on. Some of these activities will be continued; but without warning, collecting has ended, the Lannan Foundation announcing that it plans to transfer the funds ear-marked for art (some $2 million annually) to charities for the poor.

This decision was immediately hailed by the press as a "tragedy" for the art world. "The sudden shift away from a 30-year tradition of collecting art," declared Christopher Knight in the *Los Angeles Times* (January 31, 1994), inescapably represents a public loss of faith in art's power"; Knight and other reporters observed that Lannan's "decision was hard to understand."

But is it hard to understand? My own hunch, as I have met some of the Lannan staff, is that the foundation was beleaguered by the identity politics that now threatens all endowments and foundations. No doubt, they were told that there had to be a certain percentage of minority artists, not to mention the homeless and the disabled. Faced with a cry to "do something for the disadvantaged," Lannan decided to get off its ass and—do something. Not just for the poor who happened to paint but, of all things, for the poor. For who needs art, when so many people are suffering and have so little?

The Lannan decision provides us with a perfect paradigm of what will happen in the university if we are not vigilant. If "high" art is no better than popular culture, if the poetic discourse of Goethe or Yeats is just one among other cultural discourses, why should so much money go into its dissemination? And why should universities have literature departments—whether French or Chinese or Russian or even English—at all? Why art history, now labeled by theorists such as Donald Preziosi as the *coy science?* Feminist studies, gay and lesbian studies, minority studies—these could easily be incorporated into the social sciences (especially psychology and anthropology) rather than into comparative literature or even the English department. In recent years, the law school, for that matter, has sponsored some of the most interesting intellectual discussion in gender studies, race relations, and so on.

Now let us come back to the Bernheimer report and its suggestion that "literary texts" are to be approached "as one discursive practice among many others," and that "comparative literature departments should moderate their focus on high-literary discourse and examine the entire discursive context in which texts are created." For whom will such an examination be of value? Perhaps for the graduate student, but the graduate student can no longer be our central focus, given the retrenchment and attrition of graduate programs. The undergraduate, who has read precious little of that "high" literature in elementary and secondary school—and has, at best, read it uncritically—is not likely to respond well to the Marxist and Foucaultian study of cultural formations. For suppose one only takes a single literature course in one's undergraduate career and that course turns out to be, say, "Imperialism and the Modern Novel," on the model of Edward Said. Since the student in question knows nothing about the history of the modern novel, or of its categories, genres, modes, or rhetorical choices, he or she cannot exactly debate the issues likely to arise. Doctrine, as it were, replaces discipline and, not properly digested, is likely to be forgotten as soon as the course is over.

What can be done about this depressing situation? I am not advocating a return to "business as usual," for, against the conservatives in this debate— the Allan Blooms and Roger Kimballs and William Bennetts and Dinesh deSouzas—I believe that business will never be again "as usual," "usual" referring to a small elite white male university population, exposed to the small elite core course of study which is deemed "important" by its white male mentors. Those days are over, and a good thing too. It is also true that comparative literature, in its first U.S. phase, was the pursuit of a very specific Eurocentric canon and that this canon had been designed largely by a group of white male multilingual refugees from totalitarian Europe: Erich Auerbach and Leo Spitzer, René Wellek and Roman Jakobson, Renato Poggioli and Claudio Giullén, Geoffrey Hartman and Michael Riffaterre. Today, in a university where white males are the distinct minority, this situation clearly *must change* and indeed has changed appreciably. We must now provide many more options so far as national literatures and cultures are concerned and be much more open with regard to theory and methodology. It may be, then, that the Ph.D. in comparative literature will be replaced by a Ph.D. in one of many area studies—European studies, Latin American studies, Asian studies, and so on—as well as in different time frames: medieval studies, Renaissance studies, eighteenth-century studies, modernism, postmodernism. And here the sort of prescriptiveness found in the Bernheimer report seems to me self-defeating. If I want to specialize in the nineteenth-century European lyric, I should know something about Latin verse, but there is not much point learning Swahili, no matter how "multicultural" such a choice might be. It also works the other way around: if I want to study black Caribbean literature, there is not much point being forced to learn German. Or if I want to study Mayan poetics and performance theory, I must learn something about Mayan religion and anthropology, but I doubt that a knowledge of Jane Austen would be of much help.

I have not yet dealt with the most important question of all: why should we study something called "literature," comparative or otherwise, to begin with? What is the *literary* anyway? "You might think," Wittgenstein once remarked, "Aesthetics is a science telling us what's beautiful—almost too ridiculous for words. I suppose it ought to include also what sort of coffee tastes well." And he was fond of pointing out that "If I say A has beautiful eyes," B may ask, "'What do these eyes have in common with a gothic church that I find beautiful too?'"[5] But the same Wittgenstein also said, "Die Philosophie sollte man eigentlich nur dichten," which translates very roughly as "Philosophy ought really to be written only as poetry" (CV 24e). What can that possibly mean if we can't define what poetry is? Wittgenstein would have shrugged and responded that although we can't define the poetic, we all do in fact refer to it in everyday communication, and we seem to have no particular trouble in understanding one another. The word is defined by its use, by the language game in which it is played.

This everydayness of the *poetic* is an interesting phenomenon. From the philology and hermeneutics of the nineteenth century to the *Stoffgeschichte* of the early twentieth, to the New Criticism and Russian Formalism, to deconstruction and Marxist criticism and the new historicism and now cultural studies, theories of and about literature have been regularly contested, reviled, and replaced by other theories and explanatory models. The discipline itself, it seems, is always changing. But—strange as it may seem—the constant that has remained in all these disciplinary debates is literature itself. Not any one literature, not a list of "great works" that everyone must read across the board (a notion that has always troubled me in its move to "discipline and punish"), but the *literary* in its various forms—the *literary* of different centuries, different cultures, different nations; the literary in the broad sense in which Ezra Pound defines poetry as "news that stays news," or in Roland Barthes's words, "One might call 'poetic' (without value judgment) any discourse in which the word leads the idea."[6]

The word leading the idea: it is inevitable that the *poetic*, more broadly, the *literary* will return to the campus because the writers among us will see to its renewal. For of course there has never been a time, at least not since the onset of literacy, when people haven't wanted to write stories, create dialogue, or create new language fields that are poetic. And those who practice literature are naturally interested in the practices of earlier writers. As someone who works primarily on the poetry and poetics of the present, I have learned that the professoriate can't stamp the stuff out, no matter how hard it tries to do so.

Just a few weeks ago, the student representative on our departmental curriculum committee asked, much to my surprise, whether "Yeats and Eliot," which I last taught three years ago, couldn't be offered again. Perhaps, after all, "Prufrock" is more interesting than the lyrics of Madonna. Not necessarily "better"—we must avoid such value judgments, and certainly everyone needn't like Yeats or Eliot—but more interesting. A course called

"Yeats and Eliot" would not, however, speak to those who know no English. Unlike a realist novelist like Tolstoy who can, even with some loss, be read in translation, poetry in translation becomes, at best, someone else's poetry. Take the famous opening lines of Hölderlin's "Patmos":

> Nah ist
> Und schwer zu fassen der Gott.

For me those lines are almost unbearably poignant. But how would one render them using English syntax? "Near is / and hard to comprehend, God"? "Near and / Hard to grasp, the god," "Near is / God and hard to grasp?" "Near / And hard to get a hold of is God"? However one translates these eight little words, it sounds wrong. Then again one doesn't have to read Hölderlin; one might prefer Neruda or Gertrude Stein or Ingeborg Bachmann or Aimé Césaire—and that would be fine too. Flexibility, not punishment, must be at the heart of our discipline. And literary paradigms are enormously various.

What, then, can we expect of comparative literature and its offspring in the area studies of the twenty-first century? Will the study of language disappear? I think, on the contrary, language study will be more important than ever even if we can't prescribe which language is most important to whom. Will the study of literature be replaced by something called cultural studies? Hardly, no matter how much the professoriate would like it to. Indeed, one of the ironies of the current situation is that the demand for literary (rather than political or economic) study is coming from our minority professors. Robert Warrior, who teaches American Indian literature and culture at Stanford, recently remarked in an interview that "poetry represents, in [his] opinion, the widest range of creative literary expression in contemporary American Indian work."[7] Sharon Holland, our new African Americanist, writes poetry herself and is planning a book on the new poetic formations in her field. Literature, for these academics, may be just one discourse among many, but it's the discourse to which they have chosen to commit themselves. The end of "mere" literary study? Perhaps it is only in a residually Puritan nation like the United States that anyone would want such a thing.

Notes

1. René Wellek and Austin Warren, *Theory of Literature*, 3d ed. (New York: Harcourt, Brace and World, 1956), 49.

2. René Wellek, "The Crisis of Comparative Literature" (1958), in Wellek, *Concepts of Criticism*, ed. Stephen G. Nichols, Jr. (New Haven: Yale University Press, 1963), 283.

3. John Guillory, *Cultural Capital: The Problem of Literary Canon Formation* (Chicago: University of Chicago Press, 1993), 241–47 (subsequently cited in the text as CC).

4. Barbara Johnson, *A World of Difference* (Baltimore: Johns Hopkins University Press, 1987), 11.

5. Ludwig Wittgenstein, *Lectures and Conversations on Aesthetics, Psychology, and Religious Belief*, ed. Cyryl Barrett (Berkeley and Los Angeles: University of California Press, n.d.), 11; *Culture and Value*, ed. G. H. von Wright, trans. Peter Winch (Chicago: University of Chicago Press, 1980), 24e (subsequently cited in the text as CV).

6. Roland Barthes, *Roland Barthes by Roland Barthes*, trans. Richard Howard (New York: Farrar, Straus, 1977), 152.

7. *Stanford Observer*, January–February 1994, 6.

18

TELLING TALES OUT OF SCHOOL

Comparative Literature and Disciplinary Recession

MARY RUSSO

Recently, my colleague who specializes in Latin American and Latino literature and I decided to teach a new course entitled "Introduction to Comparative Literature." We regard the choice as timely, if somewhat ironic. We teach at the rare, if not the only, institution of higher education in the United States where one can simply choose to offer a course without departmental or committee approval; in fact, there are no departments, and no standing committee is charged with reviewing courses. Hampshire College was founded in the 1960s as an experiment in deregulatory, interdisciplinary education dedicated to fostering individual initiative and social change. The college slogan, "Non Satis Scire," catches the activist spirit (and something of the minimalist approach to foreign language learning) which still characterizes the institution. Contemplating the impressive accomplishments of many colleagues and former students, I would judge the experiment to have been a success—a success, I should add, due in part to the presence of the four more traditional institutions with which we form a consortium. We have needed these "disciplined" spaces nearby both to fill in our deficiencies and to distinguish us oppositionally, since the college was founded on an antidisciplinary, as well as an interdisciplinary, basis. The most repeated advice I was given thirteen years ago when I was appointed as a professor of "literature and critical theory" was that we were *not* like the nearby Amherst College English Department. The fact that the Amherst College English Department is not like the mythical "Amherst College English Department" anymore (and perhaps never was like it) has hardly diminished this oppositional rhetoric. Nonetheless, the alterity that we try to recapture from time to time, what the administrators call our "uniqueness," is increasingly elusive, as those disci-

plinary boundaries that constituted the "alternative college" threaten to re-
cede into a kind of academic *mise en abîme.* This is not to say that what I am
about to describe is typical or representative of disciplinary recession. In its
best and worst manifestations, I like to think of my place of employment as
truly exceptional. Still, in the last few years, in the aftermath of various crises
relating to programmatic, personnel, and budgetary issues at the college, I
have begun to wonder if something of the future cannot be glimpsed by
viewing my institution as a kind of limit case, since we have gone faster and
further than most in many of the directions indicated in the most recent
Report on Standards submitted to the American Comparative Literature
Association in 1993.

Before I tell a few tales out of school, and tell them in an admittedly
partial way—since I was an active participant in the incidents I am going to
recall and am drawing on only a few details from a local, and undoubtedly to
some, farfetched, context—I want to explain why a report on standards
which invites us to reflect in a general way on the state of a discipline has led
me instead to rethink some particulars. First and most obviously, I think that
these particular incidents resonate in other contexts where fields like comparative literature are in crisis. Secondly, as the Bernheimer report indicates, two
key developments in higher education, the rise of multiculturalism in various
forms and the emergence of cultural studies as an academic field in the United
States, are reshaping comparative literature and are often sources of conflict
which are subsequently exploited in attacks on higher education in the mass
media. Thirdly, I believe that these conflicts are necessary and must be lived
through and reflected upon as an integral part of what otherwise can be seen
as a kind of antiseptic Whig history, from document to document, from
report to report.

Before recounting my own stories, I want to elaborate this last point in
relation to a history of comparative literature which is likely to be drawn from
the recent report and its critical summary of the reports of the previous
committees chaired by Harry Levin (1965) and Thomas Greene (1975). Reading over these Reports on Standards successively, one is tempted to construct a
happy narrative, radiating from a narrow elitist past to a progressive, multicultural future. To do so, however, is to risk the construction of a mythical
past of comparative literature, as if these men and these ideas were entirely
representative of its practice, its function, or its constituency within all institutions of higher education, as if fields and standards in the previous decades
existed outside all "historical, cultural, and political contexts" except for the
admittedly "restrictive Eurocentrism" of the postwar/Cold War era.

In fact, the first two reports belong to a much more heterogeneous history of the field of comparative literature than is evident either in the language of their own reports or in the admirable critique of these reports by Charles Bernheimer and his committee. While it is true that the Levin and Greene reports "strongly articulate the conception of the discipline which prevailed," there were strong countervailing effects in the reception and practice of comparative literature in those decades which exceeded the standards of professional containment espoused in those earlier documents. How else to explain the large, if minoritarian, presence of, for instance, social activists—including feminists who chose and succeeded in literary study, often in a comparativist mode, as a way of transforming history and culture in the 1960s through the 1980s?

Perhaps it is worth remembering here that cultural politics and social progressiveness are never in perfect sync. Alan Sinfield's work on "left culturalism" in Britain under Thatcher, especially as elaborated by Bruce Robbins in his *Secular Vocations*, suggests the arhythmias of events and discourses in the institutionalization of literary study in the differing contexts of Britain and the United States.

Comparative literature, in particular, has had a syncopated progression because, while it certainly has had its culturally conservative moments, as perhaps manifested in the earlier reports, it has served not only as a departmental context where standards are applied but also as a kind of horizon for other disciplines, departments, and fields. Beyond what can still be experienced as the claustrophobic confines of certain national literature departments can be the vision of comparative literature as a theoretical free space and a more cosmopolitan environment for multilingual and multiaccentual community. This extradepartmental function, while it is not the focus of the reports, is an important component of the history of the discipline. The old style of "internationalism" in the university context meant that certain literatures outside of French, German, English, and Spanish—as the Bernheimer report rightly points out—were marginalized in ways that did not correspond to any cultural or geopolitical logic. One of my own "mobile homes" in the academy, Italian, is listed in the report as a European, but minority, literature, except for Dante. When I taught Italian, it was "under" French. From such subaltern spaces, comparative literature, through affiliation or even from a departmental distance, served as a vital locus of realignment and possibility.

Drawing on this past strength, the new comparativism envisioned in the Bernheimer report—with its emphasis on differences within nations, including "multiple-language use and modes of hybridization"—would open up traditional language departments such as Italian to the transmigratory aspects of its culture and language both within Italy and abroad, through immigration, colonization, cultural tourism, and global culture markets. The emergence of a multilingual literature of recent African immigrants in Italy, sometimes translated from another colonial language, sometimes written in collaboration with an Italian-born speaker (*a quattro mani*), is only one of many signs of such a contemporary reconfiguration of modern nationhood.

A focus on the shifting parameters of one country is, in my view, a crucial addition to those considerations of multiculturalism which focus on mere multiplicity and reserve discussions of heterogeneity, ethnicity, and uneven development for geopolitical locations outside Western Europe. A new comparativism, in this case, would go beyond the center/periphery dichotomies that still tend to dominate discussions of "the Third World" and "Eurocentrism."

Comparative literature, as the authors of the Bernheimer report assert, has been a privileged site for such cross-cultural reflection, but, as they also acknowledge, the multicultural recontextualization of literary study owes much to the emergence of the much larger field of cultural studies. Beginning here, with cultural studies, I offer, as promised, some brief "field notes" describing three episodes that have troubled my own understanding of disciplines and interdisciplinarity.

Postcultural Studies

Although I teach in a college where disciplinary boundaries do not exist as such, twenty of us found out that we had gone too far when we proposed a new School (the only official academic unit at my institiution) of Cultural Studies. We began by inviting members of the faculty whose work seemed to be in that area, or who thought they might be interested, to join us in planning. We did this to be *inclusive*, knowing that the first charge to be leveled against such a consolidating initiative would be (and, in truth, had been) that it was exclusive. Perhaps predictably, the shuttle began almost immediately to run in the opposite direction. Suddenly, our inclusivity threatened to overwhelm the entire college as an uncanny effect took hold: we looked simultaneously like almost everyone and like no one else. We were both indistinguishable and too distinguished. Crises of identity ensued. Colleagues who had never heard of cultural studies confessed that they could not decide whether they were in it or not. Others feared that we would all look the same from the outside if a majority of the faculty in humanities, communications, and video, along with some artists, were in cultural studies. What would happen to the four members of the humanities who were left? Since many of us wear five or six disciplinary hats at this small interdisciplinary institution, the cultural studies initiative threatened to destroy many provisional academic groupings—or to borrow Benedict Anderson's term for nationhood, "imagined communities." Even as we attempted to constitute and delimit an institutional space that would have negotiated the dilemma of scale, we were aware that no matter how big or how small, no matter how sharply defined or vague, our boundaries were going to be challenged. We withdrew our formal petition, but that was not enough. In an extraordinary parliamentary maneuver, with a small number of faculty in attendance, a vote was taken and passed to amend the dean's minutes to include a statement of intention not to discuss the cultural studies initiative anymore.

Today cultural studies continues as an unofficial program at Hampshire, and, if student enrollment is the measure, it is extremely successful, arguably the most successful student concentration we have. Yet many of us are wondering whether further efforts to institutionalize it are worth it. Is the lesson here that cultural studies is more appropriate at a larger institution, where it can be defined against individual departments? Or is interdisciplinarity in some guises more tyrannical and homogenizing than the founders of our alternative institution imagined?

Hiring and Firing

Although I would not have put it in these terms at the time, I was confronted with what seemed to me an almost totalizing interdisciplinarity some years ago when two of my colleagues in literature were not reappointed. I will not rehearse in full the merits of their cases, which were discussed widely in the national press as part of the debates around political correctness. What was not emphasized in the journalistic accounts was the extent to which judgments of their case hinged on definitions of comparative literature and disciplinarity. Before going further, I want to report that they were both reappointed eventually, through a series of appeals hearings and negotiations, which took place inside and outside the institution, and have both gone through the reappointment process again with near unanimous votes and excellent evaluations of their work. Although their scholarly interests are different, they shared a common denominator: they were both comparatists and they were both literary. Not grounds for dismissal? Let me describe, in brief, how these terms played themselves out.

In the first stage of the the reappointment process, secret ballots were cast with room for comments (a practice that was later revoked as incompatible with our "open" system). The comments on the negative ballots (four in one case and seven in the other) and the discussion by the approximately thirty voting school members focused on my two colleagues' perceived attitudes ("elitist," "arrogant," and so forth) or on the failure of candidates to teach Third World literature in a proper mode or context. Examples: In the first case, a recent Ph.D. from a leading graduate program in comparative literature (hired primarily to teach German, French, and English) explained that he taught Richard Wright's *Black Boy* in the context of his course on autobiography, drawing on the autobiographical tradition of Augustine and Rousseau. He also taught Borges in another course as an interestingly problematical example of a cosmopolitan "Third World writer." His approach to these authors was deemed "out of context" and insufficiently engaged in the college project to engage the students in Third World topics. The second case was more clearly grievous to most. A Hispanic hired to teach Latin American and domestic Latino literatures was accused, in a letter from a colleague in the social sciences, who admitted to having no firsthand knowledge of his teaching or scholarship, of emphasizing Eurocentric literary terminology, genre, and stylistic questions over representing the Third World to the Hispanic "community." *Community* is a word that circulates widely to mean the small number of minority students on campus or to mean the "Hampshire community." Despite the strong support of all the minority faculty in humanities and arts, his representativeness (in all senses) and his identity were called into question through a critique of his approach to literature, which included repeatedly bringing in European examples and theoretical frameworks.

The positive assessments of the candidates' work by outside evaluators, including many of the most distinguished members of the profession, were written off largely as elitist and/or oblivious to our internal standards. Obviously, the relative merits of teaching any particular author in one context or another, using one method or another, are debatable. It just seemed that there was no one to whom the full-time literature faculty, all of whom supported the candidates, could make a case, except on the much-expanded grounds of academic freedom or discrimination. These latter issues are far more significant in the larger context, but this was an opportunity to demonstrate the claim made by the 1993 report that comparative literature can play a pivotal role in pluralizing multiculturalism. In this case, however, I found myself appealing, mostly in vain, to professional and disciplinary standards that did not seem to obtain in these cases.

My point is that in cases in which there are no disciplinary norms, interdisciplinarity can mean that "community standards"—in this case a homogenizing identitarian model of multiculturalism from the social sciences—can take its place. In such a case, the effects on academic life can be devastating. This was not a thought I entertained before this incident when I shared the community sentiment that interdisciplinarity and multiculturalism(s) were self-evidently progressive.

In retrospect, the relationship between social change and academic standards in the United States—particularly in relation to comparative literary studies—is much more complex than our parochial version of multiculturalism allowed. But there are other developing models of comparative literature at my own institution and beyond which, in the words of the recent report, "promote significant reflection on cultural relations, translations, dialogue, and debate."

The Budget

The Bernheimer report closes with some reflections on the financial uncertainties of higher education in our time in relation to the future of comparative literature. The authors see "comparison"—defined in the report as "the wave of the future"—as being, unfortunately, held back in many universities and colleges as a conservative response to budget restrictions. Cultural conservatism is not, however, the only response to budgetary crisis. As Mary Louise Pratt argues in her MLA paper, there are many examples of more daring and resourceful strategies. In many cases, jobs will be created and sustained precisely because they revitalize the academic enterprise.

As a member of a budget committee called to respond to a deficit crisis, I was struck by the complexity of the connections between financial exigencies and the "progressive tendencies" of fields like comparative literature which potentially have great flexibility in reconfiguring their programs and staffing. "Flexibility" is the keyword here, as in "flexible accumulation" and "flexible staffing." For an institution like my own, high on standards, tuition, and multiculturalism and low on endowment and salaries, the versatility of a comparatist faculty willing to engage with other understaffed fields has meant that we are able to produce many outstanding students who go on, with great success, to graduate programs in literature (again, this is made possible, in part, by cooperating with nearby institutions with which we exchange students and courses). The chair of the Trustee Committee on the Budget, who owns a successful art supply business, identified strongly with the entrepreneurial spirit and initiative that drive small, "flexible" programs.

This is not a model I endorse. Our budget has been cut too close to the bone for anyone's comfort. The "downsizing" model is, however, a possibility, given the role that deregulation, flexibility, outcontracting, and the subsequently reduced work force have played in other sectors. Surely it is a possibility that some administrators outside my local context have recognized.

Such an administrative response is, of course, not in the spirit of the 1993 report, which looks forward to a time beyond this "transitional period" and urges an engagement with those larger economic and political issues that will determine the future of higher education. As higher education experiences what I imagine (and sometimes fear) will be a massive deregulation and "downsizing" of the humanities, these border negotiations will be worked out on an institution-by-institution basis. Public reports on the state of the disciplines help us understand the different circumstances and horizons of our local situations, but it is the daily practices of specific institutions—including curricular, personnel, and budgetary committee work—which will determine and reveal the constraints and possibilities of working in any field.

19

SINCERELY YOURS

TOBIN SIEBERS

—————

Comparatists today are riding a current that began at the end of the Second World War. Part of the symbolism of comparative literature at that time was that it would help to reunify Europe. American comparative literature students went to war in Europe, at least some of them, and they returned home to build their incipient knowledge of European cultures and languages into scholarship. Their professors were often refugees from the same European battlefields. This history is highly visible in the stories told by both the Levin and Greene Reports on Standards. What is not so visible, at least to our time, is how sincere was this effort and how important its symbolism. In a world recently torn by great wars and on the brink of greater ones—or so it seemed—comparative literature represented the spirit of peace, sincerity, reasonableness, and hope. Comparatists also saw themselves as a brain trust, for intelligence and talent were necessary to pick up the pieces and clean up the mess. Comparatists wanted to do something about this mess, and they believed that they had the intelligence to do it.

The world seems to have grown larger now, but not much has changed with regard to the symbolism of comparative literature. The Bernheimer report shows that comparatists still have huge ethical and political ambitions for their discipline. It is true that their confidence has been shaken somewhat by bad economic times and unsympathetic deans, but they still seem to believe that given enough money, they can produce the kind of people who will change the world for the better. These are the same kind of people whom comparatists have always wanted to produce: they are, in Mary Louise Pratt's words, "bicultural" or "multicultural people." Other names touching on the same vision include "global citizens" (Pratt), "cultural pluralists" (the Levin and Bernheimer reports), "internationalists" (the Levin and Greene reports), and "cosmopolitans" (the Greene report). Comparative literature remains a symbolic United Nations; it celebrates a postwar vision of world unity called for by the spectacle of the globe torn asunder by human conflict. It wants to resolve conflict among the people of the world. This is a worthy ambition, but I question whether it is a reasonable one for the discipline.

Those Wrecked by Success

Perhaps the greatest task facing comparatists in the coming years will be to grasp the underlying ethical and political symbolism of comparative literature and to decide whether they want to live or die by it. To my mind, there is no doubt that comparative literature as a discipline is dying. The irony is that it is being wrecked by its own success, and this is a difficult irony to understand.

To summarize briefly, comparative literature was an early advocate of a world-view that has found a new and more popular formulation in multiculturalism. In the cola wars between comparative literature and multiculturalism, the old brand cannot stand up to the new one, no matter how similar they really are, because multiculturalism has found a marketing strategy that makes it available to more people. Comparatists are losing their identity in the university because everyone is becoming a comparatist of a kind.

The current controversy among comparatists about multiculturalism, then, boils down to a simple choice: continue to dream the dream under the old name or dream the dream under the new name. The only difference between the dreams is one of standards. Comparatists in the classical mold believe that language proficiency is central to cultural pluralism because literatures and cultures cannot be understood in translation. The more languages one knows, then, the better. At minimum, someone in the classroom should speak the original language of each work and know something about its culture. Usually, this person is the teacher, and he or she plays the dual role of tour guide and policeman, pointing out things to see and rejecting improper interpretations. The multiculturalists believe that culture is translatable; cultural pluralism can be taught simply by exposing students to content, regardless of its form. Therefore, it is more important to give ideas and cultures a place in the classroom than to demonstrate an understanding of them. No one need know the original language and culture of the work.

Students need know only that it comes from afar. The teacher continues to play the role of tour guide and policeman, if only because he or she is the spokesperson for the underrepresented element.

Both dreams prize the same virtue of cross-cultural experience, and they share the belief that the literary works themselves hold the key to this virtue. Multiculturalism is, of course, more text bound than comparative literature, since multiculturalism does not require knowledge of languages and cultures as prerequisites to its study; it requires only that certain kinds of texts exert a symbolic presence in the classroom, which means that it enjoys a more accessible pedagogy. But access and openness are what both dreams value. If it comes down to an argument between them, then, the comparatists will always fret about their motives for holding to exacting linguistic standards. The Greene report, despite its supposed hard-line stance on standards, is in fact more worried about being humane than the other two reports. It is difficult to stay humane. The Levin and Bernheimer reports seem confident that their plans of action will do no harm, if only comparatists are given the resources to implement them.

In the final analysis, however, the disagreements between the three reports are negligible. The argument is an intramural squabble, a German quarrel, and all sides agree about what is ultimately the most dubious claim of the discipline. This is the theoretical assumption that literary works, if studied cross-culturally, will produce better world citizens.

The current debate about standards reminds me of the rival claims made by two diet plans. The first promises that you can eat all you want and still lose five pounds a week if you climb stairs for an hour a day. The second promises that you will lose the weight if you take a pill every day. Most people try the second method because it is easier. No one notices until the twenty-fifth week that there is something wrong with the theory behind both methods and that neither one works.

Conclusion #1: Comparative literature cannot compete with multiculturalism. Conclusion #2: The philosophical differences between comparative literature and multiculturalism are minimal, largely symbolic, and not worth debating because neither one can deliver on its promises. It remains to be seen whether the symbolism alone is useful.

Theory in Theory

A theory is a point of view about what is invariable. What would a theory of multiple points of view be? No doubt, it would be one point of view about what many points of view are. But it would also be a means of reducing variables, of dealing with the explosion of multiple points of view.

Literary and cultural theory in the United States and Europe, perhaps worldwide, is European theory, and its vision of what multiple points of view are remains singular. For all the talk of multiculturalism today, there is very little genuine multiculturalism going on, especially in classrooms. If I were better educated, I could provide many examples of the kinds of ideas which are outlawed by theory and its classroom politics. As it is, I will have to content myself with three illustrations.

1. The most obvious case is recitation because it is a part of the educational experience of every child in every world culture. Parents teach their children about their own cultures (and others) by telling and reading stories to them, and the children learn by retelling them. American teachers in the early grades read aloud to their classes to educate and as a reward for good behavior, which suggests that there must be something rewarding about it. College professors early in this century still included large amounts of recitation in their teaching. Certainly, in history and in world culture, recitation defines a very familiar and important means of experiencing poetry and narrative, whether oral or written.

More important, recitation in the broad sense is everywhere a central aspect of daily life. Someone tells a story, and another person responds by reciting another story. The two stories are related, apparently, for having been put together in a conversation, although it is not always clear what the relation is. What is clear, however, is that no active theoretical interpretation intervenes to connect the two accounts. Part of learning what a culture is consists of having this kind of experience many, many times every day. It produces the large cultural conversation whose webs and interstices create the context for further conversation. One needs to stress the massive scale on which this takes place. Presumably, being exposed to one or two hundred conversations will not introduce a person into a cultural conversation. I have no idea how many conversations are necessary to make someone culturally informed.

In the West we can chart when and where recitation becomes demoted as a form of knowledge. From secondary school onward, it disappears in the classroom. No university professor today would consider reading aloud to students for the entire class period or even a small part of it. Instead, reading is assigned as homework, students do some of it, and the professor spends class time explaining the work. The explanation is a way of translating content for the class, but if culture resides in the repetition of the form and baseline content, explanation must be less successful than recitation. Here is a modest proposal: perhaps this material would be better transmitted, and the exposure to different cultures would be greater, if college professors devoted all of their class time to reading aloud.

But that would not require a Ph.D.

2. Personal interpretation is taboo in the classroom. If I am a student in a literature class and I am assigned Chinua Achebe's *Things Fall Apart*, it may come alive for me only because its preoccupation with anger strikes a chord with my personal family history. But when the professor opens discussion of the novel, I will not be allowed to dwell on this correspondence. I will be cut off if I try to tell the long and complicated story about how anger destroyed my own father and how what I fear most in my life is becoming an angry man.

Surely, if I am a literary critic, this reading has no professional value. If I submit an essay about my experience to *Critical Inquiry, Representations,* or *Cultural Critique,* I will discover its worthlessness very quickly.

Nevertheless, personal interpretation is a central part of the experience of poetry and narrative. People at cocktail parties like to swap stories about what they are reading and the films they have seen because they identify with characters and use them to talk about themselves. Arguably, part of the success of film comes from the fact that people now use it as a means of self-expression. People used to talk this way about novels, just as they used to read to each other to pass the time. Personal interpretation is very much a part of cultural experience worldwide and historically. Dream interpretation, prophecy, magical ritual, astrology, games, and myths provide general symbols by which individuals explain themselves to others and to themselves.

3. Religious interpretation is extremely important historically and on a global scale. In some societies, narratives have no meaning if they are not religious. For historical and political reasons, however, religion is not part of literary and cultural studies today. It is not permissible for teachers to interpret a secular text as a religious one or to give a strictly religious reading of a sacred text. If they do, they risk being seen as fanatical or unbalanced. Anyone who teaches the Bible can tell tales about religious students who try to make themselves heard on the true importance and meaning of the word of God. These students are on the whole seen as a nuisance.

Conclusion #1: Multiculturalism is fine as long as it is the right kind of multiculturalism. Generally, the right kind derives from the European Enlightenment, which privileged hermeneutics, disinterestedness, and secular knowledge. Conclusion #2: The ethic of multiculturalism is to increase communication and understanding among people of different discourses, cultures, ideologies, races, and genders. This ethic has limited applications. See conclusion #1.

Sincerely Yours

I am afraid that I am not typical of the academy in our age, if Anthony Appiah is right that literary and cultural criticism no longer have anything to do with rationality. Mr. Appiah's statement surprises me, if only because I find him to be a reasonable man, and I wonder whether he really means what he says. Rationality is a form of action according to principles, and so if we want to act with principle—and I take it that we all do, even if we might disagree about what these principles are and the language in which they might be expressed—we need to work in the interest of reason. For me, this is the way to approach the problem of standards because standards are reasons that people have agreed to act upon in concert.

Kant made the case in the First Critique that three questions help to summarize the interest of reason. They are: "What can I know? What ought I to do? What may I hope?" I want to answer these questions in the interest of finding the connection between reason and multiculturalism. I think, however, that Kant got the order wrong, so I am going to revise it to place the question of action last (although ultimately the order is recursive, since we pose the questions anew after each action, their final purpose being happiness).

Unfortunately, a brief confession is necessary before I proceed. I am going to try to answer these questions sincerely. I know this is a problem, but I will make the effort because I believe that the question of rationality is most important today because it raises the issue of sincerity. We live in a world where skepticism is the general rule and where promises to be reasonable are thought to be the best strategy for telling lies. So it is the value of sincerity which is most on our minds when other people tell us their reasons for acting. When we ask whether something is good or good for us—and in my view we ask these questions more often than any others—we are asking a question about the kind of community we want to live in. To define that community, before we agree on what it might be, we must agree that we have a common purpose. If we refuse for any reason to believe in the sincerity of other people's desire for agreement, if we are skeptical about their motives, for example, the task of agreement will be much more difficult.

If we assumed the sincerity of everyone in the current debate about standards or at least allowed the issue of sincerity to become part of the debate, instead of embracing skepticism, we would have a much better basis for agreement and disagreement.

What Can I Know?

The short answer, compared to what I may hope for, is "Very little." Given what I am about to say, it is easy to understand the temptation to study literature in terms of aesthetic autonomy, as Michael Riffaterre does, since it defines knowledge on the basis of the formal unity of the work and in isolation from the totality of forces that produce and give it meaning. If someone who knows as much as he does takes this route, who can blame anyone else?

The task of acquiring multicultural knowledge, of becoming deeply informed about more than one literature and culture, is enormous. To understand at a basic level what a work from another culture means is extremely difficult: it requires years of language study and some familiarity with idioms and customs. To place a work in its cultural context may be impossible for a native speaker, let alone a nonnative one.

Of my nonnative languages, I am most proficient in French. I have been studying French literature, philosophy, and culture for more than twenty years, and so far I have lived in France for a total of about three years. I am in Paris on sabbatical leave as I write these words. What is it like to be an American in Paris? I buy fruit and vegetables everyday, and never is it easy. I say what I want and I get what I want in varying approximations, according to the vendor's whims. I pay with money that I understand in slow motion. A few more examples. I do not understand why the French dress the way they do or their sense of the erotic. I do not understand why one body part is obscene and another not, and when. The French often greet each other by kissing cheeks, always twice, sometimes four times, maybe more. When do they do it twice, double it, or go for broke? Does it matter whether they start on the left or right side? I can explain all of this in great detail, but I do not understand it.

I go to a French film, and the theater bursts with laughter, but I do not laugh because I did not get the joke. I go to an American film, and I laugh alone because the French audience did not get the joke.

I have been trying to understand French literary theory for twenty years. What if my disagreements are based on something as simple as not getting the joke? Am I deeply informed about French culture? I love France. I do not feel deeply informed.

I do know more about French culture than I did ten years ago. At least, I think I do. I want to return to France, to read its literature, and to continue to study its culture. I am making my children learn French. Most of my American friends think I am being cruel. It goes without saying that my French friends think I am doing the right thing.

Where does this leave me as a multiculturalist? I would like to be one, but I am not. Given my ignorance, I ought to try to stay close to what I know I know, if that is possible. I should occupy myself with what is going on in my classroom, with its culture, and its place in university culture, and try to resist any symbolism that exaggerates the analogy between my classroom and the world at large. I should set reasonable goals for learning and teaching. If my ideal is multiculturalism, what can I do today, next week, and for several weeks after that to help my students to approach that ideal? Do I see progress from week to week toward this ideal? What adjustments should I be considering to make progress, including adjustments in goals for students and myself?

What May I Hope?

I may hope against hope to know what I do not know and to come to know it. My hope is what keeps me going. I may hope to be a good teacher, to be a better teacher, to contribute to making my classroom, university, country, and the world into better places. I may hope to teach my students that what I know will be important to them, and then hope that they will learn what I teach them. I may hope to know the limits of my hope, when my hope leads me and others into the darkness instead of the light. I may hope not to allow my hope to become a substitute for what I can know—not to feed myself and others on false hopes.

Where does this leave me as a multiculturalist? I know that I am not multicultural, and my experience tells me that it is an ideal that cannot be realized, at least by me. But I also know that unrealizable ideals are useful to encourage people and that they often help us to make progress, although not always in the direction we intend. I will speak favorably about the multicultural ideal because of its hopefulness, but I also want to be reasonable about its limitations. What I may hope for is to place multiculturalism in the service of hope.

What Ought I to Do?

I must do what I know and attempt what I hope for, but I must not forget that there is a gap between what I can know and what I may hope. That gap is my ignorance. My ignorance is a form of hope and a form of counterhope. The knowledge of my ignorance pushes me forward and gives purpose to my actions. But my ignorance also tells me that there may be no path leading from what I can know to what I may hope for, that what I hope for may not be very good for me, and that the means to acquire what I hope for may bring me something else entirely—something equal, better, or worse.

Where does this leave me as a multiculturalist? I ought to teach what I can know and what I may hope but temper them by teaching students about my ignorance. This has the added advantage of not indenturing them to me. They should understand that the world is not in my classroom but outside it and that they will need to go to other teachers and other places to learn more about it.

$2 + 2 = 4$

I have just told a story about reason and the value of sincerity. There is another story to tell, but it cannot be told today with impunity. It says that sincerity is not enough. This story includes facts. It says that we need to teach humane values, but it includes among such values as peace, sincerity, reasonableness, and hope simple facts such as $2 + 2 = 4$. It is a story where simple facts contribute to humaneness as much as talk about humaneness.

Today those who think that facts get between people and those who think that facts bring people together see each other as enemies. I want to suggest, however, that both views are sincere and that their common enemy is skepticism. Skeptics are people who will not agree that agreement is a pearl of great price. What the people who believe in facts share with those who believe in values, when compared to skeptics, is the desire to do something rather than nothing, even if it turns out to be the wrong thing. People who deal in values and facts make many mistakes. This is why sincerity looks stupid compared to skepticism. This is why those who believe in simple facts look stupid compared to skeptics. The sincere are those who dare to be stupid in order to do. Please do.

NOTES ON CONTRIBUTORS

EDWARD J. AHEARN is Chair of the Department of French Studies at Brown University, where he is the Francis Wayland Professor. He published *Marx and Modern Fiction* in 1989 and is currently completing *Visionary Fictions: Apocalyptic Writing in the Post-Revolutionary Age.*

K. ANTHONY APPIAH is Professor of Afro-American Studies and Philosophy at Harvard University and the author most recently of *In My Father's House: Africa in the Philosophy of Culture* (1992). He is currently co-editing the Amistad literary series Critical Perspectives on African-American and African Writers. His second novel, *Nobody Likes Letitia*, was published in 1994.

EMILY APTER is Professor of French and Comparative Literature at the University of California–Los Angeles. Her books include *Feminizing the Fetish: Psychoanalysis and Narrative Obsession in Turn-of-the-Century France* (1991) and *Fetishism as Cultural Discourse* (1993, co-edited with William Pietz). She is completing a book entitled *Colonial Subjects/Postcolonial Seductions.*

CHARLES BERNHEIMER is Co-Chair of the Program in Comparative Literature and Literary Theory at the University of Pennsylvania. His most recent book is *Figures of Ill Repute: Representing Prostitution in Nineteenth-Century France* (1989). He is now writing a book on the idea of decadence in the European fin de siècle, *Decadent Subjects.*

PETER BROOKS is Tripp Professor of the Humanities and Chair of the Department of Comparative Literature and The Literature Major at Yale University. He recently published *Body Work* (1993) and *Psychoanalysis and Storytelling* (1994).

REY CHOW is Associate Professor of English and Comparative Literature at the University of California–Irvine. Her publications include *Woman and Chinese Modernity* (1991) and *Writing Diaspora* (1993). In 1995 Columbia University Press will publish *Primitive Passions: Visuality, Sexuality, Ethnography, and Contemporary Chinese Cinema.*

JONATHAN CULLER is Chair of the Department of Comparative Literature at Cornell University. His many books focus primarily on nineteenth-century French literature and on structuralist and poststructuralist theory.

DAVID DAMROSCH is Professor of English and Comparative Literature at Columbia University. He is the author of *The Narrative Covenant: Transformations of Genre in the Growth of Biblical Literature* (1987) and of a methodological study, *Scholarship: A Manifesto* (1994), on alienation and aggression in the university. He is now working on a book on the discipline of comparative literature.

ELIZABETH FOX-GENOVESE is Eléonore Raoul Professor of the Humanities at Emory University. Her most recent book is *Feminism without Illusions: A Critique of Individualism* (1991). She frequently writes about history, literature, and theory.

ROLAND GREENE is Professor of Comparative Literature and English at the University of Oregon and Director of the Program in Comparative Literature there. He is the author of *Post-Petrarchism: Origins and Innovations of the Western Lyric Sequence* (1991) and the forthcoming *Unrequited Conquests: Love and Empire in the Colonial Americas.*

MARGARET HIGONNET is Professor of English and Comparative Literature at the University of Connecticut. She has edited *The Sense of Sex: Feminist Perspectives on Hardy* (1992) and *Borderwork: Feminist Engagements with Comparative Literature* (1994) and co-edited three volumes of essays in feminist criticism (1983, 1987, 1994).

FRANÇOISE LIONNET teaches French and Comparative Literature at Northwestern University. She is the author of *Autobiographical Voices: Race, Gender, Self-Portraiture* (1989) and the forthcoming *Spiralling Tensions: Authenticity, Universality, and Postcoloniality.*

MARJORIE PERLOFF'S most recent books are *Radical Artifice: Writing Poetry in the Age of Media* (1992) and, with Charles Junkerman, *John Cage: Composed in America* (1994). She is the Sadie Dernham Patek Professor of Humanities at Stanford University.

MARY LOUISE PRATT is Professor of Latin American and Comparative Literature at Stanford University. She is co-author of *Women, Culture and Politics in Latin America* (1990) and recently published *Imperial Eyes: Travel Writing and Transculturation* (1992).

MICHAEL RIFFATERRE is University Professor at Columbia University and Director of the School of Criticism and Theory at Dartmouth College. His most recent book is *Fictional Truth* (1990).

MARY RUSSO is Professor of Literature and Critical Theory at Hampshire College. She is the author of *The Female Grotesque: Risk, Excess, and Modernity* (1994) and co-editor of *Nationalisms and Sexualities* (1992) and of *Designing Italy: Italy in Europe, Africa, Asia, and the Americas* (forthcoming).

TOBIN SIEBERS is Professor of English and Comparative Literature at the University of Michigan. His latest books are *Cold War Criticism and the Politics of Skepticism* (1993) and *Heterotopia: Postmodern Utopia and the Body Politic* (1994).

ARNOLD WEINSTEIN is the Henry Merritt Wriston Professor of Comparative Literature at Brown University. In 1993 he published *Nobody's Home: Speech, Self and Place in American Fiction from Hawthorne to DeLillo*. He is currently working on studies of Ibsen, Strindberg, Munch, and Bergman and on the poetics of city art.

Library of Congress Cataloging-in-Publication Data

Comparative literature in the age of multiculturalism / edited by Charles Bernheimer.
    p.   cm. — (Parallax : re-visions of culture and society)
  Includes bibliographical references.
    ISBN 0-8018-5004-5 (alk. paper). — ISBN 0-8018-5005-3 (pbk. : alk. paper)
    1. Literature, Comparative—History and criticism.   2. Literature, Modern—History
and criticism.   3. Criticism.   4. Multiculturalism.   I. Bernheimer, Charles, 1942–   .
II. Series: Parallax (Baltimore, Md.)
PN863.C586   1995
809—dc20   94-29219